WITHDRAWN

Looking at Animals in Human History

Looking at Animals in Human History

LINDA KALOF

REAKTION BOOKS

Published by Reaktion Books Ltd
33 Great Sutton Street, London EC1V 0DX, UK

www.reaktionbooks.co.uk

First published 2007

Printed and bound in China by Imago

British Library Cataloguing-in-Publication Data
A catalogue record for this book is available from the British Library.

Kalof, Linda
Looking at animals in human history
1. Animals (Philosophy) – History
2. Human-animal relationships – History
I. Title
179.3
ISBN-13: 9 781 86189 334 5
ISBN-10: 1 86189 334 5

Contents

Contents

Preface

A hopeless attempt to see things whole is at least as worthy as the equally hopeless task of isolating fragments for intensive study.[1]

As hopeless as the task may or may not be, the larger picture of animals in human history is one that I have endeavoured to see for some time now, so the story behind this book is a familiar one – it was written to fill a need. No single volume existed that synthesized the vast scholarship on animals in human history, a body of work that has been percolating for years now in ever larger quantities from a staggering array of academic disciplines. So here is my contribution – a broad historical overview and synthesis of the body of knowledge on the cultural representations of animals and how those representations have changed with changing social conditions.

I deploy the notion of 'looking at animals' as a way to trace how animals have been represented (re-presented) in a wide variety of human cultural texts, both visual and narrative. The concept 'representation' is particularly compelling, with a huge range of meanings, and I engage with many of these ways of looking at animals in this book, including their

depiction, illustration, likeness, semblance, similitude, icon, picture, portrait, painting, drawing, engraving, sketch, photograph, snapshot, image, reflection, shadow, silhouette, drama, parody, imitation, impersonation, personification, mental image, impression, concept, illusion, description, account, exposition, elaboration, recitation, and unfolding. (Modified list from Rodale 1978)

You will see that I have chosen to include those cultural representations that I found most provocative in my research looking at animals through the ages. As John Berger argues, the way we see things is profoundly affected by what we know and what we believe,[2] and what I have seen has surely been framed by my background and interests. For example, it is the sociologist in me that has described the numerous ways that animals have been used to highlight hierarchies of gender, race and class, particularly the disgrace associated with transgressing traditional social boundaries (and for women, those social boundaries are sexual borders). It was a long-standing interest in visual imagery that compelled me to spend the time and resources necessary to locate the images I have used to illustrate the story of animals in human history. My beginning with animals in prehistoric cave paintings had its roots in a unit on parietal art in a Western Civilization course I took as a teenager oh-so-many years ago, while a growing interest in ecology and the environment is responsible for my including material on outbreaks of plague and rabies, and writing an article on the display of animal bodies in trophy photography drove me to the literature on dead-animal portraiture in the seventeenth century. Alas, it was necessary for me to confine my looking to cultural accounts from the western world. I regret the implication that I believe only western history is important, because it was only a paucity of time that prevented me from researching the many important and vital stories about animals in the non-western world.

In researching this book I have consulted a very large number of books and articles. Some of that work touched only marginally on the subject of animals, but were important to my vision of the larger story, including such seemingly disparate topics as the Black Death, still life painting and charivaris. Of course I have also included the essential work of the scholars who have written entire books on animals in a particular place at a particular time in our history, such as the intensive studies of animals in France in the eighteenth century[3] and in the nineteenth century[4] and the numerous works on animals in England's history – in the early modern period,[5] during a 300-year period 1500 to 1800,[6] during the Victorian era,[7] and in the early twentieth century.[8] In addition I am also deeply grateful for Esther Cohen's work on animals in medieval rituals and processions,[9] Scott Sullivan on the Dutch gamepiece,[10] Paul Bahn and Jean Vertut on Palaeolithic art,[11] Juliet Clutton-Brock's history of domesticated mammals[12] and Eric Baratay and Elisabeth Hardouin-Fugier's history of the zoo.[13] This is a heavily documented book, a writing style that is not popular these days. My penchant for documentation is driven not only by the desire to adhere to a scholarly tradition but also to avoid the tendency lamented by Lynn White who complained about scholars who omitted their sources because they worried that their readers would not cite them but rather their sources.[14]

Finally, I gratefully acknowledge the inspiration and enthusiasm for this book from my animal kin and colleagues, particularly Thomas Dietz, Adam Henry, Alexandra Kalof, Rebecca Jones, Amy Fitzgerald, Darwin, Bailey and Maggie. I leave you with this quotation from Bruno Latour:

For every hundred books of commentaries, arguments, glosses, there is only one of description.[15]

Linda Henry Kalof
East Lansing, Michigan
April 2006

Chapter 1

Prehistory, before 5000 BC

We begin our journey by looking at the animals painted by our Palaeolithic ancestors 32,000 years ago. Nowhere is the profound and undisputed link between humans and other animals more compelling than deep inside a cave in southwestern France. Dark, wet and slippery, with shifting floor levels, sharp protruding rocks and dangerous overhangs, the Chauvet cave was decorated with stunning images of animals by a few Late Palaeolithic humans around 30,000 BC. The cave walls are filled with complex scenes – confronting rhinoceroses, snarling lions, herds of animals drawn as if rapidly moving through the cave – 420 animal images in all (and only six human images). The Chauvet cave artists used sophisticated artistic techniques to render animals spectacularly lifelike. They employed shading and perspective; they depicted images in ways that convey body motion, speed, strength and power; they incorporated convex and concave rock surfaces to provide volume and three-dimensionality; and they distorted anatomical details for some animals so that the image could only be viewed in its correct proportion if seen from a specific location in the cave.[1] Our prehistoric ancestors were not only very good at art, they also spent much of their time looking at animals.

Why? What significance did these animals have for the Palaeolithic humans? Why did they go to such great lengths to paint, draw and carve animal images inside caves? We simply don't know. But there is much speculation. Hundreds of painted caves have been discovered thus far, and it is clear that each cave tells a somewhat different story, narratives embedded in geography, climate, local culture and time. Thus, over the thousands of years of cave painting, there was no linear development of the art from simple to complex or from abstract to naturalistic, but rather a collection of artistic expressions of different cultural ideas and content.[2] For example, the depicted animal behaviours vary widely from cave to cave. At Chauvet, the animals were drawn in ways suggesting movement, speed and strength. But at the Cosquer cave (also in southern France) the positions of the animals are fixed and immobile, never leaping, running or charging.[3] At Chauvet, the animals depicted are the most powerful carnivores of the Late

Palaeolithic (bears, lions, rhinos), clearly an emphasis on large, dangerous animals. That emphasis changed around 25,000 BC when parietal art represented primarily herbivores with few detailed drawings of carnivores. While it has been argued that the stylistic difference could be a reflection of the abundant presence of animal species in the older period which later became rare in the environment and thus also in human art,[4] it is largely unknown why the art motif changed from carnivores to herbivores.

Herbivores of course accounted for most of the diet of the Palaeolithic humans. And of the numerous theories proposed over the past 125 years to account for the cave art, the most common is that the paintings and carvings of animals represent hunter art – part of a ritual in which visual representations of hunted prey ensured a successful hunt or provided a means of communicating hunting information to other humans. It has also been argued that big herds of animals withdrew to the north as the climate grew warmer, and the purpose of the paintings was to *make* animals rather than to kill them, because they were in short supply.[5] Similarly, it has long been suggested that cave art was not about hunting at all, but about fertility, with prehistoric artists drawing animals as a way of encouraging their reproduction to ensure a source of food. But there are few examples in the art that support the idea that the art was about animal fertility – rarely are animals depicted with obvious gender, genitalia or engaged in sex, and there are even fewer pictures of young animals.[6]

Others argue that the Palaeolithic representations of animals are part of a shamanistic ritual. This theory suggests that the images, particularly deep-cave paintings, are attempts to make contact with spirits or a quest for a spiritual vision, with certain geometric images representative of hallucinogenic states of consciousness and paintings that employ the cave's natural contours indicative of 'ritually materializing the animal spirits already present in the underground'.[7] For example, Lewis-Williams proposes that Palaeolithic humans established and defined social relationships through imagery, and that the ability to reach higher-order consciousness made it possible not only to create images, but also religion and social distinctions.[8] Since shamanistic cultures are usually zoomorphic, with humans seeing and experiencing the world in animal forms and animal attributes, it has been argued that the cave paintings may be representative of spirit animals rather than copies of real animals.[9]

Perhaps it was the act of *looking* that was important. For example, based on what is known about contemporary hunting cultures, Bahn and Vertut consider the possibility that the shaman's power was derived from the subsequent viewing of the images rather than from the act of drawing or painting. The artist/shaman might have been a 'master-of-animals' who

represented the life force of an animal or imparted life force to it, with
lines drawn at the nostrils and mouths of animals depicting the entrance
or exit of the animals' life forces.[10] While there is no consensus on when
language first appeared in human history, it is believed that the Chauvet
artists must have had language to be able to produce such complex representations of animals. Material representations extend the capability of
verbal imagery. Randall White argues that to be able to think visually is a
revolutionary development; visual and tactile representations are durable,
and their authority comes with the ability to 'communicate in the absence
of the communicator'.[11]

Regardless of the theory employed to explain the cave paintings, it is
clear that the people of the Late Palaeolithic were expressing admiration
for animals, and most scholars agree that the prehistoric art work is closely
linked to ritual and ceremony.[12] It is logical that we would celebrate
animals that we held in high esteem. For most of early history, humans
were more often prey than predators and occasionally scavenged off the
carcasses killed and abandoned by other, more powerful carnivores.[13]
Unambiguous evidence of hunting dates to about 400,000 years ago when
Early Palaeolithic humans appeared to have used wooden hunting spears
to hunt horses, although they were still heavily involved in scavenging off
the remains left by other carnivores.[14] Under those conditions, it is hardly
surprising that humans would venerate the carnivores who took prece-
dence in the feeding hierarchy.

At most cave sites there is no direct relationship between the species
depicted on the walls and ceilings and the bones found scattered about,
indicating that the artists did not usually draw the species eaten by the
group. For example, at Altamira they ate red deer and drew bison (see
illus. 1), and the Lascaux humans ate primarily reindeer but only one of
the pictures they drew is clearly a reindeer.[15] Thus, artistic expression at
these early times is widely considered a reflection of cultural preferences
rather than an accounting of the availability of certain animal species in
the immediate environment.[16]

The species most often depicted in cave paintings were horse (30 per cent
of all drawings) (see illus. 2, an image known as the Chinese Horse), bison
and aurochs (another 30 per cent), deer, ibex and mammoth (another 30
per cent), and bears, felines and rhinos (10 per cent).[17] One of the many
interesting aspects of how specific species are depicted in cave art is the
overwhelming coexistence of horses and bison, both drawn larger and more
detailed than other species, perhaps suggestive of a duality that formed the
basis of a 'figurative system' for the Late Palaeolithic humans, although alas
the meaning of this hypothetical system is unknown.[18]

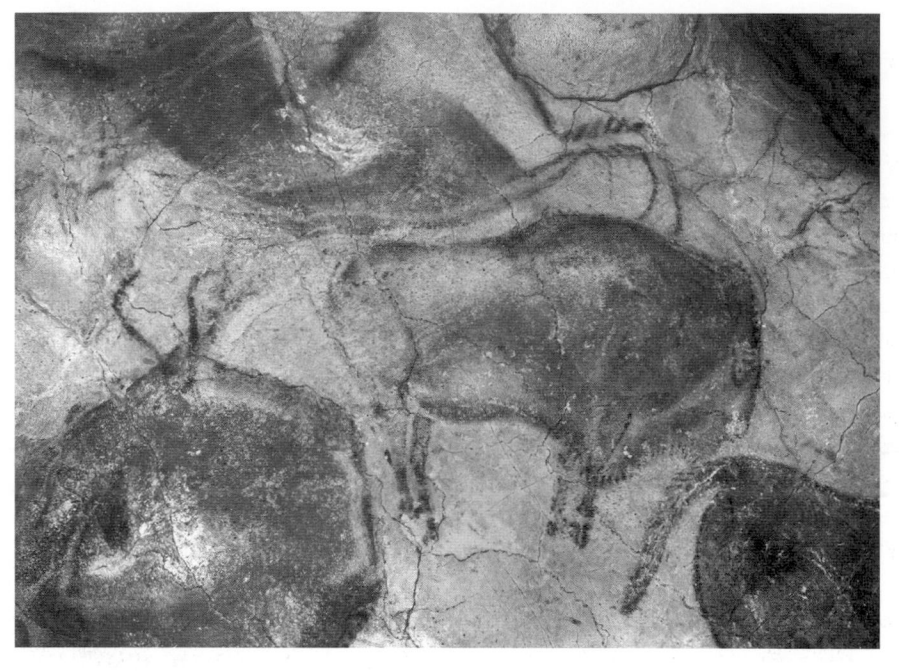

1 Bison, Palaeolithic cave painting, Hall of the Bison, Cave of Altamira, Spain, 15,000–8000 BC.

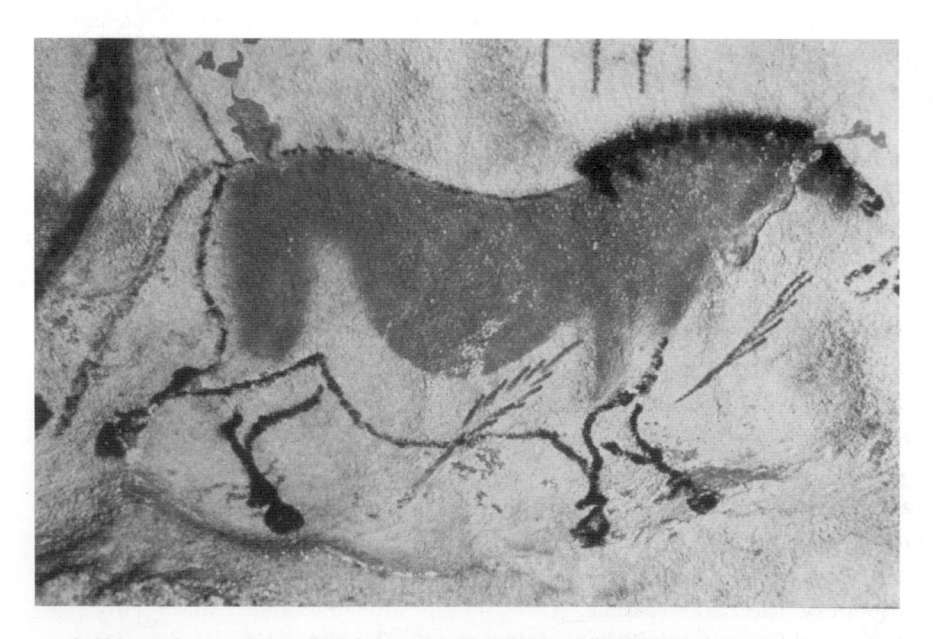

2 Chinese horse, Palaeolithic cave painting, Lascaux Cave, Perigord, Dordogne, France.

In addition, the remarkable anatomical detail of some species is evidence that prehistoric humans had substantial knowledge of certain animals in their environment. Some of the familiarity early humans had with other animals was likely the result of a short flight distance (the point at which the prey will begin to flee) between human hunters and their prey; it is only because of modern weapons that hunted animals have learned to run from a distance.[19] Thus, carnivores are consistently inaccurately represented in Palaeolithic art, probably because they were not easy to observe from short distances, as were herbivores, a more manageable prey. The most common mistake in the representation of carnivores is the incorrect position of the canine teeth (the only teeth ever depicted in carnivore images and usually exaggerated in size) in both bears and felines, with the lower canines depicted in such a way that they would come in contact with the upper canines when the animal's mouth is closed.[20]

Certainly the Chauvet artists had a keen sense of observation and substantial knowledge of animal behaviour as shown in their depictions of animal anatomy, animal-on-animal confrontations and accurate illustrations of the 'social' behaviours of certain species, emphasizing for example the difference between gregarious species such as mammoths, lions and bison and solitary species such as bear and panther.[21] Most of the animals represented in confronted situations are social animals who normally live in families or flocks, and thus their postures are usually interpreted as representative of specific behaviours.[22] For example, a kind of expressive, non-aggressive 'ritual struggle' is read into pictures of bison with raised tails, arched backs and contracted muscles and of wolves with ears upright, mouths open and noses pointed at one another; ritual display is seen in art depicting animals smelling each other; and in 'ornamental composition' animals are drawn in a balanced distribution of bodies, horns, antlers and tusks.[23]

While some animals are drawn galloping, stomping on the ground and leaping, others are depicted motionless, often with turned-up feet and protruding tongues, leading some scholars to the conclusion that the artist's detail of animal anatomy was the result of copying the image directly from animal carcasses.[24] Indeed, many of the animal images in parietal art have been interpreted as representations of dead or dying animals. For example, it has been argued that the curled-up bison on the Altamira ceiling are dead from a forced drive over a cliff.[25] On the other hand, as is often the case, scholars see different things in the same imagery. Randall White argues that in the Palaeolithic cave paintings, animals are rarely depicted in postures of suffering and pain, and 'there is an almost total absence of violence and clear acts of hunting'.[26]

Images of animals in portable art also show how Palaeolithic artists attempted to craft representations of animal behaviours. Three small figures, none longer than 2 cm and each carved from mammoth ivory, were found in 1999 in southwestern Germany: a water bird, the head of a horse and a therianthrope with human and feline characteristics.[27] Considered the oldest representatives of figurative art in the world at an age of about 33,000 years before the present, the figurines were polished from constant handling and were probably cached for later use or deliberately buried.[28] The three-dimensional animal forms were sculpted with remarkable attention to the details of animal behaviour. The bird has an extended neck suggestive of a flying or diving waterfowl, with wings close to the body and back feathers, clearly recognizable eyes and a cone-shaped beak.[29]

The last prehistoric painting ever made (at least the most recently painted piece discovered thus far) was of a horse in France at Le Portel, Ariège, created in 11,600 BC (plus or minus 150 years). With that horse painting more than 20,000 years of parietal art, some argue the most spectacular art tradition ever known by humans, came to an end.[30] It has been argued that cave art ended when social, environmental and economic conditions brought the spirit world from behind the walls of rock shelters to above ground.[31] Bears in particular appear to have had a unique relationship with our Palaeolithic ancestors. In the Chauvet cave, drawings of bears never included their eyes, and while we don't know the significance of that absence, the bear seems to have had an important role in the cave. There are traces of bear everywhere, bear prints and claw marks on the walls and hollows of the cave and many, many bear bones.[32] While humans were likely influenced by the bear's similarity to them in form (in gait, in the ability to stand on the hind feet, in a palm with five digits) and in omnivorous diet, it is also possible that the bear was perceived as a metaphysical link between the human community and the supernatural (or animal) world, as is the bear's role in Eskimo or Inuit cultures.[33]

Steven Mithen writes that the tradition of painting and carving animals disappeared virtually overnight because of global warming. During the cold climate of the Ice Age, groups joined together from time to time for ceremony, ritual, painting and the exchange of important information about the movement of animals. Cave paintings documented crucial hunting information, such as the location and movement of animals, who was living and hunting where and what to do in times of crisis. Thus, cave art, together with mythology and religious rituals, maintained the flow of hunting information, stories of survival for the unpredictability of hard living in a harsh climate.[34] But around 9600 BC the climate grew warmer, and life was not as demanding. Humans lived in small, scattered, self-sufficient groups, and there was no need to know what was happening many miles away. Since hunting could be practised anywhere, at any time and by anyone, there was no longer a need to convey hunting information.[35] The end of cave painting marked a major change in the relationship between humans and other animals.

New Relationships

At about the time we learned how to make tools and build fires for better survival during the cold climate of the last Ice Age, we began to associate with wolves. This association was most likely a hunting partnership, for there is evidence that 120,000 years ago Palaeolithic humans built shelters in caves with the skull of a wolf intentionally placed at the entrance. Juliet Clutton-Brock's description of hunting in the Palaeolithic era helps us understand the role of wolves in that important activity of humans and other animals.[36] She writes that Palaeolithic hunters in the northern hemisphere lived much like wolves, and both humans and wolves evolved as social hunters preying on the same large mammals. Humans began to reduce both the numbers and the diversity of large mammal species with the employment of wasteful hunting practices and the promotion of fire. While the wolf had been around the northern hemisphere for nearly a million years living in a balanced ecosystem in which they killed the weak, sick, old or young animals in the prey populations, Palaeolithic humans killed randomly, slaughtering more animals than were needed for survival, and by the end of the last Ice Age many large mammal species had become extinct. No longer did humans deploy confronted hunting techniques to kill the horses, bison and reindeer they used for food; now they deployed wolves, and later dogs, in cooperative hunting strategies capable of the ambush and slaughter of entire herds of animals (see illus. 3).

Thus, environmental changes, over-hunting and wasteful hunting created conditions such that by the end of the last Ice Age many megafauna species were extinct. Gone were the kangaroos, giant wombats, large ground sloths, the mammoth, the mastodon, the cave bear and rhinoceros in Europe, the horse in the Americas, the pigmy elephant and hippopotamus in the Mediterranean islands and the marsupial lion in Australia.[37]

The transition from hunting wild animals to herding tame ones was yet another important milestone in our new relationship with animals; as Juliet Clutton-Brock notes, animal ownership is the characteristic that separates hunting from herding. While it is unknown whether animals were herded or managed for food by Palaeolithic and Mesolithic humans, some scholars argue that there is evidence from depictions of horses with harnesses in portable art that the horse may have been domesticated in the Upper Palaeolithic.[38] Further, horse teeth have been found in Palaeolithic sites that appear to have been worn down from crib-biting, a restless habit that confined horses have of gnawing on their wooden enclosures.[39] On the evidence of the bone fragments and teeth of food animals uncovered by archeological excavation, it is believed that early Neolithic farmers were selectively breeding some animals, particularly those that were submissive, small, hardy and easy to feed.[40]

The introduction of animals into human culture as companions was another major change in the prehistoric human–animal relationship. Our first domesticated companion was probably the wolf, not as a source of food, but rather an animal brought into the human group, not only as a hunting aid as I mention above, but also a recipient of affection, and/or a useful forager of human debris.[41] Evidence that wolves had evolved into domesticated companion species by the Late Palaeolithic (early Natufian, about 12,300–10,800 BC) is found in the excavation of burial sites. One site uncovered a puppy curled up by the head of an elderly woman whose left hand rested on the canine's body, and at another site three humans and two canines were found carefully arranged together in a grave.[42] According to Clutton-Brock, the puppy burial is the earliest cultural evidence for the presence of a domesticated canine, although it is unknown whether the animal was a wolf, dog or jackal – the bones were in fragments and the animal was very young.[43] It can be assumed, however, that the animal was

3 Cooperative hunting of wild animals, rock painting,
Sahara, *c.* 8000 BC.

tamed and highly valued by the hunter-gatherers who lived in stone houses at that Natufian site 12,000 years ago.

It is almost certain that Late Palaeolithic humans brought young off-spring of slaughtered animals into the social group, perhaps feeding, nursing and playing with them.[44] It is common for humans to adopt orphaned or abandoned young of other species.[45] Early Neolithic humans kept animals tethered at the entrance of camps, and these animals were likely used as hunting decoys or perhaps even as status symbols.[46] And there is clear archeological evidence that some species of wild animals were tamed as early as 6000 BC. For example, a pair of mandibular bones from a brown bear was excavated from a rock shelter in France. The jaw bones show a perfectly symmetrical deformation of the bone and teeth, with no pathological features, and suggests that a thong or rope was placed around the bottom jaw when the animal was very young, and the mandible then grew around the rope as the bear matured.[47]

Animal body parts were commonly used for decoration, display and ritual. Evidence from portable art tells us much about the use of animal body parts, primarily bones and teeth, as decoration during prehistory. Bahn and Vertut provide a good summary of the archeological evidence.[48] They write that 110,000 years ago humans bored holes through the top of a wolf foot bone and a swan vertebra; 100,000 years ago humans carved and polished an ornament using a mammoth tooth; and more recently, about 43,000 years ago, pendants were made from perforated animal teeth, primarily incisors from bovines and canines from fox, stag, lion or bear. Canine teeth were very popular decorations during the Magdalenian period (15,000–8000 BC), and some bear canines were engraved with animal images, such as fish and seals.

One interesting technique used by Palaeolithic artists to make jewellery was to saw through the roots of the teeth while still intact in the animal's mouth, then cut them as a group from the jaw, a strip of gum holding the teeth together like a string of pearls.[49] Antlers were made into ibex head pendants and spearthrowers which were often decorated with leaping horses carved in relief along the shaft. Most figurines were carved from stone or ivory since carving in hard bone is very difficult, and imitations of stag canines were often made from ivory, bone or stone. Mammoth ivory was used for statuettes, beads, bracelets and armlets. Bahn and Vertut propose that early humans may have attached a mystical role to carvings or engravings on material that was once alive, particularly antler, which is impressive in its continual growth and annual shedding.[50]

As in the cave paintings, there is no relationship between the animals sculpted and those in the diet of these Late Palaeolithic artists.[51] This corroborates the widely held assertion that prehistoric animal representations are not a roster of hunted prey. Not all of the Palaeolithic portable art was carved into ivory, bone or stone. The first ceramic technology was developed 26,000 years ago (about 15,000 years before the development of agriculture), the first fired objects were of animals (mostly carnivores) and women, and it appears that a large number of the figurines were made in a purposeful ritual.[52]

Finally, just as images of animals most likely had a ritualized role in the cave art, actual animals were used in ritual and ceremony in prehistory. Excavations of 100,000-year-old burial sites show that humans were buried with animal body parts, such as the deer head and antlers placed on top of a child's body and a male with the jaw of a wild boar clutched in his hands.[53] And 60,000 years later, in the Chauvet cave, a bear skull was placed on purpose on the flat surface of a block that had fallen from the ceiling on to the centre of the chamber, another bear skull was marked with black lines, two cheek teeth were placed into small hollows in a large calcite block, and two animal forelimb bones appear to have been driven into the floor close to the cave entrance, although it is not known if by humans or by water or mud which flooded the cave from time to time.[54]

While for the first few million years of human history we made only utilitarian tools, around 40,000 years ago a cultural revolution occurred and we took up painting, engraving, sculpting, wearing jewellery and making musical instruments.[55] It is significant that the vast majority of the image-making in these early years of our prehistory was representations of animals. As John Berger notes, the first symbols for humankind were animals, the first paint was probably animal blood and for millennia the human experience of the world was charted using animal signs.[56] This reverence for animals continued for as long as humans held nature to be sacred and kept to an agrarian way of life. We see in the next chapter that both of these characteristics of human societies changed radically beginning around 5000 BC, and so also did the ways humans looked at animals.

Chapter 2

Antiquity, 5000 BC–AD 500

As we move into the earliest known civilizations to pursue the story of animals in human history, we turn our gaze to bulls. Bulls were important in prehistoric times as well – recall the overwhelming presence of bovines in cave art, a presence that accounted for almost one-third of all species represented. Archeological evidence of cattle worship in early history comes from the discovery of a cattle shrine at Çatal Hüyük, one of the first true cities that flourished around 6000 BC in the area of present-day Turkey. The shrine had horns set in clay along the side of a bench-like platform, suggesting that cattle played a ritual and ceremonial role in the Çatal Hüyük culture and that horns were associated with fertility and human figures.[1] Much of the connection humans had with other animals was realized in the process of domestication and the development of agriculture, such as the revolutionary lifestyle changes that came about for the hunter-gatherers of the Mediterranean when they began to keep goats instead of exclusively hunting wild animals.[2] But certain animals played a particularly important role in the human perception of creation, birth, life and death, and no species was so critical to human civilization as cattle.[3] The bull was the most powerful image in the art of the third millennium BC throughout most of the world, including Mesopotamia, Egypt, Anatolia, the Gulf and the Caucasus, western Central Asia and the Indus Valley.[4] There was a profound identification between the bovine and human species during antiquity, and wild bulls (large, strong, brave and libidinous) were models for male power and fertility, particularly for chiefs and early kings.[5]

Hitching the ox to the plough in 4500 BC was the first source of animal power (other than human muscle) for food production, and with that innovation it was possible to develop a surplus system that not only produced food but also a leisure class and a clearly marked social division of labour.[6] Ownership of cattle quickly became a marker of wealth. Calvin Schwabe writes that the word *chattel* is related to cattle, *capital* originally referred to head of cattle, and in Sanskrit 'to fight' meant 'to raid for cattle' and 'leader' meant 'lord of cattle'.[7] Even the origins of modern English financial terms are cattle-driven, such as stock, stock market and watered stock. Writing evolved out of the need to record cattle wealth, and the first symbol for the things to be counted as wealth was the horned bovine head (*capital*), the first letter in alphabetic writing systems and drawn in cuneiform as an upside-down triangle, on its side with curved horns as in the Greek α and in English on its back as A.[8] In Egypt during the Old Kingdom (2649–2134 BC) the official count of domestic cattle was the basis for dating the years of a king's reign.[9] Thus the bovine's importance had as much to do with fertility as it did with the strength to carry heavy burdens and pull ploughs. It therefore comes as no surprise that by the time of the rise of the ancient Sumerian civilization, the bull not only maintained his dominance in the representation of animals in pictorial art but also took centre stage in human narrative art.

Untamed Nature, Cities and War

With the creation of cities, the accumulation of wealth, increased trading and fighting, powerful animals and untamed nature began to be used to symbolize struggle, violence and war. Human representations of animals assumed a motif that emphasized animals as wild, ferocious, strong and symbolic of warring kingdoms.[10] The earliest examples of this view of animals were carved into stone cylinder seals around 3500 BC in Mesopotamia. Used to secure and record valuable materials inside containers (and, if pierced from end to end, worn on a string as decorative jewellery) these small cylinder seals are the only visual records we have of life in very ancient Mesopotamia. (We know much more about Egyptian art than Mesopotamian art because of the absence of stone to quarry in the Mesopotamian valley.[11]) Thus, cylinder seals provide an important record of Mesopotamian art for about 3,000 years and illustrate the increasing development of the perception of animals, particularly bulls, as linked to struggle, strife and victory in war.[12] Designs were engraved on the outside of the stone and an impression was taken when the stone cylinder was rolled in clay providing a continuous pattern in relief.

According to Francis Klingender, the animal images on the cylinder seals fall into three major categories:[13] (1) a symmetrical frieze in which animals are depicted moving single file in one direction; sometimes for balance two files are shown, each moving in opposite directions, one placed above the other, (2) pairs of animals and/or humans are shown in confrontation, such as the depiction of a nude hero and a bull man fighting with rampant bulls, and (3) a continuous frieze of fighting animals, often lions and other predators attacking cattle, with humans defending flocks of domesticated animals. Illus. 4 is a photograph of a

4 Sumerian stone cylinder seal depicting a continuous fight between men, beasts and a centaur, and impression made by the seal on a clay tablet, Ur, undated.

stone cylinder seal from the Sumerian city of Ur (shown on the left) and the impression the seal made when rolled in clay (on the right). The image produced is one of a continuous fight between man, beast and a therianthropic (half-man/half-beast) form. This image is also a good example of how Mesopotamian artists depicted animals in scenes reflecting the ongoing cycles of battle between the uncivilized and civilized, the wild and the tame, the unknown and the known.[14]

Along with the angular and symmetrical depictions on the cylinder seals, animals were also represented in a naturalistic style that provided details of both their physical and behavioural characteristics. As early as 2600 BC and apparently based on first-hand observations, Mesopotamian artists were creating lifelike, naturalistic sculptures of animals. Donald Hansen writes that they used skills that gave substance to individual species, such as using lapis lazuli and shell for eye inlays to give the impression of vitality and life.[15] Many animals are shown as part of larger compositions, including lions, hyena, jackal, bear and wild ass. Importantly, animal behaviours are also represented, such as constraint through harnessing and the depiction of free movement from a series of animal depictions that progress from walking to cantering to a full gallop. Some of the most widely known artefacts of the period come from royal tombs and burial sites, including elaborately decorated sculptures and musical instruments adorned with magnificent wood-core bull heads.

One famous animal representation is a sculpture of a rearing male goat with his front legs resting on the branches of a budding plant (see illus. 5).

The sculpture is also frequently referred to as 'Ram Caught in a Thicket' based on the biblical story of Abraham's discovery of a ram caught by the horns in a thicket whom Abraham disengaged and then sacrificed instead of his son. But in fact the animal depicted in the sculpture is not a ram but a goat, although he was originally 'caught' – his forelegs had been tied to the plant with a silver chain. The sculpture is believed to represent the Sumerian concern with the fertility of plants and animals.[16] The goat's rearing stance has multiple interpretations. First, the goat is very successful at reproduction, second only to the bull, and the rearing-up stance he adopts in the statue is also the position he assumes for sex. Second, the rearing-up stance has been interpreted as climbing the tree, a reflection of the goat's ability to climb trees

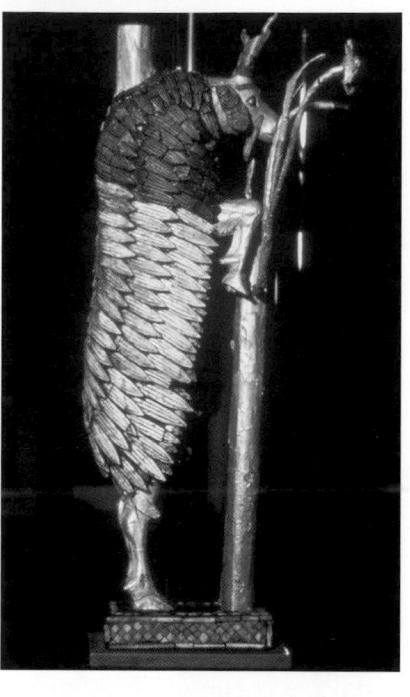

5 Male goat with his front legs resting against the branches of a budding tree, Sumerian, Ur, *c.* 2600 BC.

to feed on hard-to-reach leaves.[17] There were two statues of the rearing goat uncovered from the Ur tombs, both badly crushed and eventually reconstructed. While the gender of one of the goat statues is unknown because of damage to the underside of the body, the statue preserved at the British Museum is clearly male, with a penis sheath and gold-covered testicles.[18]

Some of the best known artefacts from the period are musical instruments decorated with elaborately modelled bull heads. Illus. 6 shows a portion of a bull head harp from Sumerian Ur that dates to about 2800 BC. Another famous harp was found in the tomb of Queen Puabi at Ur and dates to about 2600 BC. The later bull head was constructed of precious materials: most of the head and horns are made of gold sheet worked over a wooden core, the eyeballs are shell insets, the pupils, eyelids and layered tufts of hair are made of lapis lazuli (a deep-blue-coloured mineral), as is the magnificent beard of twelve locks ending in tight curls.[19] Under the bull head the instruments often had a series of panels depicting confrontational (or 'heraldic') scenes of intertwined heroic humans and animals, human-headed bulls and animals performing human behaviours such as playing musical instruments.

The depiction of confrontation between animals, again usually bulls, and between animals and men was common in Mesopotamian art. Much of this art was thought to represent the struggle between Gilgamesh and Enkidu, the main characters of the first epic poem ever written. While early versions of the story date to about 2100 BC, the best preserved were inscribed on eleven clay tablets around 1700 BC in Babylonia.[20] The poem tells the story of a friendship between a king, Gilgamesh, and a beast-(bull)-man, Enkidu. Gilgamesh befriends Enkidu, a naked wild man who has been civilized by having erotic relations with a woman, but whose animal qualities are endearing:

6 Bull's head carved on a harp, Sumerian, Ur, *c.* 2800 BC.

he is peaceful, wandering with the herds from pasture to pasture, driving away predators and freeing his friends from the pits and traps set by humans. While the 'beast-hero' motif in Mesopotamian pictorial art does not convey friendship, but rather violent confrontation between men and animals, particularly between heroes and bulls, the ancients documented many peaceful scenes of domestication and friendship between humans and animals.[21]

Domestication

Ancient limestone carvings are excellent illustrations of the human affection for domesticated animals in antiquity, particularly the Egyptians' fondness for cattle. The Egyptian word *ka* refers at the same time to man's 'animating principle', man's 'double', and 'bovine animal', and when drawn in hieroglyphic form as human arms raised overhead in imitation of the horns of a bull, the symbol suggests a bond between individual men and individual bulls.[22] There are numerous Egyptian images of nurturing and bonding among cattle, such as mother cows gazing at or licking their

7 Cattle fording a river with, on the right, a calf being carried on the back
of a herdsman, Egyptian limestone relief from the Tomb of Ti,
c. 2400 BC.

calves, and also of humans caring for bovines. For example, illus. 7 shows
some cattle being driven across a river, with one of the young animals
glancing back at mother for reassurance while being carried over the
water on a cowherd's back. Illus. 8 is another common image from antiquity that shows a calf carried protectively on the shoulders of a human
(perhaps on a journey to a sacrifice).

Animals are often represented in typical situations, such as donkeys
walking across the threshing floor or cattle grazing under trees, scenes
that document life cycle events and the daily routine of country life in
ancient Egypt.[23] Egyptians often depicted domesticated animals in groups,
and as accomplished artists they were capable of depicting remarkably
realistic plants and animals. Illus. 9 is a good example. This limestone
carving of cattle grazing under trees gives the illusion of the movement of
cattle while foraging and of the leaves overhead rustling in the wind. Some

8 Calf being carried around the
neck of a human bearer,
Egyptian, Middle Archaic,
c. 575 BC.

details of nature were drawn with such accuracy that zoologists can still recognize the species of birds and fish drawn by these ancient artists.[24] The scene in illus. 10 is a standard representation of agriculture in Egypt. A donkey (with wounds on his rump from the stick wielded by the driver pushing him on)[25] carries grain, humans carry storage baskets up to the silos and antelopes feed from mangers.

By 2500 BC domesticated donkeys and horses were commonly used for riding, carrying loads and drawing carts, sleds and chariots.[26] Cattle were used as draught animals as well, and bulls provided substantial animal power once domesticated and controlled through nose-ringing, cutting off the sharp tips (or all) of the horns and of course castration.[27] Tomb art from 2400 BC shows long-horned cattle utilized in Egyptian agriculture to pull wooden scratch ploughs, with the plough attached to their horns with a rope. By 1400 BC oxen were being used for a variety of draught tasks. They pulled carts filled with supplies to support military and quarrying expeditions; they pulled wagons filled with foreign visitors such as Syrians and women and children from foreign lands, and in one case a Nubian princess; they even pulled huge blocks of limestone on a wooden sled-like platform probably for building construction.[28]

Much like yoking the ox to the plough, mounting and riding horses brought about major social and cultural transformations. The horse's centrality to human life moved from being a primary food source in prehistory to the primary means of transport in antiquity. The horse was a source of speed and stamina for the rulers of

9 The Voyage to Punt: a herd of cattle grazing under trees, coloured limestone relief, from the Temple of Queen Hatshepsut (Maat Ka-Re) (1495–1475 BC) in Deir el-Bahri. 18th Dynasty (1554–1305 BC), New Kingdom.

cattle-rich city-states that not only surpassed the 'powerful but plodding cattle' but also provided a way to engage in long-distance trade and the conquest of foreign lands; the horse became as important to the developing city-states as the cattle had been to the creation of civilization in the early years of antiquity.[29]

Just as cattle conferred wealth on the people of the earliest civilizations, the horse became a symbol of status and wealth. The upper classes were referred to by names representing horse ownership, such as the *hippeis* in Athens and the *equites* in Rome.[30] Juliet Clutton-Brock describes the history of the horse as transport in antiquity and what is known about the use of that essential horse-riding equipment, the stirrup.[31] There is pictorial evidence that the hunters, warriors and kings of ancient Egypt, Mesopotamia and Greece rode about in chariots harnessed to small, stocky horses (harnessed in such a way that the horses' heads were pulled

10 A donkey shares with humans the labour of carrying baskets of grain,
while antelopes feed from mangers, wall painting from the Tomb of Ity,
Gebelein, Egypt, *c.* 2181 BC.

back and the neck strongly arched). But in the northern area of Scythia,
large horses were common and, according to Clutton-Brock, the Scythians
didn't use chariots but apparently rode astride their horses with the assistance of stirrups, as shown by the horsemen carved on an ornamental gold
torque that dates from the fourth century BC. The Scythians' use of a metal
hook attached to the saddle by a metal chain did not spread quickly and
not at all to the southern area of Greece, since stirrups are never represented in the visual art of the time, nor were they described by the ancient
historians, as Clutton-Brock notes: 'Xenophon would certainly have
written about stirrups if he had ever seen them'.[32]

The history of the stirrup is voluminous and beyond the scope of this
overview. But a few interesting aspects are worth mentioning here. While
Alexander the Great (356–323 BC) learned much about horsemanship in
Scythia, he never used stirrups, nor did Julius Caesar, a fact that might
explain why the cavalry was never very central to Roman military endeavours.[33] It is widely believed that stirrups were first used by the Chinese and
mentioned in narrative accounts only in 477 AD, and it took another three
centuries for stirrups to reach western Europe, arriving there in the eighth
century.[34] Thus, the history of the horse's use in battle is divided into three
periods: the charioteer, the mounted warrior who adheres to his horse
with his thighs and knees and the horseman equipped with stirrups, with

each improvement in the military use of the horse linked to dramatic social and cultural changes in human history.[35]

By 1900 BC selective breeding of animals, such as dogs, cattle and sheep, was well under way in both Babylonia and Egypt.[36] Dogs, for example, are depicted in many shapes and sizes in ancient Egyptian art – large hunting dogs that resemble the contemporary mastiff and slim dogs that appear similar to greyhounds, suggesting that these two canine breeds have continued relatively unchanged for 4,000 years.[37]

While artists continued to depict animals in outdoor settings in a variety of activities (such as harvesting, ploughing, fishing and hunting) well into the New Kingdom (1550–1070 BC), internal domestic scenes became increasingly popular, providing substantial visual evidence that Egyptians were fond of living with animals. The abused donkey in illus. 10 notwith-standing, most of the early Egyptian representations of animals reflect their affection for a wide variety of species. According to legend, Cambyses, a Persian king, was able to conquer Egypt in 525 BC by posi-tioning in front of his advancing army animals revered by the Egyptians, such as dogs, cats and ibises; fearing that harm would come to one of the advancing animals, the Egyptians stopped their defensive strategies and Cambyses's victory was won.[38] In her book on ancient Egyptian animal imagery, Dorothy Phillips writes that Egyptian artists drew pictures of dogs wearing wide collars that proudly announced the animal's name (such as 'Town Dog'). They also made toys in the shape of animals such as an ivory dog whose lower jaw could be moved by a lever, and they painted house-hold scenes depicting monkeys and cats teasing and playing with other household pets.

It well known that cats were among the most sacred of animals in ancient Egypt. The story recounted above of Cambyses's triumph has been retold as one in which each Persian soldier held a cat aloft as the army advanced into Egypt.[39] While the earliest visual evidence of cat domestication in Egypt is around 1600 BC, cats were probably tamed and lived with humans much earlier.[40] According to Herodotus (484–425 BC) it was forbidden to kill a cat, and if one died of natural causes members of the household were required to shave their eyebrows. Some cat-killings did take place and probably for sacred reasons. For example, close examination of mummi-fied cats at the Natural History Museum revealed that many were young and had been deliberately killed by having their necks broken, perhaps so that they could be sold as votive offerings.[41] A wide variety of animals were mummified in ancient Egypt – bulls and huge numbers of cats and birds. At the end of the nineteenth century, shiploads of cat mummies were sent to England to be ground into fertilizer, and miles of tunnels at Saqqara were carved with thousands of niches, each containing a mummified bird.[42]

As the Egyptians began to illustrate domestic scenes that embraced animals, so also did artists in Minoan Crete decorate mansions with gay frescoes, coloured reliefs and vase art illustrating a keen observation of animals. Cretan palaces were open, unfortified (Cretan naval fleets could repel any attack on the island), bathed in sunlight and adorned with frescoes reflecting a wonderful world of colour, refinement and graceful movement.[43] Minoans were particularly fond of sea creatures, and the beautiful dolphin fresco from the Palace of Knossos in Crete (illus. 11) is an excellent example of their artistic talent in depicting the graceful movement of animals of the sea.

Animals in ancient Greek art were often shown in such lifelike representations that one can readily discern the animal's emotional state. Some animals were cast as decidedly unbeautiful, sick or deformed, such as the famous sculpture of a sick greyhound carved in marble around 200 BC.[44] The dog's pain and discomfort is conveyed very well by his facial expression, the awkward position of his body and his lowered head. Another good example of realistic expression of emotion in the depiction of animals is a horse and jockey sculpture that dates to about 140 BC (see illus. 12). This bronze statue of a galloping horse ridden by a young jockey

11 Dolphins and other fish depicted on a Minoan fresco, Knossos, *c.* 1500 BC.

12 Leaping horse ridden by a young jockey, bronze statue, *c.* 140 BC.
Archaeological Museum, Athens.

emphasizes movement in the horse's flexed muscles and the front hooves
raised off the ground, and on the horse's face we see passion and perhaps
agony in the marked contractions of the cheek muscles, laid-back ears,
wide eyes, flaring nostrils and open mouth. This is a horse that is being
ridden hard and fast by the young jockey sitting astride him, cast as if
holding reins in the left hand and a whip in the right.

The Greeks sculpted many beautiful animal images in marble and stone,
primarily as tomb adornments. Most of the images are partnered with
humans (who are often cast as gods or goddesses): animals sleep alongside
children, dogs gaze lovingly up at their human companions and birds and
hares are carried about. Birds appear to have been particularly important
to the ancients as childhood companions, or perhaps as toys – there are

numerous statues of children holding a bird in one hand and of adults offering birds to children. Along with the animal representations in domestic scenes, there are also numerous images of animal violence and death: bulls and rams being led to sacrifice, lions attacking sheep, and children holding dead pigs and goats aloft for display after the kill.

Domesticated animals were frequently deployed as weapons, equipment and decoys in ancient wars. The Greeks often used elephants as war equipment. Intended primarily to terrify the enemy, elephants were elaborately decorated with ornaments, such as headpieces and clanging bells and occasionally given fermented wine to drink, thus encouraging ferocious behaviour.[45] The use of elephants on the front lines was probably more a display of strength than of their practical use as a war animal. Elephants are not effective in fighting human wars; if bombarded by arrows, an elephant will simply turn around and retreat, often inflicting more damage on his own army than on the enemy.[46] Further, a female elephant will refuse to fight if separated from her young, and she would immediately abandon all military duties and rush to the rescue if her offspring squealed when wounded or trampled upon.[47]

While the Greeks used elephants for display in war, the Romans exploited elephants in public shows and entertainment, taking pleasure in publicly humiliating the animals they considered unfaithful and untrustworthy because of their tendency to depend on instincts in stressful situations.[48] Other species were used as war equipment in antiquity. In 217 BC, strategizing a way to bypass Roman resistance to his march through a guarded area, Hannibal had his troops tie bundles of sticks to the horns of 2,000 bovines captured during the Carthaginians' trek through Italy.[49] Come nightfall they set fire to the 2,000 bundles and herded the cattle toward the enemy. As the animals moved on, the surrounding trees and bushes caught fire from the burning bundles, and when the fire reached the heads and ears of the animals, they began to panic and run wildly about. While the Romans were busy dealing with the assault of fire and animals running berserk, Hannibal and the Carthaginians sneaked past the enemy and continued their march through enemy territory.

Hunting

During the New Kingdom (1550–1070 BC), Egyptian art motifs became increasing varied, often representing personal aspects of the lives of important or wealthy individuals, such as tomb paintings that included imagery celebrating the status of the tomb's owner.[50] Many of these visual representations were devoted to hunting, with the animal prey symbolic of the human enemy. The palace of King Ashurbanipal (sometimes spelled Assurbanipal) at Nineveh provides elegant illustrations of royal conquests and valour in depictions that show kings hunting wild beasts as if on a battlefield around 650 BC. Typical scenes in the chronicles are gruesome pictures of animal slaughter, with lions leaping at the king's chariot, vomiting blood and dragging their wounded bodies across the battlefield. Noting that these picture chronicles are good examples of the Mesopotamians' skill at boasting and propaganda, E. H. Gombrich writes that in their glorification of ancient campaigns, the monuments suggest that 'war is no trouble at all . . . the enemy is scattered like chaff in the wind'.[51]

Hunting in antiquity has often been closely linked to battle by scholars of the ancient world. An association between hunting and war is depicted in the visual representations of hunting in the southern Greek societies of Mycenae[52] and Sparta.[53] And in a study of 121 examples of non-mythological boar and deer hunts depicted on Greek vases painted between 600 and 425 BC, one scholar concluded that, as an activity of the wealthy that asserted social dominance and elite interests, hunting in ancient Greece was a rite of passage to adulthood, prepared elite youths for warfare and civic responsibilities and was often linked with athletics such as boxing which helped to train warriors.[54]

Ancient hunting is also associated with political upheaval and sexuality. Hunting iconography increased as official power decreased during the rise of democracy in Athens when the aristocrats' rule was in peril, and depictions of hunting in Greek vase painting were visual metaphors for sexual courtship, particularly pederastic relationships.[55] It is possible that hunting representations declined because they were appropriated by the non-elite, reducing the appeal of the imagery for the aristocrats.[56]

When animals and humans are shown in hunting and other scenes of struggle, animal suffering and death is often depicted alongside human serenity, as in illus. 13. Hunting in antiquity was also a spectator sport and used captive and trapped animals as prey. Indeed, as early as 2446 BC, hunting in Egypt often occurred in confined areas, and royal hunters slaughtered wild animals driven to the site and corralled by attendants.[57] The stone reliefs from King Ashurbanipal's palace discussed above are spectacular illustrations of ancient hunting as a public exhibition. As early as 859 BC the Assyrians built large animal parks to enclose free-roaming lions and gazelle, and Egyptian art often depicted wild gazelle being lassoed or hunted in the desert.[58] When the king wanted to hunt, he would hide in a pit while his assistants released the animals from wooden cages with sliding doors. The assistants would drive the animal toward the hiding king who

13 A lion trapped by hunters wielding swords, pebble mosaic,
Macedonia, *c.* 300 BC.

simply waited for the animal to come close enough to be killed. Meanwhile, crowds of people watched the hunt from the sidelines. The hunt was not only a spectator sport for the public, it was also a public display of the king's power.[59] Some rulers employed particularly cruel hunting methods, such as Domitian, a Roman emperor in the first century AD, who was described by the Roman biographer, Suetonius:

> He was incapable of exertion and seldom went about the city on foot, while on his campaigns and journeys he rarely rode on horseback, but was regularly carried in a litter. He took no interest in arms, but was particularly devoted to archery. There are many who have more than once seen him slay a hundred wild beasts of different kinds on his Alban estate, and purposely kill some of them with two successive shots in such a way that the arrows gave the effect of horns.[60]

Wild animals were often kept in enclosed areas in antiquity. Large walled-off areas called 'paradise parks' kept animals for royal hunts, processionals and to accommodate gift animals from foreign leaders. Early empires such as Assyria, Babylonia and Egypt had such parks, and the idea of a royal 'paradise' which served as a model for the Garden of Eden continued in the West until the end of the Roman Empire and in China until the 1800s.[61] Paradise parks were usually situated close to landowners' estates so that owners could hunt whenever they wished and so the animals could be easily observed. In one ancient account the estate staff trained animals to appear at a certain location for food, delighting the owner and his guests as they observed the animals' feeding activities from the dining room:

. . . a trumpet was sounded at regular hours and you saw boars and wild goats come for their food . . . at Hortensius's place at Laurentum, I saw the thing done more in the manner of the Thracian bard . . . as we were banqueting, Hortensius ordered Orpheus to be summoned. He came complete with robe and lute, and was bidden to sing. Thereupon he blew a trumpet, and such a multitude of stags and boars and other four-footed beasts came flooding round us that the sight seemed as beautiful to me as the hunts staged . . . in the Circus Maximus – at least, the ones without African beasts.[62]

While in myth Orpheus was able to civilize and pacify wild animals with his music (see illus. 14), the overall purpose of the training was to make the animals easy to kill.[63] Thus, argues Shelton, the rural hunts were carefully staged events; Roman hunters simply waited for the animals to assemble for their regular feeding, with the kill rather than the pursuit providing the thrill of the hunt. The countryside park hunts and the infamous Roman arena hunts were similar in that they both provided the opportunity to see wild animals destroyed by humans, affirming the superiority of culture over nature.[64]

14 Orpheus charming the animals with his lyre, Roman mosaic
from Blazny, fourth century AD. Musée Municipal,
Lacon, France.

Slaughter as Spectacle

For more than 450 years (according to public records, beginning in 186 BC and ending in 281 AD) the public slaughter of animals (and humans) was a celebrated form of Roman entertainment. Public slaughter events were so popular and so widespread that there were few Roman cities that did not provide such entertainment.[65] As patrons of the Roman social hierarchy, emperors sponsored lavish and exotic spectacles to please the public and ensure their own popularity with the Roman people. While associated with a form of emperor worship, the shows provided the opportunity for public participation in Rome, and Cicero noted that the wishes of the Roman people were expressed in three places: public assemblies, elections and plays or gladiatorial shows.[66] Keith Hopkins writes that as citizen participation in politics declined under emperor rule, the arena shows and games provided opportunities for regular meetings between emperors and the masses. Rome was unique among the large empires of antiquity in allowing the dramatic confrontation of the rulers and the ruled, and the amphitheatre was the people's parliament.[67] With several months of every year devoted to celebrations, Rome had many festivals lasting several days at an interval, and the emperor and the public spent about a third of their time together as spectators at the shows.[68] The shows became a political arena, a place where, face to face with their emperor, the Roman crowd could honour him, or demand that he grant them pleasures, or let him know of their political demands. When the crowd applauded the show it was a celebration of the emperor; when they booed, they berated him.[69]

Roman spectacles of slaughter have long captured the attention of scholars, generating numerous theories to account for the public killing of exotic animals. It has been argued that animals were publicly slaughtered in Rome to establish a sense of control over the strange and the spectacular,[70] to display exotic animals as the novel booty of foreign exploits,[71] to legitimately kill less powerful beings,[72] to prove wealth by destroying exotic and expensive animals,[73] to fulfil a desire to watch animals by combining the pleasure of killing and torture with the pleasure of watching the swift and spirited activity of wild beasts,[74] and to promote the spread of agriculture by reducing the number of crop-destroying animals.[75]

In fact, the Romans had a tradition of killing large numbers of wild animals in public spectacles long before the arena slaughters, particularly in rural areas where predators of livestock and agricultural pests were killed in public spectacles and festivals. According to Alison Futrell, animals were used in rituals as both sacrificial victims and as active participants in Roman festivals and holidays, such as the *Ludi Taurei*, the *Cerialia* and the *Floralia*.[76] During the *Ludi Taurei*, bulls were released and hunted, some of whom may have been set on fire; the *Cerialia* was an event that honoured the goddess of Italian agriculture and during which foxes were set loose with flaming torches tied to their backs; and in the *Floralia*, hares and roebucks were hunted in commemoration of greater control over gardens and cultivated lands.

In addition, the animal shows in urban Rome had their beginnings in rural hunts, a leisure activity of wealthy men. Jo-Ann Shelton writes that the spectacles were staged in part to earn the votes of urban citizens who had neither the opportunity nor the financial means to hunt. In this way, men desiring political office brought the experience of hunting to the urban areas so that all could participate in the sport, at least as spectators.[77] In the Roman arena, actual hunting experiences were recreated in the deployment of hunters and weapons, the construction of natural, wooded scenery and the resistance of dangerous and wild animals to the chase.[78] According to Shelton, the Latin word *venatio* eventually took on a double meaning – the hunting of animals in a rural area and the urban spectacle of killing animals in public.[79]

Most of what we know about the Roman displays of animal slaughter is derived from ancient narrative accounts. Surviving documents record the number of animals killed (3,500 during the reign of Augustus; 9,000 during the reign of Titus; 11,000 butchered by Trajan to celebrate a war victory). Other records detail the elaborate construction of arena scenery to simulate the animals' natural habitat, details of ingenious technological apparatus capable of elevating animals or humans into the air and descriptions of the reluctance of some animals to fight in the arena.[80] For example, the record of the last animal show in AD 281 documents that 100 maned lions were slaughtered at the doors of their cages because they refused to leave.[81]

Curiously, there are no records to account for how the Romans disposed of the thousands upon thousands of dead animals after their slaughter. We know that the carcasses were removed from the arena through the Doors of the Dead which were situated under the seating area of the ruling elite.[82] Donald Kyle speculates that the disposal of many thousands of corpses and carcasses over hundreds of years must have been extremely important to the Romans in efforts to avoid pollution. While fire was not an efficient means of disposal, some bodies were probably thrown into the River Tiber, some unclaimed corpses of social marginals and other outcasts were probably dumped in a field and exposed to dogs and birds, and some of the animals slaughtered in arena combat were probably eaten by the Roman people: thus, Kyle notes, '[i]f the games led to distribution of meat, the emperor/patron as a master hunter was providing game as well as games for his people'.[83]

While the disposal of dead animals is the subject of much speculation, we know quite a bit about the capture and arrival of living animals destined for combat in the arena. There are numerous descriptions of the hunt and seizure of wild animals and their transport to Rome. Some of these details are embedded in mythological narratives, such as the goddess Diana's collection of animals for the amusement of the Romans:[84]

> Whatsoever inspires fear with its teeth, wonder with its mane, awe with its horns and bristling coat – all the beauty, all the terror of the forest is taken. Guile protects them not; neither strength nor weight avails them; their speed saves not the fleet of foot. Some roar enmeshed in snares; some are thrust into wooden cages and carried off. There are not carpenters enough to fashion the wood; leafy prisons are constructed of unhewn beech and ash. Boats laden with some of the animals traverse seas and rivers; bloodless from terror the rower's hand is stayed, for the sailor fears the merchandise he carries. Others are transported over land in wagons that block the roads with the long procession, bearing the spoils of the mountains. The wild beast is borne a captive by those troubled cattle on whom in times past he sated his hunger, and each time that the oxen turned and looked at their burden they pull away in terror from the pole.[85]

In an examination of the correspondence of some notable authors of the time, George Jennison describes how wild animals were captured and conveyed to Rome for the shows.[86] Imperial officials charged with obtaining animals for the arena probably hired professional hunters, and soldiers were likely also deployed to capture animals since hunting was considered good training for war. The two main methods for capturing large wild animals were the pit and the net. The pit method consisted of driving a pillar into the middle of an excavated hole, on the top of which was fastened an animal (usually a kid, lamb or puppy) in such a way as to make him howl from pain, thus the lion or leopard would be attracted by the decoy's vocal struggle. A wall or fence was erected around the pit so that as the predator ran up to snatch the prey, he would not see the pit and in jumping to reach the decoy, fall into the hole. A cage baited with meat would then be lowered into the pit, and when the beast entered the cage for the meat, he would be caught and hauled to the surface. In the net method of capture, animals were driven into runs or alleys, and then captured at the dead end with nets. After capture, large carnivorous animals were likely kept in dark, narrow boxes, an enclosure that would keep them quiet and less likely to bring harm to themselves during their journey to Rome; 'inoffensive animals' may have been allowed to roam about the ship or trained to follow caravans.[87]

Dragged into Rome, caged and kept out of sight in the dark cellars of the amphitheatre, the wild animals were often reluctant participants in the arena shows. Jennison recounts one of numerous strategies devised to get recalcitrant animals from their cellar quarters out into the arena.[88] The animals were kept in cages under the arena and either hoisted up on to the stage or transferred to a series of underground cages and at show time released into a passage and forced to move to the surface. Upon release, the animals often huddled against the back of their cages or took refuge under a wooden barrier. Burning straw or hot irons were used to make them leave their cages, the fronts of which were made to open wide and at the rear of the top of the cage, there was a small square opening to insert the blazing bundle of straw. Jennison quotes a line from Claudian that captures the moment illustrated in illus. 15: 'The wild beasts, looking up mistrustfully at the thousands of spectators, become tame under stress of fear'.[89]

15 Jean Léon Gérôme, *The Christian Martyr's Last Prayer*, 1863–83, oil on canvas. Walters Art Museum, Baltimore. A lion pauses at the entrance to the arena, apparently no less reluctant to engage in fighting than his huddled Christian victims.

Occasionally the animals' reluctance to partake in the games was an added attraction for the spectators. For example, the rhinoceros was one of the most popular animals to place in combat with another species because of his reluctance to fight. When prodded by an arena attendant to engage in combat, the rhinoceros would become angry, and once angered, he was invincible, tearing bulls apart and throwing bears into the air.[90] One of the most often repeated stories of animal resistance to fight in the arena is based on a spectacle in 55 BC of a combat between elephants and humans. The elephants abruptly ceased fighting their human tormentors, turned to the audience, trumpeted piteously and appeared to beg for mercy, bringing the spectators to tears and to their feet cursing the triumvir (Pompey) for his cruelty. A retrospective account of the event was recorded by Dio Cassius:

> . . . eighteen elephants fought against men in heavy armour. Some of these beasts were killed at the time and others a little later. For some of them, contrary to Pompey's wish, were pitied by the people when, after being wounded and ceasing to fight, they walked about with their trunks raised toward heaven, lamenting so bitterly as to give rise to the report that they did so not by mere chance, but were crying out against the oaths in which they had trusted when they crossed over from Africa, and were calling upon Heaven to avenge them. For it is said that they would not set foot upon the ships before they received a pledge under oath from their drivers that they should suffer no harm.[91]

But the audience rarely protested against the public slaughters. The seating arrangement of the arena, with the spectators seated safely in tiers away from the kill floor of the amphitheatre, served as a distancing mechanism from the carnage. Keith Hopkins writes that crowd social psychology may have provided some release from individual responsibility for the arena activities and/or an opportunity for spectators to identify with victory rather than defeat. Brutality was an integral part of Roman culture; owners had absolute control over slaves, fathers had absolute power over life and death in a strict patriarchal society, and state-controlled legitimate violence was established late in the empire, with capital punishment introduced in the second century AD.[92] In addition, Roman citizens had been active participants in battle for centuries, and the popularity of the gladiatorial contests was a residual of war, discipline and death. Public executions served as reminders that those who betrayed their country would be quickly and severely punished, with public punishment re-establishing the moral and political order and reconfirming the power of the state.[93]

The games were wildly popular. Evidence of just how enjoyable the spectacles were for the Romans rests, according to K. M. Coleman, not only in the endurance of the shows for four centuries but also in how much they liked to look at the images in their everyday experiences. The visual representations of arena scenes were standardized imagery in both inexpensive objects and in works of art for the wealthy, with depictions of the games recorded as mosaic decorations on the floors and walls of villas and on domestic objects such as lamps, ceramics, gems, funerary reliefs and statues.[94] For example, a scene depicted on a Roman lamp illustrates the wide appeal for innovative combative situations between humans and animals: a lion lunges up a ramp toward a prisoner who is bound to a stake on top of a platform, just out of reach of the animal, thus increasing the uncertainty of the outcome, the frenzied actions of the animal and the enjoyment of the audience.[95]

In an extensive study of the visual representation of Roman arena scenes, Shelby Brown argues that domestic mosaic representations of the events illustrate how the Romans viewed the institutionalized violence. Scenes of blood, panic and death depicted in mosaics not only decorated the houses of the wealthy but also emphasized the distance of the audience from the death of animals (and disenfranchised humans).[96] The recreations of particular spectacle events are particularly well preserved in private houses and villas in North Africa and Gaul where there was a thriving mosaic industry. The mosaic art typically shows an animal or a human killed or in a soon-to-be-killed situation, and most arena mosaics identified with a specific house or villa were decoration for the reception-dining room. According to Brown, animal representations in the mosaics consist of four different visual contexts: inactive or calm animals, active but not attacking (or fleeing) animals, carnivores and other strong animals attacking weaker herbivores, and animals of equal aggressiveness attacking each other. Fear and suffering are represented in the animals' faces and body positions: bears, large cats and dogs are shown with ears back and teeth bared. While animals are shown suffering, fearful or ferocious, with anguish and pain emphasized, human faces are shown without facial expression, emphasizing a calm unflappability, an expression characteristic of gladiators whose faces were exposed in the arena and of hunters on horseback in rural settings in the act of capturing animals for the arena or killing for sport.[97]

As in the staged hunts, visual representations of combative encounters between humans and other animals were designed so that humans would win, with the emphasis on the fatal blow, the time of maximum excitement and danger just before the animal dies, with spears protruding from animal bodies and dripping blood forming puddles on the ground.[98] Similar representations of animal slaughter are found in mosaic decorations throughout the Mediterranean. Floor mosaics in an ancient villa in Armerina, Sicily, tell the story of the hunt and capture of wild animals in North Africa, their journey by ship to Rome and their death in the arena. A mosaic from Tunisia shows two prisoners, arms tied to their sides, being pushed towards their assailants by arena attendants in protective clothing, one of the prisoners is being mauled in the face by a leopard, the other stares in wide-eyed terror at his animal attacker.[99] Coloured tiles from Zliten in Libya depict a victim gripped by the hair and thrown to a lion by a man with a whip in one hand to either incite or control the animal; two other victims are tied to stakes on wheels with long handles so that they can be driven toward the animals.[100] The Zliten mosaic illustrates the complex nature of the shows as a spectacle put on with numerous 'miniperformances' taking place at the same time. The mosaic shows humans and dogs killing horses, antelope, and wild boar in a hunting scene, a fight between a bull and a bear who have been chained together, three humans being mauled by a lion and leopards, and all the while an orchestra is playing.[101]

Baiting humans and other animals for sport and entertainment did not begin (nor did it end) with the Roman games. Several Etruscan wall paintings from a 510 BC tomb in Tarquinia illustrate a 'beast-master' character, called 'Phersu', in scenes that depict bloody competition, some between humans and animals.[102] In one painting, the masked and bearded Phersu, dressed in a multicoloured shirt and a conical hat, incites a vicious dog to attack a wrestler who wields a club but is handicapped with a sack over his head. Phersu holds a length of rope intended to entangle the human as the dog attacks and tears into the flesh of the profusely bleeding wrestler. It is believed that this scene depicts a funereal event at which staged games and athletic contests were customary. The Romans perceived their gladiatorial shows as distant descendents of these Etruscan funereal combats.[103]

In addition, bullfight scenes were popular decoration in Egyptian tombs of the Old and Middle Kingdoms (beginning around 2600 BC and continuing until about 1600 BC). The bullfight motif was linked to both farmyard life in ancient Egypt and to funerary texts celebrating the deceased's status as victor over a challenge by another potential leader.[104] Pliny the Elder claimed that the Thessalians of ancient Greece started killing bulls for sport by racing a horse alongside and twisting the bull's neck by grabbing his horns and that Julius Caesar staged similar contests in Rome.[105] There is evidence that in 1450 BC bulls were used in sporting spectacles in

16 An athlete tumbles gracefully over the back of a prancing bull,
toreador fresco from the palace at Knossos, Minoan, *c.* 1450–1400 BC.

Knossos when the Minoans participated in bull-leaping contests (see illus.
16). Bull-leaping or bull-jumping appears to have been a form of Minoan
sport entertainment that demonstrated agility, bravery and strength. The
extant illustrations of bull-leaping show that both men and women participated in the event, and there is no evidence that either bulls or humans
were harmed. It is clear, however, that bull-leaping was a forerunner of the
arena combats between beasts and humans, and the event certainly antic-
ipates the Spanish bullfights.

Menageries and the Exotic

Animals were also displayed in more passive conditions in menageries and
animal parks. Early menageries appeared with the rise of urbanization
which provided the large number of skilled labourers and artisans
required to manage the animals.[106] In addition, encounters with wild
animals were not considered a novelty until the development of cities, and
thus the rise of cities may have created a yearning for wild nature and the
menagerie became a kind of 'art form' of encounters with the wild.[107]

The earliest evidence of exotic animals in Egypt comes from a 2446 BC
limestone tomb carving of three Syrian bears. Shown with slight smiles on
their faces, collars around their necks and tethered to the ground by short
leashes, the bears were likely taken captive by Egyptian trading expeditions

to the Phoenician coast or obtained through trade with Asians.[108] Numerous illustrations of tame Syrian bears held on leashes by foreigners are found on the walls of Theban tombs, and while it is believed that they were brought to Egypt as curiosities, there is no evidence that they were performing animals – the first performing bear in Egypt danced during the Roman period.[109] Elephants were popular as exotic animal performers, and some Romans were impressed with their intelligence. According to Pliny the Elder:

> It was a common trick for them to throw weapons through the air – the wind did not deflect them – and to engage in gladiatorial contests with each other, or to play together in light-hearted war-dances. Later, elephants even walked tightropes, four at a time, carrying in a litter a woman pretending to be in labour. Or they walked between couches to take their places in dining-rooms crowded with people, picking their way gingerly to avoid lurching into anyone who was drinking. It is a known fact that one elephant, somewhat slow-witted in understanding orders, was often beaten with a lash and was discovered at night practising what he had to do. It is amazing that elephants can even climb up ropes in front of them, but more so that they can come down again when the rope is sloping! . . . Mucianus (has) . . . seen elephants at Puteoli, when made to disembark at the end of their voyage, turn round and walk backwards to try to deceive themselves about their estimate of the distance because they were frightened by the length of the gangplank stretching out from the land.[110]

Rare animals and plants were transported back to Egypt from an expedition to Somalia organized by Queen Hatshepsut (1495–1475 BC). Exotic animals and animal products were depicted in wall scenes, including baboons, leopards, cheetahs, monkeys, giraffe, elephant tusks, giraffe tails and ostrich eggs.[111] Some of the animals probably became part of her palace menagerie and members of the royal household – one wall painting shows a pair of beautiful cheetahs wearing collars and being led about on leashes. Queen Hatshepsut's predecessor Tuthmosis III also had an impressive collection of exotic plants and animals supposedly brought back to Egypt from military ventures into western Asia. The walls of his temple at Karnak show approximately 275 specimens of plant life, 38 birds, 13 mammals and even a tiny insect – a 'kind of natural history museum in stone'.[112] While most of the plants were imaginary forms created to indicate a totally alien environment, the animals depicted are similar to those seen in traditional Egyptian pictorial representations, including foreign species and common farmyard 'freaks' such as two-tailed and three-horned cattle.[113]

The Egyptian Kings Ptolemy I (367–280 BC) and Ptolemy II (309–247 BC) founded a research institute, the Museum of Alexandria, that maintained a large zoo exhibiting a variety of exotic species, such as elephants, antelope, camels, parrots, leopards, cheetahs, a chimpanzee, twenty-four 'great' lions, lynxes, Indian and African buffaloes, a rhinoceros, a polar bear and a 45-foot long python.[114] The collections were acquired through special expeditions, such as Queen Hatshepsut's ventures, and as gifts from Indian and Greek merchants and ambassadors. When the Emperor Augustus conquered Egypt he probably took the Ptolemaic menagerie animals back to Rome to be killed in the arena in celebration of his military victory.[115]

The Romans also liked to view animals destined for the arena in holding areas called *vivaria* where they awaited exhibition, and some animals were put on display at slaughter-free Roman celebrations and games.[116] J. Donald Hughes notes that a thirst for blood went hand in hand with scientific curiosity in ancient Rome. Galen, the famous physician of antiquity who lived between AD 130 and 200, wrote that after their slaughter in the arena, elephants (and probably other species as well) were dissected by physicians to satisfy anatomical curiosity.[117] Galen is also known as the father of sports medicine, having gained experience in trauma and sports medicine as physician to the gladiators from AD 157 to 161.[118]

Aristotle's (384–322 BC) writings on animal biology and zoology describing three hundred vertebrates were based on observations of captive animals in a Greek zoo that was stocked by Aristotle's student, Alexander the Great. Alexander sent animal specimens to Greece from his military expeditions, and it is possible that Aristotle also participated in animal dissections.[119] The Greeks exhibited a variety of small exotic animals, and the public was charged admission to visit the collections, the earliest recorded 'gate fee' in history to see animals on display.[120] The Greeks had a general scientific interest in animals: they performed experiments on captive quail-like birds and school children took field trips to observe small animal collections.[121]

While watching animals slaughtered in the arena was a favourite pastime for the Romans, they also liked to observe animals in aviaries, fishponds and small parks. Indeed, their penchant for watching animals in different contexts gave rise to opportunities for satisfying the Roman obsession for elaborate spectacle. For example, Pliny the Elder gives a first-hand observation of how the emperor Claudius put on a spontaneous spectacle involving a trapped whale:

A killer whale was seen in Ostia harbour . . . It had come when . . . [Claudius] was building the harbour, tempted by the wreck of a cargo of hides imported from Gaul. Eating its fill of these for many days, the whale had made a furrow in the shallow sea-bed and the waves had banked up the sand to such a height that it was absolutely unable to turn round; its back stuck out of the water like a capsized boat. Claudius gave orders for a number of nets to be stretched across the entrances of the harbour and, setting out in person with the praetorian cohorts, provided the Roman people with a show. The soldiers hurled spears from ships against the creature as it leapt up, and I saw one of the ships sink after being filled with water from the spouting of the whale.[122]

Staged displays on land and water became 'multi-dimensional spectacles'.[123] Good examples of these multi-dimensional displays are the elaborate aquatic spectacles put on by the ancients and carefully described by K. M. Coleman.[124] To celebrate the inauguration of the Flavian Amphitheatre in AD 80, Titus filled the arena with water and staged complicated aquatic displays, including naval combats, re-enactments of myths in a marine context, water-borne banquets, and according to Dio, horses, bulls and other domesticated animals taught to perform in water everything they could do on land (although that probably consisted only of rearing on hind legs and goose-stepping). Augustus flooded the Circus Flaminius in 2 BC and exhibited thirty-six crocodiles, which were netted in the dug-out basin, dragged on to a platform in view of the spectators and then released back into the water;[125] another report has it that the crocodiles were promptly killed after their exhibition.[126] Nero flooded a wooden amphitheatre with seawater, filled it with fish and other marine animals and staged a mock sea-battle between Athenians and Persians, after which he drained the water and brought in the infantry to continue the battle. While it has been argued that these aquatic displays did not take place in water at all, but were only mimed performances, many of the reported spectacles could have taken place on platforms which were slightly submerged and thus not seen by the spectators.[127]

The ancients were fascinated by the spectacles of nature. They believed that animals were naturally violent and aggressive, and watching their combative behaviours was appropriate human activity.[128] Indeed, watching animal-on-animal struggle was enjoyable for Pliny the Elder who was fond of providing narratives that detailed the spectacles of nature embedded in his encyclopedic descriptions of animal physiology and behaviour. Here is his account of a combat between an elephant and a large snake:

The sagacity which every animal exhibits in its own behalf is wonderful, but in these [elephants] it is remarkably so. The dragon [a huge
snake] has much difficulty in climbing up to so great a height, and
therefore, watching the road, which bears marks of their footsteps
when going to feed, it darts down upon them from a lofty tree. The
elephant knows that it is quite unable to struggle against the folds of
the serpent, and so seeks for trees or rocks against which to rub itself.
The dragon is on its guard against this, and tries to prevent it, by first
of all confining the legs of the elephant with the folds of its tail; while
the elephant, on the other hand, endeavours to disengage itself with
its trunk. The dragon, however, thrusts its head into its nostrils, and
thus, at the same moment, stops the breath and wounds the most
tender parts. When it is met unexpectedly, the dragon raises itself up,
faces its opponent, and flies more especially at the eyes; this is the
reason why elephants are so often found blind, and worn to a skeleton
with hunger and misery. What other cause can one assign for such
mighty strifes as these, except that Nature is desirous, as it were, to
make an exhibition for herself, in pitting such opponents against each
other?[129]

In another account, Pliny records a spectacular event of cooperative
fishing between humans and dolphins:[130]

There is . . . a lake . . . where dolphins fish in company with men . . .
multitudes of mullets make their way [from the lake] into the sea . . .
[swimming] with all speed towards the deep water which is found in a
gulf in that vicinity, and hasten to escape from the only spot that is at
all convenient for spreading the nets. As soon as ever the fishermen
perceive this, all the people – for great multitudes resort thither, being
well aware of the proper time, and especially desirous of sharing in the
amusement – shout as loud as they can . . . sooner than you could have
possibly supposed, there are the dolphins, in all readiness to assist.
They are seen approaching in all haste in battle array, and, immediately taking up their position when the engagement is about to take
place, they cut off all escape to the open sea, and drive the terrified
fish into shallow water. The fishermen then throw their nets, holding
them up at the sides with forks, though the mullets with inconceivable
agility instantly leap over them; while the dolphins, on the other hand,
are waiting in readiness to receive them, and content themselves for
the present with killing them only, postponing all thoughts of eating
till after they have secured the victory. The battle waxes hot apace, and

the dolphins, pressing on with the greatest vigour, readily allow themselves to be enclosed in the nets; but in order that the fact of their
being thus enclosed may not urge the enemy to find additional means
of flight, they glide along so stealthily among the boats and nets, or
else the swimmers, as not to leave them any opening for escape. By
leaping, which at other times is their most favourite amusement, not
one among them attempts to make its escape, unless, indeed, the nets
are purposely lowered for it; and the instant that it has come out it
continues the battle, as it were, up to the very ramparts. At last, when
the capture is now completed, they devour those among the fish which
they have killed; but being well aware that they have given too active
an assistance to be repaid with only one day's reward, they take care to
wait there till the following day, when they are filled not only with fish,
but bread crumbs soaked in wine as well.[131]

Pliny the Elder's detailed descriptions of animals' physiology and behaviour were cut short by his untimely death at age 55 during the eruption of
Vesuvius in AD 79. In his desire to observe the volcano at close range he
travelled by small boat to Stabiae and on landing he was overcome by
sulphurous fumes.[132] He was a prolific writer and left a huge body of work.
According to Pliny the Younger, the Elder worked all of the time, slept very
little and was carried about Rome in a sedan-chair to save walking time; he
believed that any time not devoted to work was time wasted. Pliny the
Elder's work was to have a substantial influence in the Middle Ages, a time
of reliance on the observation of others as sources of instruction. Indeed,
his first-hand observations, such as that of the whale in Ostia harbour, were
to be the last written or visual records based on looking at real animals for
the next 1,100 years.

Chapter 3

The Middle Ages, 500–1400

Looking at the medieval horse is a good way to begin the discussion of animals in the Middle Ages. The horse was the most highly valued animal in a social and economic system that was initially a military arrangement designed to supply and maintain warriors on horseback – 'feudalism'.[1] In the mid-700s, the agricultural economy of Gaul depended on large plots

17 Farmers with a plough yoked to four oxen in a decorative bas-de-page from the Luttrell Psalter, East Anglia, c. 1325–1335. British Library, London.

of soil, mounted warriors could only be supported by landed endowment, and a landowner gave land to supporters on condition that in return they serve him on horseback.[2] Ownership of a trained battle horse was a mark of status, every nobleman had a horse, and the knight's constant companion was his horse.[3] The close relationship between horse and rider is documented in many medieval narratives, such as the story of the saintly man's horse who ceased to live after his beloved master died, the battle-weary marquis who accidentally slipped into a deep hollow with his horse so they died together while being pelted with spears and arrows, and countless noblemen who died doing what they did best, riding horses, either in battle or while out hunting.[4]

While the military horse was central to medieval society, it was another use of horses that revolutionized economic and demographic growth in medieval Europe – the application of horse power in agriculture. Oxen had been used as draught animals since the invention of the plough, but

they were slow. The horse had replaced the ox as the primary draught animal in France by the late twelfth century, but in England the ox continued to be used to work the fields into the late Middle Ages (see illus. 17). Lynn White writes that this 'technological lag' in England was in part the result of an intentional 'slow-down' by ploughmen reluctantly ploughing land under manorial obligation (see illus. 18). While in thirteenth-century France the possession of land was moving away from manorial labour services towards a rental system, there was a revival of the old exploitative system in England; in the words of a medieval agricultural writer: 'the malice of the ploughmen does not permit a horse-drawn plough to go any faster than one pulled by oxen.'[5]

Replacing oxen with horses as the primary plough animal dramatically changed peasant life in the eleventh century, just as substituting horses for oxen as transport animals revolutionized life in the ancient world. But similar to the way stirrups enhanced the warrior's ability to stay on top of his horse, special equipment was needed before the horse could be used as an effective draught animal – a non-choking harness and nailed horseshoes. Lynn White describes the

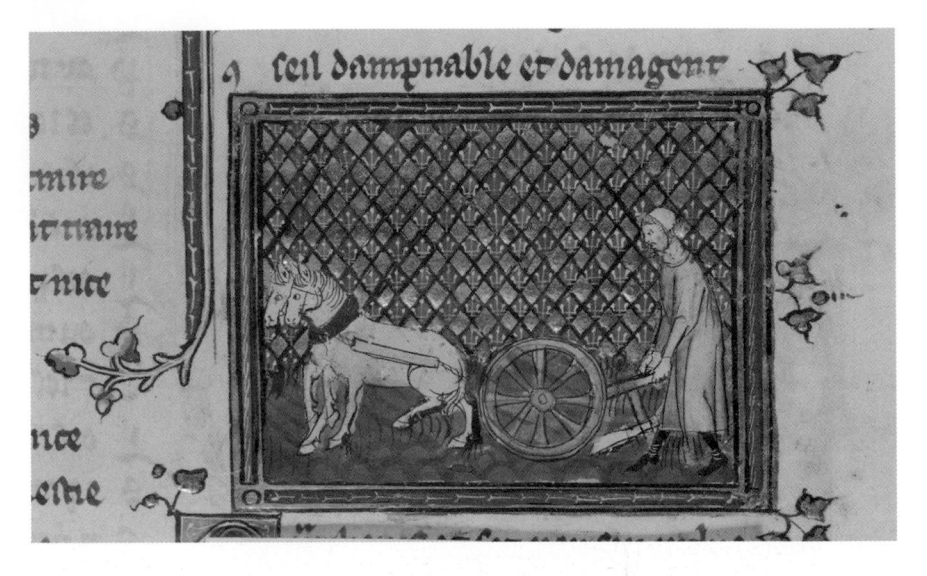

ol fecil dampnable er damagenr

18 The Man Obliged to Work for a Living': a peasant's wheeled plough
is pulled by two horses equipped with padded collar harnesses and
iron horseshoes, French School, fourteenth century, on vellum,
text by Chrétien Legouais.
Bibliothèque Municipale, Rouen.

horseshoe and harness innovations in the development of horse power
in the Middle Ages.[6] While the Greeks and Romans used hippo sandals
and a kind of slipper attached with wire either for decoration or for
healing a damaged hoof, their horses were not shod. The development
of the nailed horseshoe in the ninth century solved the problem of
horses' hooves becoming soft and easily broken in the moist climate of
northern Europe, and by the eleventh century even peasants were
probably using iron for shoeing their horses. But as White notes, 'even a
shod horse is of little use for ploughing or hauling unless he is harnessed
in such a way as to utilize his pulling power', and by the ninth century
horses were harnessed with a rigid padded collar rather than the suffocating yoke harness used for oxen.[7] White writes that horses were ineffi-
ciently harnessed in antiquity, with a yoke harness attached with two
flexible straps from each end of the yoke to encircle the belly and the
horse's neck. When the horse pulled, the strap pressed on his jugular
vein and windpipe, suffocating the poor animal and cutting off his blood
flow. The collar harness, in contrast, rested on the horse's shoulders and
in addition to allowing for adequate breathing and blood circulation, the
collar was attached to the load so that the horse was able to put his entire
weight into pulling.[8]

19 Ambrogio Lorenzetti (fl. *c.* 1311–48), detail from a fresco
showing the effects of good government in the country.
Palazzo Pubblico, Siena.

The shod and harnessed horse not only made ploughing easier but he
was also capable of carrying goods to market and peasants back and forth
to distant fields from urban areas.[9] Horses were better than donkeys in
hauling goods to town (see illus. 19). As the primary farm animal, the
horse was central to the urbanization of agricultural workers, particularly
in northern areas where the climate allowed adoption of the triennial
rotation system that was necessary to produce the quantity and quality of
surplus food (particularly oats) needed to keep horses.[10]

Changing Relationships

Agricultural and technological innovations in the Middle Ages also brought about a substantial shift in attitudes toward nature. According to Lynn White, humans were part of nature when they were limited to scratch ploughs and square fields and working just enough land to sustain a family unit (subsistence farming). With the development of the heavy plough in northern Europe, medieval peasants pooled animals and ploughed together, creating a cooperative plough-team. Land was now distributed according to a peasant's contribution to the team, and cooperative ploughing encouraged the distribution of land according to the ability to till the soil rather than the subsistence needs of a family.[11] White argues that attitudes toward the natural world were also changed by the religious fervour of Christianity, which dismantled the assumption that nature was spiritual and encouraged humans to exploit the natural world.[12]

By the late Middle Ages, the relationship between people and animals in Europe had changed radically. As more and more land came under cultivation, the wilderness receded, the size of a forest was no longer estimated according to the number of pigs it could support, the enclosure replaced the open land of the countryside and animals were kept close to the villages.[13] Animals were also being heavily exploited for their skin, wool and flesh and under these exploitative conditions sheep became particularly important. The price of wool is believed to have driven the widespread conversion from plough land to meadow because one or two men could easily herd hundreds of sheep.[14] Before being slaughtered for food, sheep could give years of high-quality wool, billions of pounds of which was exported, and by the mid-fourteenth century 5 per cent of the Crown's income was derived from the export tax on wool.[15]

While horsemeat provided a substantial part of the European's diet throughout the Middle Ages, particularly in France,[16] eating horses was unpopular with the English.[17] Horses were too expensive to raise for food, the flesh of old worn-out horses was tough and suitable only for the peasant's table (and the peasants resented food spurned by the wealthy), but most importantly, the horse was noble and considered too close to humans to eat.[18] Further, the prohibition on eating horses applied to clerics and nobles, not peasants, a difference that was a reflection of the different attitudes toward the riding horse and the farm horse.[19] Riding horseback brings humans into close body contact with the animal, an intimacy that is not experienced by the farmer and his working animal; the horse was often anthropomorphized and regarded as more 'human' than pigs or oxen, animals that were often slaughtered for food (see illus. 20).[20]

20 Fattened pigs being slaughtered for food in December,
illumination in the Playfair Book of Hours, late fifteenth century, Rouen, France.
Victoria and Albert Museum, London.

Medieval animals in general were often anthropomorphized and even endowed with spiritual characteristics. For example, in Bavaria it was common to hold a mass for horses, and the French celebrated the Feast of the Donkey by parading a donkey first through the Church and then through the town.[21] Peasants attempted to cure sick horses with holy water, and as a contraceptive measure women exposed their genitals to the smoke of a burning hoof from the sterile mule.[22]

But along with these examples of anthropomorphism and transcendence, there was a medieval preoccupation with maintaining a sharp distinction between humans and animals. This anthropocentrism is well conveyed in the thirteenth-century encyclopedic writings of Bartholomeus Anglicus. In his *De proprietatibus rerum*, he claims that all animals were created to be used by man – deer and cattle were for eating; the horse, donkey, ox and camel were for helping; the monkey, songbird and peacock were for amusement; bears, lions and snakes existed to remind humans of the power of God and lice and fleas were around to remind humans of their own fragility.[23]

22 A hyena devouring a corpse in its open coffin,
from a Bestiary, 1200–10. British Library, London.

Animals and Devalued Humans

The bestiary's characterization of the hyena as a sinful, double-sexed creature was a reference to Jews who were considered beasts feeding on anti-Christian doctrine.[32] In her essay on sex in the medieval bestiaries, Debra Hassig writes that medieval anti-Jewish attitudes often found their way into bestiary symbolism, as did hostility toward women. Misogyny and anti-Jewish imagery existed alongside pictures and narratives about animals, texts that were actually 'de facto expressions of hostility toward women and Jews, albeit marketed as moral guidance'.[33] Female sexuality in the bestiaries was often linked to small furry animals, such as squirrels and cats and commonly associated with prostitution. Hair-combing sirens (primping in front of a mirror was symbolic of the medieval sin of lust) have been depicted next to half-human/half-animal centaurs, hybrids notable for their lecherous behaviour.[34]

Jews and women were not the only medieval groups whose devaluation earned them an association with animals. Freedman writes that peasants were described using animal metaphors, and servitude was often linked to sin and bestial characteristics.[35] Peasant physical appearances were characterized as animal-like (teeth like a wild boar, a nose like a cat, a wolf-like snout); peasant behaviour was described as stupid, foolishly violent and associated with excrement; and peasant labour was regarded as similar to that of domestic animals, useful but needing coercion since, as Freedman notes, it was commonly believed that like donkeys and nuts peasants had to be beaten into productivity.[36]

Domestication

Not all of the medieval representations of animals were symbolic and connected to religion, humiliation or degradation. While rare, there is some visual record of the daily activities of animals, servants and nobility in the Middle Ages. For example, domestic scenes fill the margins of the Luttrell Psalter, an illustrated devotional book that dates to the mid-1300s and provides a superb source of pictorial information about medieval rural life in England. The Luttrell Psalter has many nature motifs that depict animals in everyday activities as both primary subjects and as filler and accessories in the manuscript's margins.[37] Dogs are depicted harassing peddlers, chasing birds, fiercely guarding the master and sitting on women's laps; cats worry birds, rabbits flee a warren invaded by a fox and another fox trots along carrying a dead duck in his mouth. The artist's depictions of animals was remarkably lifelike: one can easily make out the whiskers and stubbly snout of a bull, a boar's bristly coat, the heavy working shoes on the hooves of draft animals and the crowded conditions of sheep penned up together in a sheepfold. The detailed illustration of a medieval sheep pen is one of the best-known images from the Luttrell Psalter (see illus. 23). Twenty sheep are crowded into a pen held together at the corners with rope. One of the sheep is being milked by a woman, while another appears to be taking some medicine administered by a man. Two women walk away from the pen carrying on their heads containers probably filled with milk.

Medieval humans and animals lived together in close proximity. Keith Thomas writes that in many parts of medieval England humans lived under the same roof with cattle. Men and cattle slept in a 'long house' until the sixteenth century when humans and animals began to live separated by walls, separate entrances or separate buildings out in the farmyard.[38] Robert Gottfried writes that diseases were often transferred to humans from animals in the Middle Ages, and animals play a substantial role in the spread of disease; humans share 65 different diseases with dogs, 50 with cattle, 46 with goats and sheep, 42 with pigs, 35 with horses, 32 with mice and rats and 26 with poultry.[39]

23 A sheep pen, from the Luttrell Psalter, East Anglia,
c. 1325–35. British Library, London.

Animals, Humans and the Plague

Close living conditions between animals and humans is widely regarded as
responsible for the spread of the Black Death, which began in Sicily in
1347. Fleas carrying plague bacilli lived on the backs of black rats, who in
turn lived in the thatched roofs of peasant houses and in the dark corners
and roof beams of urban dwellings; plague-carrying fleas could also live on
the bodies of all domestic and barnyard animals except the horse (fleas
were repelled by the smell of horses).[40]

The Black Death had its beginnings one hundred years earlier when
environmental change brought cold, wet weather conditions and alter-
ations in insect and rodent ecology to medieval Europe. Robert Gottfried's

analysis of the social and agricultural effects of the environmental changes that preceded the Black Death emphasizes the deleterious influence of poor weather on agricultural production and animal husbandry.[41] Farmable land became scarce, bringing a decrease in food surplus, land was over-farmed for high-yield wheat fields, and by the end of the 1200s the population increase was greater than the increase in food production. As the weather deteriorated, a series of famines struck Europe in the late 1200s. By 1315 medieval Europe was starving, and Clive Ponting describes the widespread effects of the famine:[42] with wheat prices soaring from poor weather conditions and low harvest yields, there was no food to buy even for those who had some resources. Huge numbers of animals were killed as their feed supplies ran out, and animal diseases were rampant, killing 70 per cent of the sheep in some areas and two-thirds of the oxen in Europe over the four-year period 1319–1322. Starving peasants roamed the countryside and people resorted to ever more desperate measures to fill their stomachs, such as mixing bread with pigeon and pig droppings and eating the carcasses of diseased animals which in turn brought about new outbreaks of disease in humans.[43] The devastating blow came with the spread of the Black Death across Europe in 1348, killing a substantial number of the population.

One human–animal relationship that has recently gained currency as an explanation for the medieval plague is eating tainted animal flesh. Graham Twigg, a zoologist, has argued that the plague that hit Britain in 1348 was the spread of a rare virulent form of anthrax.[44] As more and more land came under cultivation and the supply of wild game decreased, Europeans turned to raising herds of beef cattle in congested conditions as a source of red meat. It was in the process of eating other animals that the plague spread. Norman Cantor cites research of two reports of medieval cattle murrain that are closely connected to the Black Death.[45] The first report came from an archaeological excavation close to Edinburgh that uncovered three anthrax spores from a human waste cesspool in an area that included a mass grave for Black Death victims outside a medieval hospital. The second connection was a contemporary document that claimed that in the years before the Black Death, meat from cattle dead of murrain was being sold in local markets. In Cantor's words: 'Eating tainted meat from sick herds of cattle was a form of transmission to humans just as eating chimpanzees in what is today the Republic of Congo is believed by scientists to have started the AIDS disease in East Africa in the 1930s . . . [and the] "mad cow" disease . . . [was] transmitted to humans by eating tainted meat.'[46]

Hunting

The relative scarcity of wildlife led not only to more consumption of animals raised in confined spaces but also to the establishment of enclosed parks and forests for the hunting pleasure of the nobility. The first known hunting reserves in medieval Europe were established in the seventh century and reflected the feudal organization of the society, the importance of land ownership and the exercise of rights on that land.[47] According to Jean Birrell, royal forests and private deer parks were actually multipurpose enclosures used for hunting wild animals, grazing domestic animals and gathering precious resources such as wood.[48] In the thirteenth century deer were 'farmed' in parks, where, unlike the forests where animals had a largely natural existence, human intervention was necessary to provide food and protection for the survival of large numbers of animals in small enclosed areas.[49] Deer-farming practices included the provision of deer houses or sheds in winter, excluding other animals from roaming in the park to preserve the meagre resources and providing hay and oats for feeding in mangers or troughs. Also, while hunting privileges in the forests and private deer parks were strictly regulated to royalty and the owners of the deer parks, most of the hunting that took place was done by servants or hired hunters to provide venison for the owners' tables.[50]

As in antiquity, hunting in the Middle Ages was an elite activity that served as a marker of physical and moral stamina, military prowess and sport for spectators. Medieval hunting methods were many and diverse. Marcelle Thiébaux writes that game was stalked on foot, approached in a camouflaged cart, trapped in pits, driven into nets, hunted with birds of prey. The best and noblest method of all was the stag chase with horse and dogs.[51] There are many pictorial representations of the medieval hunt and

24 Hunting deer with horns and hounds, from an early fifteenth-century
French manuscript. British Library, London.

the ceremony and preparation associated with the dispatch of a hunting
party (see illus. 24).

When the nobles went on a hunt, it was a highly ritualized activity with elaborate displays for participants and spectators. Lords were followed in the
hunt by crowds of people providing the nobles with an enthusiastic
audience, and long hunts might include the entire court with servants to
perform chores such as erecting night-time mosquito nets.[52] Hunting was
also a pastime for medieval women. A manuscript drawing from the early
1300s depicts a women-only hunting party in which elaborately dressed
women hunt stag with bow, arrows, dogs and horses.[53] In an essay on
medieval hunting rituals, Thiébaux describes the chase, the kill and the
'breaking' (dismemberment and gutting) of the stag.[54] First, the hunting
party gathered in the forest talking, eating and enjoying nature while the
presence of deer was confirmed and the area marked off as having been
reconnoitred and off limits to other hunters. At the sound of a horn, the
hunting party departed on the chase to drive the stag from the forest into the
open country. The smell of the stag's sweat and froth from the mouth during
his frantic run intensified the excitement of the hunting dogs, and the stag
would plunge into a stream to cool himself and cover his scent. This plunge
signalled that the chase was nearing the end. When thoroughly exhausted,
the stag would wheel about to face the encircling dogs, and the hunter could
then move in to kill the animal by driving a sword into the heart from behind
the shoulder or piercing the animal between the horns and the neck, cutting
through the spinal cord. The dogs were allowed free access to the animal's

25 Detail of a dead deer from the Devonshire Hunting Tapestries, the Netherlands, fifteenth-century. Victoria and Albert Museum, London.

body for a while before the breaking ceremony. Breaking the stag consisted of placing the dead animal on his back with the antlers fixed into the ground. The right foot was hacked off and presented to the highest-ranking person in the hunting party, the testicles were removed and the carcass flayed. The hide was left under the carcass to catch the blood, the belly was slit open, the entrails removed and either saved for later or eaten immediately by esteemed members of the party, and the haunches and head were removed last. Throughout the breaking ceremony the hunters drank wine, blew horns and continued the hunting cries. As a final reward, the dogs got to eat titbits of the body or blood-soaked bread arranged on the animal's hide (see illus. 25). Finally, the rest of the carcass was trussed and carried back to the lord's estate amid continued fanfare. On the march home the hunting party carried the butchered carcass in the form of the whole deer – first they carried the head with the antlers, followed by the breast, the legs and ribs, the hide and finally special body parts (such as the testicles, tongue, liver, and heart) impaled on a forked stick.

The special role of dogs in deer-hunting and their privileged treatment at the breaking ceremony illustrate the high value placed on hounds in the Middle Ages. Manuscript illustrations from the time show the elaborate efforts taken in caring for hounds, soaking their sore, tired paws in tubs, spreading hay for their beds and grooming their coats with two-sided combs (see illus. 26).

The law on hunting prohibited the ownership of hunting dogs by those below a certain social level, and thus the status of dogs was clearly determined by the status of their owners.[55] By the twelfth century, canine breeds other than the hunting hound had achieved valued status, particularly the English mastiff. The mastiff's strength and courage were symbolic displays of English masculine valour, both to the English themselves and their foreign visitors.[56]

Introduced to England in 55 BC by invading Romans, the mastiff was a familiar human companion. Representations of mastiff-like dogs with short, large muzzles, lop ears and long tails have been depicted in figurines, statues and stone reliefs that may date from as long ago as 3000 BC.[57] Highly regarded for his ferociousness by the medieval English, the mastiff could attack deer, men and, if wearing a spiked collar, even predatory wolves and wild boar.[58] Allowed to roam in forests only if their feet had been maimed so that they could not run with any speed, the mastiff was the descendent of the 'bandogge', a dog who was collared or banded and tied up during the day, but allowed loose at night to protect property.[59] Intensely loyal and roaming only his master's land, the mastiff was more useful as a protector of people and private property than a village constable.[60]

26 Men caring for hunting dogs, manuscript illumination of a text by Gaston Phoebus. British Library, London.

27 Dogs baiting a chained bear in an illumination from the Luttrell Psalter, East
Anglia, *c.* 1325–35. British Library, London.

The strategy for training mastiff dogs to be capable of killing a man in
defence of a master was to use a bear as a human substitute (see illus. 27).
Bears were good stand-ins for humans because of their size and upright
fighting stance, making them ideal fighting partners for the mastiff.[61] As a
training exercise for dogs belonging to the aristocracy, bear-, horse- and
ape-baitings were elite activities during which the gentry would bet on their
own dogs in fights with several bears and a chimpanzee riding a horse (the
chimp, too small to fight a dog, was a surrogate for a human and tested the
dog's ability to attack a man on horseback).[62]

Fear

It comes as no surprise that medieval people went to such lengths to ensure protection of family and property. Fear was their constant companion. In the early Middle Ages, wilderness and wild animals were sources of fear and anxiety. At that time there were vast areas of wilderness, and what cultivated land there was consisted of small patches at the edge of dense forests, wild areas that were perceived as dangerous, dark, ominous and unknown.[63] In both rural and urban areas, cottages, gardens and fields were enclosed against intruders and wild animals by protective fences and hedges, suggesting that the medieval population lived in a constant state of alarm and insecurity, and that people considered it normal to live in this way.[64] As agriculture expanded, predatory animals were driven from the wilderness into the towns and villages, and sometimes attacked humans if their usual supply of prey animals was depleted. As a result wolves were hunted ruthlessly and so loathed that they were often strung up alive.[65]

By the late Middle Ages, fear took the form of anxiety over the stunningly rapid spread of the plague. The Black Death and subsequent recurrent epidemics were devastating ecological disasters, killing as many as 70 or 80 per cent of the people in cities and villages from England to Italy, and by 1420 Europe had only one-third of the population it had in 1320.[66] Among its many social, political and economic consequences, the Black Death displaced the traditional sense of community with an emphasized individualism. People increasingly turned to violence to resolve disputes, and in spite of the general drop in population, there were about twice as many homicides in England from 1349 to 1369 than there were between 1320 and 1340.[67] Death was perceived as unnatural, grotesque and horrifying, and animal imagery was often a part of the medieval preoccupation with heaven, hell and judgement.[68] A good example is a fifteenth-century wall hanging (illus. 28) depicting two human thieves lying face up in hell, arms tied behind their backs, their bodies being devoured by dogs (perhaps following Dante's scene from the *Inferno*). Symbolizing the power and energy of evil, and the tearing and eating away of human flesh, it is easy to see the representation

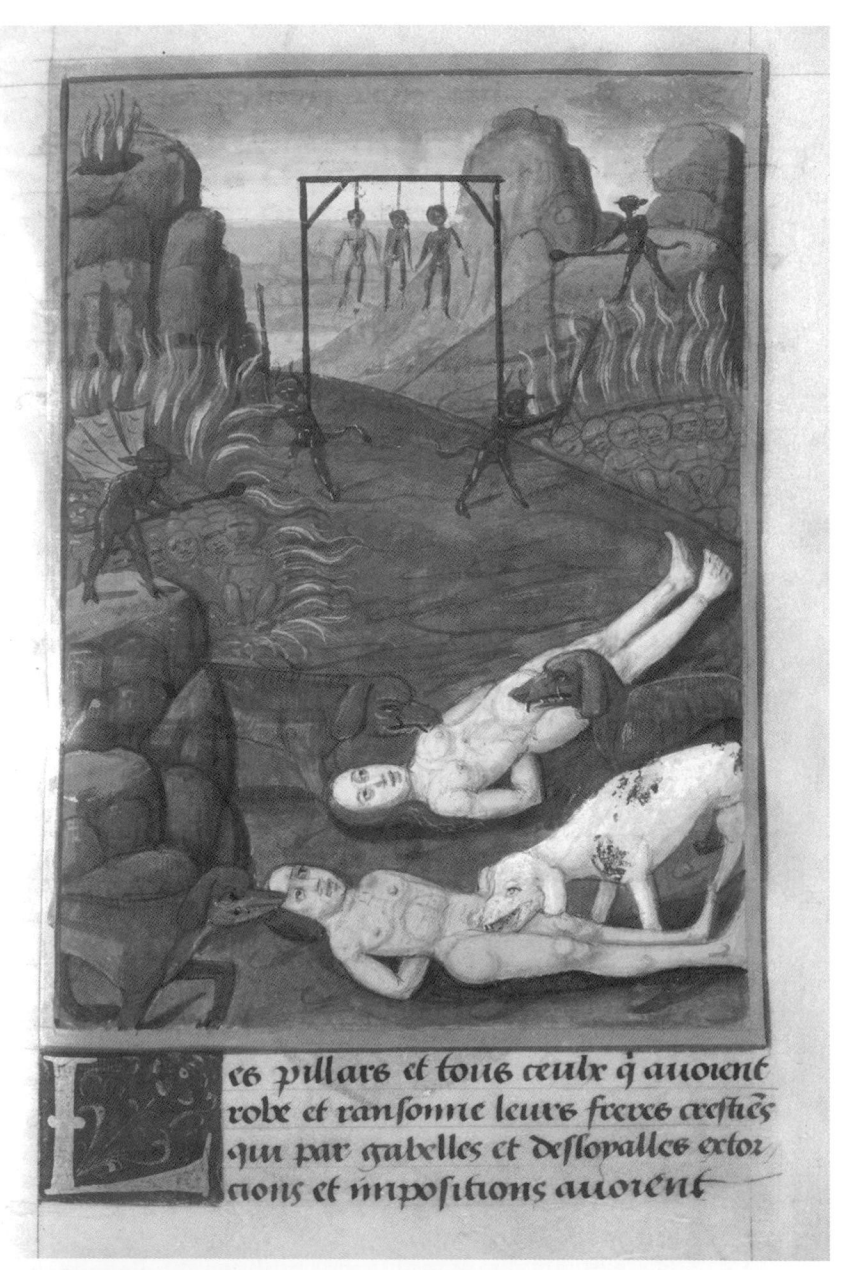

es pillars et tous ceulx q auoient
robe et ransomne leurs frexes crestes
qui par gabelles et desloyalles extor
cions et impositions auoient

28 Thieves are torn apart by dogs in this French fifteenth-century
manuscript illumination of the torments of hell, from Jean Gerson,
Le Trésor de Sapience.

of the Black Death in such imagery. Scholars have argued that the plague changed artistic expression. A deep psychological fear gave rise to a macabre vision of death in the art and literature of the 1300s.[69] Artists emphasized death as an untamed ravishing monster associated with pain, pessimism and naked, decomposing corpses.[70]

Plague and panic further isolated already marginalized groups from those in the cultural majority, and relationships with strangers, lepers, beggars and Jews became ever more violent. Fear united people with common interests and sometimes against a common enemy, usually social outsiders and other marginalized groups, and discontent was easily deflected on to scapegoats, such as women and Jews.[71] Indeed, some individuals gladly assumed the role of scapegoat. Flagellants who marched through cities in flamboyant processions 'scourging themselves in expiation for their own sins and those of society' provided highly visible and frequent 'dramatic theatre' performances that took on unprecedented scope with the Black Death.[72]

Public Processions and Rituals

Animals were particularly popular scapegoats, and as such they had pivotal roles in the dramatic theatre of the Middle Ages. In an essay on the display of animals as scapegoats in medieval public processions and rituals, Esther Cohen argues that animals were important to the definition of what it meant to be human and that the only alterity for people in the later Middle Ages was the animal other.[73] She notes that the presence of animals in medieval public rituals was always as substitutes for humans, and the public death of innocent domestic animals was useful in cleansing the community of guilt.[74] Cats were often the victims in scapegoating ceremonies. The second Wednesday of Lent was celebrated with a public procession that ended with hurling cats from a tower, and a cat-burning ceremony in Paris marked the St John's day bonfires during which the king and nobility watched from special gallery seats while dozens of cats were hung in bags over a pyre and burned.[75]

Animal imagery was also central to the medieval carnival and in mummings during which people disguised themselves with masks, donned the skins and heads of animals and paraded about in processions and rituals. As part of the New Year festivities humans wore antlers and horns, as early as the end of the seventh century.[76] Horns were symbolically significant in rituals and processions to disgrace women who transgressed sexual boundaries.[77] Writing in the early 1800s, Joseph Strutt gave this retrospective account of medieval mummings and disguisements:

There was a sport common among the ancients . . . It consisted in mummings and disguisements; for the actors took upon themselves the resemblance of wild beasts, or domestic cattle, and wandered about from one place to another; and he, I presume, stood highest in the estimation of his fellows who best supported the character of the brute he imitated . . . [some dressed] themselves with skins of cattle, and put upon the heads of beasts . . . at new year's eve, in the hall of castle of the laird, where at festivals there is supposed to be a very numerous company, one man dresses himself in a cow-hide, on which other men beat with sticks; he runs with all this noise round the house, which all the company quits in a counterfeited fright; the door is then shut, and no readmission obtained after their pretended terror, but by the repetition of a verse of poetry, which those acquainted with the custom are provided with.[78]

It was also common for people to dress themselves as specific animals according to their social position, with the upper classes identifying with strong sexual birds of the air and the poor identifying with land animals or flightless birds, such as the castrated capon.[79] According to Esther Cohen, these inversions strengthened pre-existing categories 'by the very attempt to ridicule them . . . At a time of total (though temporary) structural breakdown, the choice of an animal disguise was a statement of identity, not a loss of identity . . . [and this symbolism] could only function in a society which possessed a rich and permanent vocabulary of animal associations and symbolism.'[80]

In expressing loathing of devalued categories of people, animals were often utilized as instruments of humiliation during the Middle Ages, much as they were in the Roman arena. Esther Cohen provides excellent descriptions of the numerous medieval rituals of disgrace and punishment that involved animal themes.[81] For example, the 'backwards ride' was a pre-execution ritual during which criminals rode to the gallows sitting backwards on a donkey or a sick horse (or a ram for sexually promiscuous women). The punishment meted out to those who killed a father or a mother (parricide) was to be sewn into a bag with a dog, a monkey, a snake and a cock, with each animal standing in for a specific symbolic meaning associated with the crime, such as the monkey who symbolized similarity to human in form but not human in deed or heart. Animal imagery was often used in cases that were not penalized by law but that the community felt needed to be punished, such as requiring a man to draw a cart as if a horse or attaching a horse saddle to the back of an insurgent serf who was required to walk barefoot to the lord's estate to try to get a pardon for rebellious behaviour. Animal mutilations enhanced the humiliation in public rituals. For example, having lost a battle in the mid-ninth century, the Archbishop of Ravenna was paraded through the streets on a donkey whose tail and ears had been cut off.[82]

In a thematic essay on humiliation and symbols of evil, Ruth Mellinkoff provides a detailed description of the history of the backwards ride and the denigration of Jews through their association with animals.[83] She writes that the backwards ride has been a widespread and persistent ritual since 742 when the Byzantine emperor Constantine V had a false patriarch whipped, stripped and paraded naked while sitting backwards on a donkey. Artistic representations of the ritual have been found in contemporary popular culture in US political cartoons and, far from being contained to Europe, the backwards ride has been described in historical documents and folklore in India, Turkey, Persia, Egypt, Mexico and the US. The purpose of the backwards ride was to ridicule and mock, thus exacerbating the punishment of a wide range of offenders, such as traitors, heretics, adulterers (usually women), husbands who had been beaten by their wives, and even the incontinent. The intensity varied from a public parade to a ride to the gallows. Usually the backward riders depicted in medieval art and sculpture were nude women (symbolic of lewd behaviour) and apes (symbolic of Jews). Nude women rode backwards on rams, and apes rode backwards on animals thought of as filthy, evil or undesirable, such as pigs and goats (see illus. 29). According to Mellinkoff, the persistent appeal of the ritual of the backwards ride comes from its connection with the principle of amusing by abusing and the human ambivalence and alienation linked to a world turned upside down.[84]

The late Middle Ages was a period marked by judicial cruelty, and executions and torture were 'enjoyed by the spectators like an entertainment at a fair'.[85] Many of the public executions included animals in ritualized punishment, such as 'upside-down hanging', in which dogs or apes were often hanged with the criminal:[86] this was a form of execution normally reserved for Jews. The upside-down hanging was a spectacular and slow punishment reserved for marginalized 'others' including animals who killed humans. Women were rarely hung or executed, but instead were either buried alive or burned. Because women were associated with supernatural powers including returning to haunt the living, measures were taken to ensure that female criminals did not leave their graves. It was necessary to 'dispose of the dangerous dead female body' by drastic measures, usually by burning the body to ensure total extinction or driving a stake through her heart before covering the grave.[87] The denigration of Jews

29 An ape riding backwards on a goat, intended to signify abject humiliation, in an illumination from a Book of Hours, 1310. British Library, London.

also included being required to take oaths while standing on a bloody pigskin or being dragged to the gallows on the skin of a pig.[88]

Animal Trials

Deploying animals in displays of unusual public punishment were in the Middle Ages what they were in Antiquity – visual displays of the power of the rulers and the legal system, or 'spectacles of suffering'.[89] For example, the criminal trials of poorly behaved animals were public punishment rituals, and consisted mostly of cases in which domestic animals were tried for bringing injury to a human. Trials of animals followed the same legal procedures as trials of humans, including defence attorneys, the same range of punishments (such as excommunication and execution), and the possibility of a pardon.[90] There was a strong perception that the animal criminal deserved full justice, and regardless of whether the animal lost or won, it was his right to live in nature, even occasionally being assigned a piece of land upon which he could live in freedom and not prone to pestering others.[91] Most animal trials were held before secular courts, and the animal was usually put to death by hanging or live burial, with the sentence sometimes including some form of mutilation (which may or may not have been combined with the death penalty).[92] Animal trials also included the excommunication and exorcism of a wide range of bothersome animals, including small insects such as flies, grasshoppers, locusts and worms, and for a wide range of offences, such as eating a child (for which a pig was burned in public in 1266) and disturbing religious ceremonies (for which swallows were prosecuted in the tenth century).[93]

One important function of the trials was to send a message that animal owners must control their charges. Free-roaming and of a size that could cause substantial damage, pigs accounted for half of all recorded animal executions.[94] Pigs often brought harm to unattended children, and for killing a child in 1386, a French sow was dressed in human clothes, mutilated in the legs and head and then publicly executed.[95] Cohen notes that there was a sharp distinction between animal species in the likelihood of going to trial and in the type of punishment given for a crime. One fourteenth-century law stated that if a horse or an ox committed homicide, a trial was not necessary, and the animal would be returned to the lord on whose land the crime was committed to be impounded or to be sold. But if another animal or a Jew committed the crime, the punishment would be hanging by the rear legs, a reference to the traditional upside-down hanging of Jews.[96] Cohen argues that the explanation for the species difference in punishment was due to the special role draught animals played in medieval peasant society. The ox and horse were harnessed and under control of humans at all times, and thus their subjection was clearly evident, unlike the pig or sheep whose digressions needed ritual reaffirmation because their control by humans was not as explicit.[97]

Finally, it is widely believed that the animal trials were based on a literal reading of biblical passages and a hierarchical world view in which animals were beneath humans and should be punished for trying to change this order. However, Cohen argues that the trials were indicative of a 'progressive demonization of the animal kingdom' and there was a strong connection between animal trials and witch trials, in which both animals and women were perceived to exist in the realm of the supernatural and thus to be in need of expulsion.[98] Finally, Dinzelbacher notes that in order to understand medieval animal trials we must take into account the degree to which the Middle Ages was a time of crisis that required extreme measures to maintain order and the changed human–animal relationships that were taking place at the time.[99]

Entertainment

After Rome fell in AD 476, roving animal trainers and performers travelled the countryside with exotic animals, trading on the nostalgia for the Roman circus.[100] Itinerant animal acts performed at medieval fairs, and local governments provided opportunities to view animals kept in moats, cages and pits.[101] With the collapse of the Roman Empire and the emergence of the feudal period of relative economic decline, extravagant animal spectacles were no longer affordable.[102] But using animals to entertain humans continued, albeit at a less excessive level. For example, animals, particularly bears and apes, were often trained to imitate humans, and manuscript drawings from as early as the tenth century illustrate bears falling to the ground on command, doing headstands and dancing with monkeys on their backs.[103] Horses are shown dancing on ropes, dancing to music, beating drums and pretending to attack humans, and monkeys and apes also performed human-like actions, tumbling over chains held by jugglers, drinking ale and smoking tobacco 'as well as any Christian'.[104]

Dogs were often used to bait other animals. Deploying dogs to attack and fight a tethered or handicapped opponent has a long tradition, dating at least to 510 BC, as noted in Chapter 2, and also to protect property from human invaders, as noted earlier in this chapter. According to Joseph Strutt, regular animal-baitings provided amusement in late medieval London, and a fourteenth-century manuscript from the Royal Library depicts a horse being baited by dogs, a sport that continued into the 1600s often justified under the pretence that the horse had killed a human.[105] Rarely trained to perform tricks, medieval dogs were instead trained to attack baited animals, and the most common animal-baiting events of the time were bull-baitings.

William de Warenne, 6th Earl of Surrey, is credited with discovering the entertainment value of bull-baiting during the early 1200s.[106] According to William Secord, the Earl was watching two bulls fighting when a group of dogs belonging to the local butchers began to chase one of the bulls; the bull ran furiously through the town with the dogs yelping at his heels, and the Earl was so delighted with the scene that, in return for providing a mad bull at Christmas time every year, he would donate to the butchers the land upon which the bulls were first discovered fighting. The bulldog was bred specifically as a baiting animal; with physical characteristics to ensure that she would be able to grasp the baited animal's nose, and not let go, with her under-jaw projecting beyond the upper (thus enabling the dog to grasp the baited animal's flesh with a firm hold) and the top of the nose inclining backwards (to allow the bulldog to breathe while holding on to the victim).[107] Over the years, bull-baiting came to be associated with a method of tenderizing the animal's flesh before slaughter, with the frenzied exercise ostensibly making the meat more digestible, as described in the following sixteenth-century essay on improving health:

Bull Biefe, unless it be very young, is utterly unwholesome and hard of digestion, yea almost invincible. Of how hard and binding a nature Bull's blood is, may appear by the place where they are killed: for it glaseth the ground and maketh it of a stony hardness. To prevent which mischief either Bulls in old time were torne by Lions, or hunted by men or baited to death by dogs, as we use them; to the intent that violent heat and motion might attenuate their blood, resolve their hardness, and make their flesh softer in digestion. Bull's flesh being thus prepared, strong stomachs may receive some good thereby, though to weak yea to temperate stomachs, it will prove hurtful.[108]

Thus, Brownstein argues, medieval animal-baiting was associated primarily with festivals and the preparation for feasts. Boars, bulls and bears were baited before dinner on feast days, and some guild feasts required a bull as payment of an entrance fee for foreigners.[109]

Medieval Menageries

When the Roman provincial animal collections were dismantled, European royalty and other wealthy individuals took over the practice of maintaining animal collections, for instance Charles the Great (742–814) who kept animals in numerous locations throughout his empire, including bears, lions, monkeys and falcons. The mixture of secular and religious symbolism was critical in the establishment of royal menageries filled with animals brought back to northern Europe from the Crusades, and as a collection of live trophy animals kept on the grounds of the royal palace, the medieval menagerie continued its tradition as an illustration of the importance of the ruler and the empire.[110] According to Vernon Kisling, in the eleventh century William the Conqueror seized Britain's game reserves and began a collection of exotic animals which was eventually moved to the Tower of London by Henry III in 1235.

The royal menagerie in the Tower of London actually had its beginning three decades earlier when three crate-loads of exotic animals arrived in England with King John in 1204.[111] Tower documents show that wages were paid to lion-keepers in 1210,[112] fourpence a day was paid for upkeep, muzzle and chain for a white bear belonging to the king in 1251, and a house 40 × 20 feet was built for the king's elephant in 1254.[113] A gift to Henry III, an elephant arrived in England in 1255 and lived in the Tower of London for two years in the special elephant house which was completed just in time for his arrival.[114] Hahn claims that Henry's elephant was buried on the Tower grounds in 1257, only to be dug up one year later, most likely for his bones and ivory.[115] However, it appears that two years was time enough for the elephant to wear holes in the stone wall with his large tusks, inserting them into the wall for head support while sleeping in the standing position he preferred.[116] Two years was also long enough for the elephant to be more than an exhibited and displayed exotic animal. He gave medieval artists the opportunity to observe live animals, initiating an interest in scientific observation that had been sorely missing for most of the medieval period.

The authority of the ancients regarding animal behaviour and anatomy went unquestioned for most of the Middle Ages. Indeed, until the 1200s, artists did not even conduct first-hand observations to create their work, and often made exact copies of earlier models.[117] It was the lack of first-hand knowledge of animals that helped to perpetuate their symbolic meaning. In the absence of factual observation, allegorical roles increased unrestrained and the symbolism became more complex.[118] Concerned primarily with salvation, medieval artists produced a 'shadow-art' that distorted natural forms to reveal supernatural meaning, with the third dimension eliminated because eternity exists outside time and space creating a flat, disembodied type of representation.[119]

Since they were both shrouded in religion, science and philosophy were kindred intellectual endeavours. David Herlihy writes that in the late Middle Ages writers began to critique pre-plague philosophical ideas, such as Thomas Aquinas's assertion that there was an order to the universe and that humans could gain at least some understanding of its structure. In the late medieval period, nominalists proposed that the universe had no natural order but instead was dominated by arbitrariness and disorder.[120] Salisbury writes that Aquinas summed up much medieval thought about animals in his argument that the central purpose of animals was to benefit humans, particularly as food, and that animals could be killed without concern.[121] But Aquinas also wrote that cruelty to animals is wrong because it leads to cruelty to other humans.[122]

Indeed, Keith Thomas has argued that animal welfare issues were very much a part of medieval thought. St Neot saved hares and stags from hunters, St Godric of Finchale went outside in his bare feet to release birds from snares, and an early fifteenth-century moral treatise on the ten commandments, *Dives and Pauper*, prohibited killing animals out of cruelty or vanity.[123] Here is Chaucer on the cruelty of keeping birds in cages:[124]

> But God knows well that nothing man may do
> Will ever keep restrained a thing that nature
> Has made innate in any human creature.
> Take any bird and put it in a cage
> And do your best affection to engage
> And rear it tenderly with meat and drink
> Of all the dainties that you can bethink,
> And always keep it cleanly as you may;
> Although its cage of gold be never so gay,
> Yet would this bird, by twenty thousand-fold,
> Rather, within a forest dark and cold,
> Go to eat worms and all such wretchedness.
> For ever this bird will do his business
> To find some way to get outside the wires.
> Above all things his freedom he desires.

Finally, one of the great thinkers of the Middle Ages, St Francis of Assisi (1182–1226), argued that our first duty to animals is not to bring harm to them. Further, he is credited for having claimed that if animals are excluded from the circle of human compassion and pity, so also will humans exclude other humans from that circle. St Francis's followers recorded many accounts of his love of animals and nature, such as the story of his friendship with the fierce wolf of Gubbio, who devoured both animals and humans and was greatly feared by the citizens of the city. St Francis confronted the wolf and struck a deal with him. Calling him Friar Wolf, and noting that the only reason he resorted to killing was because he was hungry, Francis assured the wolf that if he refrained from further killing, St Francis and the people of the city would guarantee him food for the rest of his days.[125] Francis is reported to have had special relationships with cicadas, worms, frogs and many species of birds; he spoke to animals in his travels; when given a fish, Francis slipped it back into the water, when given a pheasant for dinner, Francis tamed the bird instead of eating it, and after rescuing some turtle doves from a trap and making nests for them, the birds raised their young close by for generations.[126] There is some doubt that the stories of St Francis's encounters with animals were anything more than sentimental folktales and his negotiations with wolves allegorical, but because Francis was from the country, it is argued that he had a special relationship with nature and consideration for animals as fellow creatures before God.[127] While concern for the welfare of animals was to become widespread in the upcoming centuries, it is notable that, as Thomas writes, 'at the very beginning of the fifteenth century we have a clear statement of a position which differs in no respect whatsoever from that of most eighteenth-century writers on the subject'.[128]

In the thirteenth century first-hand observations of animals finally began to be used again to generate scientific knowledge and works of art. In 1230 Villard de Honnecourt sketched exotic animals (probably from observations at Frederick II's menagerie) and proudly labelled his work: 'Know well that this was drawn from life'.[129] Villard's lion (see illus. 30) illustrates the power of artistic tradition and the difficulty medieval artists had in overcoming the conventional ways of depicting nature. While he sketched from first-hand observation, the artist seemed to have difficulty depicting realistic anatomical detail, a difficulty that was typical of much art during the Middle Ages. For example, as late as 1445, elephants were drawn with trumpet-like trunks, sharply curved boar-like horns, and cloven hooves (see illus. 31).

30 Villard de Honnecourt (*fl.* 1190–1235),
a lion and a porcupine sketched from life, pen and ink on paper.
Bibliothèque Nationale, Paris.

31 Elephants with cloven hooves and trumpet-shaped trunks being attacked by
knights in an illustration from the Talbot Shrewsbury Book
of Romances, Rouen, France, before *c.* 1445. British Library, London.

Some 150 years earlier than the trumpet-trunked elephants a far more
realistic depiction of the elephant was drawn by historian and artist
Matthew Paris (see illus. 32). Paris went to the Tower of London and made
sketches of King Henry's elephant (the elephant discussed above who
lived in the Tower for two years). In these drawings, made from first-hand
observation about twenty years after de Honnecourt's lion sketches, pro-
portional relationships are depicted accurately (in one sketch Paris drew
the elephant's keeper much smaller than the elephant himself) and
careful attention was given to detailing the animal's flexible trunk and
jointed legs. The side-by-side illustration of two views of the trunk, each
view at a different position indicating motion, will be used time and time
again in the Renaissance, as we shall see in the next chapter.

Paris's ability to make naturalistic drawings of animals from observation was revolutionary, and by the fourteenth century more and more
artists were able to make realistic and accurate representations of
animals, particularly birds. Birds were considered relatively free of symbolism and thus were central to the development of animal imagery
based on observation.[130] The scientific observation of birds was also the
passion of Frederick II (1194–1250), who was credited with producing
the first scientific treatise on animals during the Middle Ages. Frederick's
work on ornithology was based on systematic scientific observation that

32　Matthew Paris, Henry III's elephant at the Tower of London, sketched from life, St Albans, 1250–54. British Library, London.

classified and described bird behaviour, anatomy and diseases, and he conducted experiments to test his conclusions.[131] One of Frederick's experiments established that vultures located meat not by smell but by sight, a hypothesis he tested by sewing shut the eyelids of vultures (keeping the nose clear) and observing that they did not smell the meat thrown before them.[132]

Indeed, Frederick II's callous treatment of the vultures to test a scientific hypothesis is indicative of the major change that took place in medieval science and art. There was a transformation in attitudes from a symbolic–subjective to a naturalistic–objective view of the natural world, creating a new science devoted to the exact imitation of nature, a passion that dominated western art for the next seven hundred years.[133] In the next chapter we will see how animals were framed in that cultural passion for naturalistic representations.

Chapter 4

The Renaissance, 1400–1600

Our discussion of animals in the Renaissance will begin with the rhinoceros. Not just any rhino, but Albrecht Dürer's 1515 woodcut of a famous rhinoceros from India who had emerged victorious from a fight with an elephant. Drawn with heavy armour plates, scaly legs and a small horn on the shoulder, Dürer's rhinoceros was the standard visual representation of the exotic animal for almost two hundred years (see illus. 33). Unfortunately, it was an incorrect representation. Dürer did not draw the animal from his own observations, but rather based his work on a description of an exotic rhinoceros provided by a contemporary who had the opportunity to see the animal in a private zoo. Dürer's rhinoceros is a famous example of the reproduction of errors in natural history illustrations – the Indian rhinoceros does not have a second horn on his shoulder.[1] Dürer's mistake was reproduced over and over by scientific illustrators as they copied the master's work, and the non-existent horn appeared on the shoulders of rhinoceroses in natural history works until the nineteenth century.

Taking his inspiration from a printed source rather than from first-hand observation was highly unusual for Dürer. He is best known for his spectacular depictions of animals and plants in meticulous, analytical detail, creating a realistic and precise image of nature and the natural world. Many of his drawings of animals were collections similar to the medieval specimen books that provided pictures used regularly over decades for a variety of different themes, with scenes of animals or nature providing a flexible design structure.[2] Dürer's stunningly realistic 1502 drawing of a hare (see illus. 34), one of the most popular of all animal images in art, illustrates the artist's desire to mirror nature through patient and faithful representations.[3]

The penchant for realistic representations of animals was driven by the development of the printing press in 1450 and by European exploration. Careful observation of nature was in line with the critical stance supported by the scientific revolution and later, in the eighteenth century, direct observation was the mark of scholarly credibility, with exotic animals sometimes,

Int Iaer ons Heeren 1515 den eerften dach Mey, is den Coninck van Portugael tot Lifbona gebracht uyt In-
dien een aldufdanigen dier geheetē *Rinocherus*, ende is van coleure gelijck een fchiltpadde met ftercke fchelpen becleet, ende is vande
groote van eenen Oliphant, maer leeger van beenen, feer fterck ende weerachtich, ende heeft eenen fcherpen hoorn voor op fijnen neufe, dien wettet
hy als hy by eenige fteenen comt, dit dier is des Oliphants doodt-vyandt, ende den Oliphant ontfieget feere, wantals dit dier den Oliphant aen comt, foo loopet hem metten hoorn
tuffchen de voorfte beenen, ende fcheurt hem alfoo den buyck op, ende doodt alfoo den Oliphant: Dit dier is alfoo gewapent dat hem den Oliphant niet mifdoen en can, oock iffet
feer fnel, lichtveerdich, ende daer by liftich, &c. Defen voorgeftelden *Rinocherus* wert van den voornoemden Coninck gefonden naer Hoochduytflant by den Keyfer *Maximilianus*,
ende vanden hoogh-geroemden *Albertum Durer* naer t'leven geconterfcyt aifmen hier fien mach.

1515
RHINOCERVS

33 Albrecht Dürer, *Rhinoceros*, 1515, woodcut print given to Maximilian I
(1459–1519) by the King of Lisbon (1495–1521) and based on contemporary reports
that described the animal as being covered with thick scales.

according to Baratay and Hardouin-Fugier, classified based on whether or
not the animal had been personally observed and dissected, personally
observed but not dissected, or neither observed nor dissected.[4] Indeed,
Dürer sketched many of his animal images in his studio using as models the
bodies of dead animals, such as 'The Dead Blue Roller' and 'The Dead
Duck'. One of the most striking of Dürer's dead animal images is the 'The
Stag's Head' (1504), a large painting of a decapitated head of a stag, with
an arrow imbedded deep into his skull next to the eye. 'The Stag's Head'
was one of numerous drawings of animals that were probably sketched using
stuffed specimens as models from a 'chamber of curiosities'.[5]

Curiosity cabinets were the precursors of the modern natural history
museum and gained popularity with the increasing interest in the natural
world and in the collection and classification of all sorts of 'objects', from
exotic animals to exotic humans. In the century that followed the discovery of the New World, natural oddities were displayed in museum-like

34 Albrecht Dürer, *Hare*, 1502, watercolour and gouache on paper,
based on first-hand observation.

cabinets usually housed in private homes, inaccessible to the public, and
designed primarily to preoccupy the owner and his friends.[6] The oddities
included anything abnormal and strange, such as two-headed calves,
horned horses, stags' heads with deformed antlers and the bodies of dodos
and polar bears who had been previously exhibited at 'raree-shows'.[7]
While deformed animals were particularly fascinating to the collectors of

the sixteenth century because they served as evidence of nature's vigour, exotic animals exemplified the variety that existed in nature and increased the value of the collection.[8] Small species and the body parts of larger animals were valued because they were easy to collect and preserve, such as the skeletons and bones of dolphins and whales, tortoise shells, dried crocodile skins, crustaceans, insects and birds, and the teeth, horns and bones of larger mammals including elephants and rhinoceroses.[9]

With the onset of the scientific revolution, the curiosity cabinets tended to focus less on the abnormal and strange and more on the laws of nature, but the desire to look at exotic animals was still very strong.[10] Indeed, it was the direct observations of animals and live animal collections that were essential to the advancement of knowledge; live animals were critical in any study of animals beyond description and taxonomy.[11] While the live collections were few in number compared with the curiosity cabinets, royal menageries had large collections of many species through their contacts with Arab animal traders, and as Europe expanded exploration activities in the fifteenth and sixteenth centuries, the small royal, municipal and monastic collections of the Middle Ages also expanded.[12]

While the sixteenth-century menageries and curiosity cabinets were not open to the public, scientists and artists regularly observed animal collections, taking notes and making sketches of animal anatomy, movement and behaviour. As a result Renaissance artists produced remarkable animal images, all carefully detailed, with meticulous, almost scientific accuracy. Some of the most strikingly realistic animal images from this period are of domestic animals. For example, Antonio Pisanello, the first great Renaissance artist of animals,[13] sketched stunningly naturalistic animal representations, as can be seen in his drawing of the head and neck of a horse (see illus. 35). The image shows the artist's keen concentration on the contour and shape of the horse's head, the depiction of his body hair, and the realistic flowing hair of the mane and the shorter hair of the muzzle whiskers and eyelashes.

Leonardo da Vinci was also an avid sketcher of horses: horses rearing up on hind legs, horses drawing chariots, horses carrying riders, horses pulling carts. Charles Nicholl writes that Leonardo had an affinity for animals that developed during his rural childhood, and he was capable of illustrating horses as individuals with unique behaviours, such as a startled horse drawn with eyes alert and ears pricked.[14]

Leonardo's penchant for considering animals as subjects of a life is most clearly evident in a series of Aesopian-like fables that he wrote in the 1490s. Embedded in images of country life, the fables are 'brisk narratives, some only a few lines long, in which animals and birds and insects are given a

35 Antonio Pisanello, *Head of a Horse*, c. 1433–8,
pen and ink on paper, drawn with fine attention to realistic detail. Louvre, Paris.

voice, with a story to tell'.[15] Some of Leonardo's animal fables are remarkably descriptive accounts of the world from an animal's point of view,
indeed so much so that I include three of his animal fables here to illustrate his unique mastery of the animal's perspective:

A dog lying asleep on the fur of a sheep, one of his fleas, perceiving
the odour of the greasy wool, judged that this must be a land of better
living, and also more secure from the teeth and nails of the dog than
where he fed on the dog; and without farther reflection he left the dog
and went into the thick wool. There he began with great labour to try
to pass among the roots of the hairs; but after much sweating had to
give up the task as vain, because these hairs were so close that they
almost touched each other, and there was no space where fleas could
taste the skin. Hence, after much labour and fatigue, he began to wish
to return to his dog, who however had already departed; so he was con-
strained after long repentance and bitter tears, to die of hunger . . . A
rat was besieged in his little dwelling by a weasel, which with unwearied
vigilance awaited his surrender, while watching his imminent peril
through a little hole. Meanwhile the cat came by and suddenly seized
the weasel and forthwith devoured it. Then the rat offered up a sacrifice to Jove of some of his store of nuts, humbly thanking His provi-
dence, and came out of his hole to enjoy his lately lost liberty. But he
was instantly deprived of it, together with his life, by the cruel claws
and teeth of the lurking cat . . . A Spider found a bunch of grapes
which for its sweetness was much resorted to by bees and divers kinds
of flies. It seemed to her that she had found a most convenient spot to
spread her snare, and having settled herself on it with her delicate
web, and entered into her new habitation, there, every day placing
herself in the openings made by the spaces between the grapes, she
fell like a thief on the wretched creatures which were not aware of her.
But, after a few days had passed, the vintager came, and cut away the
bunch of grapes and put it with others, with which it was trodden; and
thus the grapes were a snare and pitfall both for the treacherous
spider and the betrayed flies.[16]

Leonardo's visual depiction of nature and animals was also compelling in
its liveliness. Kenneth Clark writes that while other artists of his time
painted nature with accuracy and decoration, none had Leonardo's ability
to so vividly interpret nature's moods.[17] Leonardo's visual depiction of
animals was also emotional and moody. To illustrate this we return to
Leonardo's beloved horses, who, according to Giorgio Vasari, were drawn

in battle scenes as if playing a part in a drama 'for rage, hatred, and revenge are seen in them no less than in . . . men'.[18]

However, Leonardo's behaviour toward animals was somewhat contradictory. He created beautiful visual and narrative images of active, alert animals with emotion and feeling. He did not eat animals and was loath to 'wear something dead'.[19] But his artistic expression was rooted in the science of anatomy. He probably dissected animals, and produced a complex and anatomically precise treatise on the anatomy of the horse which was unfortunately destroyed in Milan in 1499.[20]

Leonardo's dabbling in dissection was in keeping with the increasing Renaissance fascination with the 'inward animal'. With scientific dissection, the classification of animals shifted from outward appearance to internal anatomy.[21] The Flemish anatomist, Andreas Vesalius (1514–1564), emphasized animal vivisection in his work and concluded his anatomical atlas *On the Fabric of the Human Body* with a chapter describing the dissection of living animals.[22] Vesalius embraced the popular tradition of direct observation rather than the acceptance of authority, or second-hand assertions of knowledge. Although he criticized the authority of the ancient physician Galen (130–200) for confusing human and animal anatomy (human dissection was not allowed in the second century AD), Vesalius used animals to illustrate much of his anatomical atlas, such as the larynx of an ox (because the hanged human larynx is destroyed by the noose) and the eye of an cow (because a large eye made it easier for the audience to see the dissection).[23]

Death, Disease and Dead Animals

Dependent on the climate and the ecological conditions for rodents and insects, outbreaks of the plague continued to recur into the fifteenth century.[24] Depopulation and labour shortages brought substantial social and economic changes to Western Europe. Both serfdom and the manorial system were dismantled; people continued to move from the country to urban areas, causing a shortage of agricultural workers and the abandonment of rural villages, and the return of forests and woodland areas to their original state, which had begun that after the Black Death, continued unabated.[25]

Animals played an important role in this transitional period. Since there were no workers to farm grain, landowners increasingly turned to raising animals as a way to make a profit from their land. Holders of small plots of land used animals for dairy farming, and large landholders raised sheep and cattle.[26] Sheep were valued for their wool, and cattle for their skin. In 1456 it took the hides of 5,000 calves to print approximately thirty vellum copies of the Gutenberg Bible.[27] But cattle and sheep were valued mostly for their flesh. With the rise in living standards that came from high wages and low prices, there was an increased consumption of meat; in some areas the amount of meat consumed more than doubled between the fourteenth and fifteenth centuries.[28]

With the onset of the plague in the mid-fourteenth century, art and literature became preoccupied with cadavers and death – woodcut panels depicted 'The Art of Dying', fresco paintings illustrated 'The Triumph of Death' and even religious portraiture reflected a lack of sympathy, a sternness and distance between mother (Mary) and child (Christ), motifs very different from the religious depictions before the plague.[29] It is reasonable to assume that the plague epidemics of the fourteenth and fifteenth centuries had a similar impact on the cultural representation of animals in the Renaissance. For example, beginning around 1500, animals are usually represented in art as dead, dying or waiting for human consumption, visual depictions that are strikingly and overwhelmingly morbid.

The increasingly commodified relationship between humans and other animals is evident in the aesthetic illustration of food animals that began to take form in the sixteenth century. In addition to raising livestock, food surpluses were produced with enhanced agricultural knowledge (the first husbandry handbook was printed in 1493) and intensive use of arable land. The increase in food production was often expressed in sixteenth-century art, with lavish market and kitchen scenes of ostentatious displays of food abundance.

Best understood in the context of the social and economic changes of the time, the artistic representation of food abundance illustrates the changing relationship between people and commercial products and the objectification of agricultural produce.[30] Nowhere is this objectification more evident than in the cultural representation of dead animals in butcher's shop scenes. For example, one of the most famous paintings of the mid-sixteenth century was Pieter Aertsen's 'Meat Market' in which the religious narrative of the Flight into Egypt is almost entirely buried in the background of a display of butchered animals and animal body parts, including decapitated heads, dismembered feet, dead chickens and fish, a flayed pig, unidentified slabs of meat, fat, sausages and animal entrails (see illus. 36).

Norman Bryson notes that while the background scenes in Aertsen's 'Meat Market' have been interpreted as representations of solemn, mysterious, sacred events (Mary handing out nourishing bread), the middle distance and foreground depict the 'profane, lower terms of life', such as the shop attendant busy with everyday chores and the depiction of 'animal

36 Pieter Aertsen (Lange Pier), *Flight into Egypt* (*The Meat Market*), 1551,
oil on panel. Uppsala University Collection, Sweden. The religious subject is framed
by a display of foodstuffs, butchered animal
parts and peasants at work.

matter'.[31] More important, however, is the discourse of the painting that
associates human body functions (consumption and ingestion) with the
bodies of animals.[32] The kitchen and market scenes are also reminders of
the carnal desires of peasants and the lower class who are often depicted
going about their daily chores such as drawing water from a well (as in
Aertsen's 'Meat Market') or engaged in morally and socially inferior
activities such as trading in vegetables, fish and meat, or absorbed in erotic
heterosexual behaviour.[33]

It was common for sixteenth-century religious leaders to link the slaughter of animals to eroticism and the temptations of the flesh.[34] Slaughterhouse and butcher's shop paintings have often been interpreted as religious critiques of abundance and hedonistic behaviour.[35] This connection is also illustrated in the kitchen and market scenes of the sixteenth century, such as those painted by Aertsen's nephew, Joachim Beuckelaer. Beuckelaer created market and kitchen scenes in which the religious motif was largely absent, although the aesthetic connection between slaughtered animals and the temptations of the flesh continued to find artistic expression. Beuckelaer's paintings highlighted the strikingly productive new agricultural methods and abundant harvests, as in illus. 37.[36]

In addition to their representations as food abundance, animals also began to appear as major subjects in paintings of the landscape and countryside in the 1500s. City dwellers enjoyed artistic depictions of farm animals, an interest that was popular in Venice, a city sharply separated from the rural countryside.[37] Artists began to show an interest in animals and scenery that eclipsed any religious implication, such as Francesco Bassano's 1570 painting of animals herded to market by peasants, giving a dignified head nod to religion in its title, 'The Departure of Abraham for the Promised Land'. All religious pretences were abandoned in the landscape paintings of Pieter Bruegel the Elder, and while he was well known for his paintings of peasants in the countryside, he also painted animals in the landscape, as in illus. 38, one of a series of six panels depicting the seasons of the year.

The kitchen and market paintings of the 1500s were precursors to the gamepiece, paintings of dead animals in hunting scenes. While the genre reached its peak in the mid-1600s with the work of Frans Snyders (whose dead animal paintings I discuss in the next chapter), the first still life painting that concentrated solely on game and hunting equipment was Jacopo de' Barbari's 1504 painting of a dead partridge, a pair of iron gloves and the bolt of a crossbow hooked to a wall. The work probably adorned the walls of a Renaissance hunting lodge and, when displayed on the same wall upon which dead animals and hunting objects were also hung, the piece served as illusion for the amusement of viewers.[38]

37 Joachim Beuckelaer or Bueckelaer, *Kitchen Interior*, 1566,
oil on panel. Louvre, Paris. A sensual display of harvest abundance relating
slaughtered game to the pleasures of the flesh.

Dead game paintings convey messages of aristocratic privilege and
power in the masculine sphere of hunting, and the Barbari still life is a
good example of the iconography of masculine attributes that are
removed from the domestic sphere, the 'trivial culture' of the table, the
kitchen and the market.[39] In the lower right corner of the painting is a slip
of paper inscribed with the author's signature and the date, the piece of
paper appearing to have been recently dropped into the picture, an

attempt to deceive the eye, or produce a *trompe-l'œil* effect. While it is argued that there is little connection between the dead partridge and the iron gloves because hunters did not dress in armour, but rather in soft sporting clothes,[40] there is evidence that poachers did indeed dress in war gear, as I discuss below. Nevertheless, Barbari's painting of dead game with hunting equipment serves as an early representation of military valour and hunting skills, pleasures of the aristocracy since the earliest times.

Hunting

Throughout the Renaissance, hunting retained its traditional symbolic form as a ritual display of power and aristocratic ceremony. By the 1400s, wildlife was so scarce in Europe that hunting methods became increasingly artificial, and most hunting consisted of slaughtering animals by driving them into nets in enclosed deer parks.[41] Nevertheless, the nobility continued to hunt in parties that included servants and tenants, and the ritual undoing (or breaking) of the deer continued into the early seventeenth century.[42] Rituals centred around the blood of the fallen animal were customary, such as allowing the most important member of the hunting party (participant or observer) the honour of cutting the throat of the fallen deer or smearing the dead stag's blood on novice hunters, a ritual called the 'blooding'.[43]

The forests laws establishing the hunting preserves of the royalty were largely obsolete by the end of the 1500s, and former royal forested areas became parks and chases granted to loyal subjects.[44] Resolved to bring back royal protections for game, James I (1566–1625) raised the property criteria for hunting, held magnates responsible for preserving game for his personal hunt and gave noblemen and courtiers special hunting rights and the authority to enforce game laws, thus encouraging the practice of rewarding peers and followers with hunting privileges.[45]

In addition to its traditional recreational role for the nobility, hunting also provided opportunities for military exercise and training, and the vigorous display of military skills and, during the relatively peaceful reign

38 Pieter Bruegel the Elder, *The Return of the Herd*, 1565, oil on panel.
Kunsthistorisches Museum, Vienna, November, in a series on the seasons.

of James I, illegal hunting served as a substitute for war.[46] Feuds between
the English gentry were acted out by poaching game from the rival's deer
parks, and illegal hunting took on a ritualized form of traditional land
warfare, with the gentry dressed in full war attire, including chain mail and
helmets.[47] Manning writes that these subtle forms of rebellion were similar
to the use of plays, masques and entertainment to air political grievances
and engage in controversy, and poaching was considered preferable to
the more overt violence of late medieval England.[48] When applied to the

practice of poaching as warfare, Manning notes that the military term 'havoc' means to spoil and pillage, for example, to completely destroy the deer in a hunting park. Employing the hunting party as a cover for military action was the subject of sixteenth-century ballads such as 'The Hunting of Chevy Chase', a song about a fictional poaching event first printed in a minstrel book in the mid-1500s.[49]

Large panoramic paintings of the sixteenth century provided 'a visual seal for the new legal conditions' of hunting and documentary evidence of what transpires during the hunting event.[50] For example, in a painting entitled 'The Staghunt' by Cranach the Younger, the stages of the hunt are shown from left to right on the canvas. First, one sees a herd of deer chased across a clearing by dogs followed by a hunter on horseback. The middle scene shows that the end of the hunt is near with the stags in the water trying to rid themselves of their scent of sweat and fear that attracts the dogs, and several deer are lying on the ground surrounded by dogs and hunters on horseback. Finally, in the left bottom corner a boat carries the bodies of dead stags from one shore to another. The panorama also includes depictions of the hunting party with finely dressed ladies blowing hunting horns, dogs tended by servants, and the grand house in the background.

While the large panoramic scenes of the 1500s told the story of hunting in great detail, simple and realistic close-up depictions of dead game became popular in the next century. Still life paintings of dead animals, an art form that appears to be insensitive to animal life and suffering,[51] shows dead and dying animals lovingly and carefully placed among beautiful displays of fruit and vegetables in routine domestic spaces or, later in the eighteenth century, charming landscape and outdoor scenes. In illus. 39, dead game is shown as part of a colourful table display beside cherries and other fruit in a bowl, a large glass of red wine, and a plucked pink rose lying on its head in the foreground. While the beauty of the fruit and flower is notable, it is the positioning of the game that is most compelling visually. Dead birds are carefully draped

39 Christoffel van den Berghe, *Still Life with Dead Birds*, 1624, oil on canvas.
The J. Paul Getty Museum, Los Angeles. In this hunting trophy the fruit and wine
are overshadowed by the game.

across the table. Three large birds are positioned at the centre of the
piece, the one in the foreground propped on the chest of another with his
feet sticking up in the air. A small bird lies upside down at the front of the
painting, her feet curled and head lolling over the table's edge. While we
observe splendid light and shadows and a variety of shapes and textures,
the scene is overwhelmingly centred on death.

The depiction of food wealth and elaborate gamepieces did not mean
that there was plenty for everyone to eat or that just anyone could go out
and kill food for the table. Only the rich were able to afford the exorbitant
market prices for meat and produce,[52] and hunting of course was reserved
for the aristocrats and nobility. Indeed, people were starving throughout
Europe, and famine was particularly devastating at the end of the sixteenth century, as documented in the parish records of Orslosa in western
Sweden:

In 1596 at midsummer-tide the land was abundantly covered with
splendid grass and much corn, so that everybody thought that there
would be sufficient corn in the country. But . . . when the people were

at Skara market, there came so much rain and flood that all the bridges floated away. And with that same flood . . . the water went over the fields and pastures, so that the corn and the grass were ruined, and thus there was little of both grain and hay . . . In the winter the cattle fell ill from the rotten hay and straw which was taken out of the water . . . It went the same way with the cows and the calves, and the dogs which ate their dead bodies also died. The soil was sick for three years, so that it would bear no harvest. After these inflictions it happened that even those who had good farms turned their young people away, and many even their own children, because they were not able to watch the misery of them starving to death in the homes of their fathers and mothers. Afterwards the parents left their house and home going whither they were able, till they lay dead of hunger and starvation . . . People ground and chopped many unsuitable things into bread; such as mash, chaff, bark, buds, nettles, leaves, hay, straw, peatmoss, nut-shells, pea-stalks, etc. This made people so weak and their bodies so swollen that innumerable people died. Many widows, too, were found dead on the ground with red hummock grass, seeds which grew in the fields, and other kinds of grass in their mouths . . . Children starved to death at their mothers' breasts, for they had nothing to give them to suck. Many people, men and women, young and old, were compelled in their hunger to take to stealing . . . At times these and other inflictions came and also the bloody flux which put people in such a plight that countless died of it.[53]

Social Disorder and Animal Massacres

Not only did artistic expression change dramatically with the onset of the plague, Gottfried argues that much of the violence and cruelty of the fifteenth century is best understood in a context of the ever present possibility of sudden death.[54] Violence was a part of daily life in the early modern period – endorsed by the church, and regularly used by the more powerful against the less powerful, including the poor, the young and domestic servants[55] and, of course, animals. Violence against animals was widespread, and some claim that there was more tormenting of animals for sport in sixteenth-century Britain than at any other time in history.[56] Cats were particularly maligned. The French tortured cats for amusement,[57] and the English burned them, hunted them with hounds and roasted them on a spit.[58]

Dogs were also mass-slaughtered on a regular basis. Much of the regularity of the slaughter of dogs and cats coincided with outbreaks of the plague. Jenner argues that animal massacres are best understood as attempts to combat plague within a framework of the historical sociology of risk and the attempt to maintain social order.[59] While the insect and rodent population had everything to do with the spread of the plague, rodents were not associated in the public mind with the spread of disease before the twentieth century; instead dogs and cats were slaughtered when an outbreak of plague was anticipated (3,720 were killed in one city in May 1636), in effect removing the main predator of the real culprit, the rat (and her fleas).[60] According to Jenner, the slaughters had a cultural logic: roaming animals (particularly dogs) were singled out for slaughter because they were visible sources of disorder, out of control and unsanitary, but more importantly, they were without a master and not visibly and physically fixed in a social relationship. Everyone was required to have a parent or master in a culture centred on the household, and a greatly feared menace was a masterless individual woman or man.[61] In addition, Jenner argues that wandering dogs were worrisome in a society anxious about dangerous and unregulated social interaction. Not all canines were subject to the round-up; the lapdogs and hunting dogs of the aristocracy were excluded from the massacre because isolation at home was an important response to the plague, and pet animals were kept at home and off the streets.[62]

Pet-keeping was popular, and in the sixteenth century pet animals were established as part of the middle-class household, particularly in urban areas where animals had little functional value and more people could afford the upkeep of pet rabbits, squirrels, otters, tortoises and monkeys.[63] But the most cherished pet in the Renaissance was the dog. As Keith Thomas notes, dogs were everywhere in early modern England and lived in close quarters with both the aristocracy and the impoverished; estate halls were covered with bones and swarmed with hounds, and even the dog massacres during the plague did not permanently affect their numbers.[64] Katharine MacDonogh claims that the custom of keeping unnecessary pets began at court, as reflections of display and prestige and as emotional outlets for lonely and privileged royalty; royal pets were not just anthropomorphized, they were considered superior to humans.[65] Finally, in addition to their role as companions and hunting partners, dogs were also of substantial entertainment value during the Renaissance, serving as the main protagonists in the animal-baiting exhibitions that swept the country in the fifteenth and sixteenth centuries.

Animal-baiting

The medieval aristocratic practice discussed in the last chapter, using bears as bait to train dogs in the art of attacking humans while protecting home and hearth, evolved into a full-scale blood sport of immense popularity during the Renaissance. Perhaps the gruesome practice continued to be justified as a training exercise. Keith Thomas argues that, similar to the valuation of hunting as a representation of war, animal-baiting was considered of benefit because it simulated private combat.[66]

According to Brownstein, baiting as a money-making event in London and the first permanent baiting arena dates from 1562. He argues that references to commercial baiting any earlier than 1562 are unfounded, including the scholarly rumour that by 1393 Paris Garden was a public baiting place.[67] Once institutionalized, however, animal-baiting quickly became a favourite pastime. Blood sport enthusiasts were not confined to England; animal-baiting was also part of the cultural violence against animals throughout Europe, including Italy, Spain and France.[68]

Many animals were tied to a stake and tormented by dogs, including lame horses,[69] lions, badgers and of course bulls. In bull-baiting a shallow ditch was sometimes provided as additional entertainment for spectators to watch the bull shove his nose in the small ditch trying to avoid the attacking dogs.[70] But alas, easy to breed with flesh enjoyable to eat, bulls were often tormented to death at the stake.[71] While bears were rarely killed, they were often blinded since the dogs were trained to latch on to the bear's eyebrows or nose, and once blinded, bears were usually flogged by humans as entertainment.

Perhaps because of their similarity to humans, bears were the bait animal of choice in early modern England. Bear-baiting events were enormously popular; as one scholar put it, as essential a spectacle for London tourists as St Paul's Cathedral, the royal palaces and the lions in the Tower of London.[72] Bear-baiting was also popular in areas outside London, including the English countryside. For example, in Somerset, court records from the sixteenth and seventeenth centuries indicate that animal-baitings were important events at church ales (parish fund raisings), and baitings were used to attract drinkers who would spend their money on ale brewed by the churchwardens for the event.[73] Baitings in the countryside were central entertainment for all classes of people, providing a communal and social dimension, celebrating old traditions and bringing people outdoors to congregate comfortably (most recorded baitings were held between May and October).[74]

Cultural Analyses of Animal-baiting

A large body of literature has recently emerged on blood sport in the Renaissance. We know much more about the leisure time of early modern Englanders primarily because they left written records of their experiences, including flyers, posters and other mass-produced documents thanks to the invention of printing with moveable type in 1450 by Johannes Gutenberg. Scholars have analysed references to bear-baiting in early modern literature, including Shakespeare, Ben Jonson and Thomas Dekker;[75] accounts of attendance at baiting events in the letters and diaries of noted individuals such as Samuel Pepys, John Evelyn and Henry Townshend;[76] court records of bull- and bear-baiting in the English provinces;[77] and the connection between the staged baiting events and the English theatre where bear-baiting and acting occupied the same physical space, the London stage.[78]

Scholars have noted that the theatre and animal-baiting were similar cultural events, sharing a circular architectural style and prohibitive ordinances, such as no exhibitions or playing on Sunday or during times of severe plague.[79] They also had similar opponents (mostly religious people who condemned play-acting because of its popularity and bear-baiting because it took place on the Sabbath) and proponents (common Londoners, nobles and monarchs, and courtiers).[80]

Numerous theories have been put forward to explain the English penchant for animal-baiting in the early modern period. For example, it has been argued that the popularity of animal-baiting was based on an interest in studying animal nature and temperament, with the bear pit serving as a 'psychological anatomy theatre' that exposed not only the courage of the animals but also their basic character.[81] Also at the end of the 1500s, the comedy of humours became a popular dramatic theme. Drawing on the ancient medical theory that four humours or bodily substances determined personality, humours comedy offered a dissection of individual characters singled out by an internal humoral nature, a particular trait or habit of speech that disclosed the private self, stripped of surface pretensions.[82] The link between humours comedy and bear-baiting lies in the degrading treatment of the humorous individual and that the humours characters are forever trying to prove themselves.[83] In addition, Englishmen's sympathy with the mastiff's masculine courage and valour made blood sport and bear-baiting events spectacular displays of masculine bravado.[84] Baiting spectacles were supposedly based on animal natures, with both baited and baiter trained to display what was perceived as wild and uncontrolled behaviour.[85]

Eye-witness descriptions of baiting have been read by contemporary scholars as festive and comical events that, in spite of the cruelty involved in the sport, gave spectators great pleasure from the excitement of the frenzy and noise of the baiting.[86] Baiting events have been described as choreographed theatrical games that were 'more circus-like than desperate, more substantial than roguish', with an atmosphere that could light up an otherwise dull Christmas season.[87] Chroniclers of the time wrote about the physical appearance and power of the animals in the baiting ring, the bravery, endurance and strength of the bear who was also clumsy, ill-tempered and morose; the contradictory characteristics ascribed to the bear's human-like features that make her both admired and ridiculed.[88] Crowds also had their favourite bears, elevated to celebrity status after having survived at the stake time and time again, such as Harry Hunks and Tom of Lincoln, suggesting that an effective match was one that ended in a stalemate, with neither winner nor loser.[89] In addition, some first-hand accounts of baiting in the early 1600s describe the animals as reluctant to fight, acting offstage like good friends.[90] Some bears were literally dragged to the stake, and recalcitrant bulls hunkered down and refused to fight, a situation that required lighting a fire close to the animal's stomach to keep him from lying on the ground.

Not all of the eye-witness accounts were so sanguine about animal-baiting exhibitions. Drawing on the few written accounts that express reservations about the sport, Erica Fudge argues that expressions of sympathy for bears suffering at the stake is evidence that some spectators perceived themselves as similar to animals, with a diminishing of the human–animal boundary. She writes: '[t]he Bear Garden emerges as a place of immense contradictions: the place which reveals the difference between the species also reveals their sameness . . . Baiting is the most explicit and spectacular site of anthropocentrism in the early modern period, but . . . [also a] site of humanity's confusion about itself.'[91]

Bear-baiting has also been connected to the need to dominate others. For example, it has been argued that a similar ideology of domination justified animal-baiting and the emerging practice of English colonialism in the early modern period.[92] Links between baiting activities and social inequalities are also part of the historical record. Bulls were sometimes described as authority figures, and dogs were likened to the mob and the underclass. Baiting was also used as a metaphor in the abuse of women, such as the report of a man who threatened to tie his wife to a ring and beat her with dogs and another of two men who broke into a house and took a woman to be their bear, parading a scrap of her clothing through the town as a flag, crying that their bear was overheated and must be cooled, then pouring beer over her bare tail.[93]

Perhaps living in a state of psychological and moral crisis in a context of omnipresent disease and death caused people's fear and anxiety to be manifested in the enjoyment of animal torment. While one or even two plague epidemics might have left the population relatively unfazed psychologically, a hundred years of recurring epidemics had a substantial effect – people lost faith in traditional values, and Europe entered a state of moral crisis.[94] The breakdown of the traditional community that began in the late Middle Ages was speeding up in the sixteenth century. Labour became less scarce, agricultural products brought increased profits, religious changes from the Reformation penetrated into remote rural areas and the traditional authority of the local lord was being replaced by bureaucrats.[95] For about a hundred years, disorder prevailed in the local villages; people became involved in hostility, turmoil and aggressive behaviour, making accusations of witchcraft and lashing out at 'helpless neighbors whom they blamed for an unease they could not resolve'.[96]

Huizinga described late medieval customs and manners as violent, motley and riddled with the contrast of cruelty and pity.[97] David Herlihy adds that people were driven to an eat-drink-and-be-merry-for-tomorrow-we-die philosophy, and joking, dancing, fighting, playing 'unseemly games', orgies and prostitution were all common behaviours that took place at burials and in graveyards.[98] A keen sense of the fragility of life was not only reflected in people's behaviour but also in literature and art. Theodore Rabb writes that in 'nearly all of Shakespeare's plays we find ourselves in a world where the comfortable old values, the traditional verities, are no longer secure . . . [and] in the dominant forms of painting . . . Nothing seems solid or dependable'.[99] And particularly relevant to the observation that much of the enjoyment of animal-baiting was in looking at raw animal courage, there was an ever-present duality between courage and weakness in early modern Europe.[100]

When these behaviours, fears and insecurities are added to the already tense relationships of the late Middle Ages (the isolation from and anxiety about things different and strange, the search for scapegoats, the dramatic theatre) it comes as no surprise that animal-baiting spectacles would be frequent, frenzied spectacles that blended cruelty with pity. The disengagement with traditional values, the increase in individualism, the pursuit of leisure and pleasure in the face of the always present threat of disruption, disease and death might have been the foundation upon which the torment of animals was built in the early modern period.

Ceremony and Ritual

The significance of blood sport as a backdrop to drinking, festivities and raising money for churches should not be underestimated. While the medieval parish church was the centre of a ritual world that structured community activities (including plays, pageants, dancing, music, games and drinking), with the rise of Protestantism the communal function of the local church came under attack for promoting superstition and traditional rituals and entertainment.[101] In the fifteenth and early sixteenth centuries special church houses were able to hold traditional festivals, usually at the edge of the churchyard, and by 1600 a substantial number of these houses had evolved into drinking establishments.[102] By the 1630s, the parish alehouse was the principal centre for communal games and entertainment, such as football, morris dancing, New Year mummers and, most important for the representation of animals, feasting, betting (both for drink and for money) and animal-baiting.[103] In the late 1600s, outdoor gambling and gaming activities were transformed into spectator sports, and competing alehouses contributed to the commercialization of leisure by holding bear-baitings, cock-fights and horse races, and the occasional display of novelties such as ancient relics or humans with abnormal physical characteristics.[104]

As in the Middle Ages, animals and animal body parts were used to shame those who had violated the norms of the community, such as women who challenged partriarchal authority. Underdown argues that public shaming rituals were particularly effective in controlling those challenges. Punishment for women who transgressed patriarchial norms was more likely to occur in regions of England that were dairy- and clothing-based, industries that gave women employment and responsibility outside that provided by husbands and fathers, and the skimmingtons and other rituals to shame unruly women were expressions of increasing male insecurity as women became more independent.[105] Both skimmingtons and charivaris were commonly used to punish scolds (women who were accused of constantly rebuking or reprimanding) or cuckolded husbands. The term cuckold is itself a cultural representation of an animal: it comes from the cuckoo, a brood parasite with the annoying habit of leaving eggs in the nests of other birds to be raised by the nest parent.

Horns, Masculinity and Honour

Animal horns, a symbol of cuckoldry, were used in public displays to ridicule a cuckolded husband and shame the wife. Horns were attached to the victims' pew in church, tied to the necks of geese, attached to the heads of horses and hung on the church gate at the wedding of mismatched couples.[106] Linked historically to hunting metaphors in rituals and ceremonies, E. Cobham Brewer claimed that

> To wear the horns means to be a cuckold . . . In the rutting season, the stags associate with the fawns: one stag selects several females, who constitute his harem, till another stag comes who contests the prize with him . . . If beaten in the combat, he yields up his harem to the victor, and is without associates till he finds a stag feebler than himself, who is made to submit to similar terms . . . As stags are horned, and made cuckolds of by their fellows, the application is palpable.[107]

In the Mediterranean code of honour, the deceived husband is identified with the horns of the billy-goat (becco, cabrón, cabrão in Italy, Spain and Portugal) because, like deceived husbands, billy-goats allow other males sexual access to the females in their group, unlike the ram who tolerates no sexual rivals.[108] Anton Blok writes that power and honour are associated with rams and shame with billy-goats, with the two serving as complementary oppositions. Sheep milk is usually made into cheese, while goat milk is often directly consumed; in some cultures sheep are milked exclusively by men and goats by women; and in Sicily in particular men rarely drink milk, preferring cheese instead. Milk is only good for the weak – women, children, the elderly and the ill.[109] Anton Blok provides the following dualistic characteristics as symbolic of the Mediterranean code of honour:[110]

rams – billy-goats
sheep – goats
honour – shame
men – women
virile man – cornute (becco, cabrón, cabrão)
virility – femininity
strong – weak
good – evil
pure – unclean
silence – noise

Shame, dishonour and noise were central to ritual life in the Renaissance. David Underdown has provided a good description of the charivari, or rough music processional, staged against unfaithful or violent wives and the animal imagery associated with the ritual.[111] A rough music procession headed by a drummer and a man wearing horns marches to the offender's house. If the violation was infidelity, a pole (draped with a chemise and mounted with the head or skull of a horse with horns attached) was shaken in front of the house while the rough music played. If the violation was female dominance, such as husband-beating, surrogates for the offenders acted out the shameful behaviours, the 'husband' holding a distaff (the symbol of female subjugation) rides backwards on a horse or donkey and the 'wife' (usually a man in women's clothes) beats him with a ladle. The term 'skimmington' comes from the skimming ladle, a kitchen tool women used in making butter and cheese.[112]

Looking Toward Animal Welfare

In spite of the animal-baitings, the deployment of animals in shaming ceremonies and the numerous widespread massacres of cats and dogs, there were some voices raised in defence of animals during the sixteenth century. The most well-known pro-animal voice of the time belonged to Michel de Montaigne (1533–1592) who made an eloquent case for animal concern in *An Apology for Raymond Sebond*:[113]

> *Of all creatures man is the most miserable and fraile, and therewithall the proudest and disdainfullest.* Who perceiveth and seeth himselfe placed here amidst the filth and mire of the world, fast-tied and nailed to the worst, most senselesse, and drooping part of the world, in the vilest corner of the house, and farthest from heavens coape, with those creatures that are the worst of the three conditions . . . he selecteth and separateth himselfe from out the ranke of other creatures . . . How knoweth he by the vertue of his understanding the inward and secret motions of beasts? By what comparison from them to us doth he conclude the brutishnesse he ascribeth unto them? When I am playing with my cat, who knowes whether she have more sport in dallying with me than I have in gaming with her? We entertaine one another with mutuall apish trickes. If I have my houre to begin or to refuse, so hath she hers . . . The defect which hindreth the communication betweene them and us, why may it not as well be in us as in them? It is a matter of divination to guesse in whom the fault is that we understand not one another. For we understand them no more than they us. By the

same reason, may they as well esteeme us beasts as we them. It is no great marvell if we understand them not: no more doe we the Cornish, the Welch, or Irish . . . We have some meane understanding of their senses, so have beasts of ours, about the same measure. They flatter and faune upon us, they threat and entreat us, so doe we them. Touching other matters, we manifestly perceive that there is a full and perfect communication amongst them, and that not only those of one same kinde understand one another, but even such as are of different kindes . . . By one kinde of barking of a dogge, the horse knoweth he is angrie; by another voice of his, he is nothing dismaid. Even in beasts that have no voice at all, by the reciprocall kindnesse which we see in them, we easily inferre there is some other meane of entercommuni-cation: their jestures treat, and their motions discourse.

Silence also hath a way,
Words and prayers to convay.

It is clear that Montaigne not only considered animals no more 'brutish' than humans, but also as participants in cross-species communication and capable of acts of kindness and reciprocity. However, Montaigne's proposal that animals were bearers of communication skills and sensibility was drowned out in the next century by followers of a very different way of looking at animals.

Chapter 5

The Enlightenment, 1600–1800

In the Age of Enlightenment, we look at animals as philosophical and ethical subjects. There was more philosophical discussion about animals in the seventeenth and eighteenth centuries than at any other time in history before the 1970s. The discourse was fuelled in part by three rapidly spreading trends: the popularity of vivisection in the new experimental science, increasing urbanization and commodification of animals for food and labour, and the widespread availability of print media. In the arena of science, debate swirled primarily around the similarities and differences between humans and other animals in rationality and morality. Peter Harrison captured the polemic well in his observation that once Montaigne claimed that animals were more moral and rational than humans, in the next century René Descartes 'not to be outdone, put forward the even more contentious counter-proposal that animals were not only neither rational nor moral but that they were not even conscious'.[1]

In Descartes's words,

I cannot share the opinion of Montaigne and others who attribute understanding or thought to animals . . . all the things which dogs, horses, and monkeys are taught to perform are only expressions of their fear, their hope, or their joy [Descartes calls these qualities 'passions']; and consequently they can be performed without any thought. Now it seems to me very striking that the use of words, so defined, is something peculiar to human beings . . . there has never been known an animal so perfect as to use a sign to make other animals understand something which expressed no passion; and there is no human being so imperfect as not to do so, since even deaf-mutes invent special signs to express their thoughts. This seems to me a very strong argument to prove that the reason why animals do not speak as we do is not that they lack the organs but that they have no thoughts.[2]

While Descartes was convinced that 'speech is the only certain sign of thought hidden in a body . . . [and] can be taken as a real specific difference between men and dumb animals', he did not deny that animals had sensation, 'in so far as it depends on a bodily organ', and he argued that his 'opinion is not so much cruel to animals as indulgent to men . . . since it absolves them from the suspicion of crime when they eat or kill animals'.[3] Descartes was in fact quite fond of animals, or at least his dog, Monsieur Grat, who, according to Peter Harrison, accompanied him on walks (and these 'were not walks to the dissecting room, as some have suggested').[4]

Regardless of Descartes's personal attitudes toward animals, what eventually became known as 'Cartesian philosophy' sparked discussion about the relative morality and rationality of humans and other animals that engaged scientists, philosophers, artists and the public in an ongoing deliberation that lasted for almost two centuries after Descartes's *Discourse on the Method* was published in 1637. According to George Heffernan, *Discourse* was 'not Descartes's most important work, nor his most philosophical work, nor even his most methodological work, (but) it is his most representative one'.[5] In considering the historical representation of animals, *Discourse* is representative of the 'beast-machine' theory, a philosophical argument that animals were nothing more than machines. Here is Descartes's reasoning:

> . . . although there might be many animals that show more skill in some of their actions than we do, one still sees that the same animals do not show any skill at all in many other actions – in such a way that that which they do better than we do does not prove that they have any mind; for, in that case, they would have more of it than any of us, and would do better in everything; rather does it prove that they do not have any mind at all, and that it is nature that acts in them according to the disposition of their organs – just as one sees that a clock, which is composed only of wheels and of springs, can count the hours and measure the time more accurately than we can with all our wisdom.[6]

The view of animals as machines was consistent with the new scientific method sweeping Europe at the time. Theodore Brown wrote that 'Robert Hooke in England, Christian Huygens in France, Jan Swammerdam in Holland, and Marcello Malpighi in Italy all learned . . . [a] new, settled consensus of orthodox mechanical/experimental science'.[7] Descartes's mechanical philosophy accomplished a number of things bedevilling the seventeenth century. For example, the celebration of rationality (mind) over corporeality (body) gave women the opportunity to fight against their status as second-class citizens since their biology and associated capacity for reproduction could no longer be used against them.[8] The mechanical philosophy also justified animal vivisection.[9]

Dissecting animals while still alive was a practice justified by the view that 'animals do not feel pain, since pain could exist only with understanding, which animals lack . . . [t]hey only exhibit the external manifestations of pain, which are purely mechanical responses to stimuli'.[10] The vivisection of animals was a public event. Anita Guerrini notes that since experimenting on live animals required the verification of results by 'an audience of witnesses', public experiment was a prominent form of ceremony and display. Vivisections peaked in the mid- to late 1660s, when approximately one-third of the vivisections performed by the Royal Society took place in front of the assembled members; by 1670 vivisections were mostly private events.[11]

Not only were animals objectified in the new experimental science, they were also corporealized in one of the most popular artistic expressions of the seventeenth century – paintings of dead animals in kitchen and market scenes and in the gamepiece. In considering the early modern vision of aesthetically appealing depictions of death, Nathaniel Wolloch writes that while dead animal corpses are presented as objects of beauty, the value of animals is placed far below that of humans, reflecting an anthropocentric view of nature and animals and a tendency to simultaneously appreciate and exploit nature.[12]

Dead Animal Portraiture

As discussed in the previous chapter, the aesthetic illustration of food animals began in the 1500s as the relationship between humans and other animals became increasingly commodified. The tradition of painting dead animals in kitchen and market scenes popularized by Aertsen and Beuckelaer was taken up in the early 1600s by Frans Snyders. Snyders was a prolific painter of dead animals, primarily as food for humans and as dead game.

'The Butcher's Shop' is a particularly interesting and gruesome representation of dead animal bodies and body parts in the process of food preparation (see illus. 40). In the foreground is a bloody bowl filled with the severed heads and feet of a variety of animals (a cow, a few sheep and an unidentified animal, possibly a deer), a string of dead birds hangs from the rafters, along with a gutted large bristly animal (perhaps the body belonging to the boar head lying close by), slabs of meat, a roebuck lying on his back, one limb up in the air. The butcher concentrates on removing

40 Frans Snyders, *The Butcher's Shop*, *c.* 1640–50, oil on canvas.
Pushkin Museum, Moscow. The butcher tenderly peels back skin and fat
from a hanging carcass.

the skin and fat from an animal, his knife clamped between his teeth.
A woman works in the background next to a flayed ox.

The tradition of displaying animal body parts in butcher shops continued in graphic paintings of individual slaughtered bodies, particularly the
flayed ox. Probably inspired by an earlier painting of a slaughtered pig
by Beuckelaer, Rembrandt's 'Slaughtered Ox' is the best known of these
images (illus. 41).

The hunting still life, or gamepiece, emerged from the market and
kitchen scenes of the sixteenth century and the political and religious

conditions of the time that made still life painting a safe artistic endeavour. E. H. Gombrich writes that with the Protestant Reformation (which took place over a period of two hundred years, 1500–1700) came the objection to pictures and statues in churches, eliminating the best source of income for painters in the northern Protestant countries of Holland, Germany and England – painting church altar-panels.[13] While painters in most Protestant regions turned to illustrating books and painting portraits, 'art fully survived the crisis of the Reformation' in only one Protestant country in Europe – the Netherlands.[14] Instead of concentrating only on portrait painting, artists there specialized in an array of subjects that would not be considered objectionable by the Protestant Church, such as scenes of nature, daily life and other 'genre pictures' which illustrated their skill at representing the 'surface of things', particularly in the depictions of nature and animals[15] such as dead game trophy art.

In an extensive study of the Dutch gamepiece, Scott Sullivan writes that the demand for gamepiece paintings in Holland increased with economic and cultural expansion which saw an expanding middle class assume the fashion and pastimes of the artistocracy, including the purchase of country estates outside the city and paintings to hang on the walls of their new houses.[16] Since the rising middle class was not allowed to hunt prized game, the next best thing was to own a gamepiece, a general representation of the sport of hunting and proof of the rising social status of the owner.[17] The popularity of gamepiece art in France followed a similar trajectory in the eighteenth century: as the bourgeoisie became more prosperous, gamepieces were seen as fashionable.[18] Dead animal trophy art in the seventeenth century continued the hunting narratives that began in the 1500s with the large panoramic hunting scenes, but in the detail of a still life painting. Following an artistic tradition traced to ancient Greece and panel paintings of small game, fruit

41 Rembrandt van Rijn, *The Slaughtered Ox*, 1655, oil on canvas. Louvre, Paris. Stripped of head and hooves, the ox hangs on a sturdy frame.

and bread that adorned villa walls, the first game still life composition was Barbari's 1504 painting of a dead partridge hung beside hunting equipment discussed in the last chapter.[19]

The early gamepieces from the first half of the seventeenth century were painted by Peter Paul Rubens and Frans Snyders. Both artists used similar animal representations in their work, such as an open-winged swan and a snarling boar's head.[20] Snyders also often used human positions to pose dead animals – lying on their backs, legs crossed, heads canted to the side, necks stretched out from the body – much like 'fallen warriors'.[21] Illus. 42 is a good example of the mimicry of human posture (and of the use of a white swan to centre the picture). The human stallkeeper appears to be cradling a large dead bird (perhaps a peacock) much as a human body might be held in death. While there are a few live animals in the painting (besides the human), a few chickens and two curious dogs, most of the animals are dead game – the centring swan, a gutted deer, a rabbit, numerous birds of all sizes, and the head of a boar with mouth gaping open, tongue hanging out.

The gamepiece is a display of the animals that only the nobility were allowed to hunt, such as stag, boar, roe deer, hazel hens, pheasant and swan.[22] These prized game animals displaced the common domestic animals in the kitchen and market scenes of the sixteenth century, replacing the mundane with 'aristocratic elegance'.[23]

Aristocratic splendour, luxury and extravagance were also central to the representation of animals in display meals and table decorations.

42 Frans Snyders, *A Game Stall, c.* 1625–30, oil on canvas.
York Art Gallery, York Museums Trust. A splayed dead swan forms the
centrepiece of the stallholder's packed display.

Seventeenth-century aristocratic feasts and *entremets* often included artistic creations, such as bejewelled stuffed swans as decoration for the top of pies or rare foods, pies that enclosed complete orchestras, full-rigged vessels and exotic stuffed animals such as monkeys and whales, and table decorations that depicted hunting scenes or wild animals roaming about in the woods.[24]

Snyders's gamepieces are completely devoid of blood and evidence of death by hunting, attributes central to his earlier butcher's shop and kitchen scenes. For example, in illus. 43, the boar's head has made yet another appearance, but this time without any blood or tongue-hanging, and in 'The Fish Market' (illus. 44), a wide variety of fish are spread across the canvas, some still alive, some clearly dead, but no blood. It has been suggested that the tendency to eliminate blood and gore from the dead animal paintings was an early sign of a prohibition on displaying the aspects of killing animals that might be perceived as horrible or revolting.[25]

Sullivan writes that until the mid-1600s gamepiece art was mostly culinary. But after 1650 the genre became more trophy-like, with paintings focused on dead animals, hunting weapons, sporting dogs and landscapes,

43 Frans Snyders, *Pantry Scene with a Page, c.* 1615–1620, oil on canvas.
Wallace Collection, London. The page gazes thoughtfully over freshly killed lobster,
peacock and other game.

44 Frans Snyders, *The Fish Market, c.* 1618–1621, oil on canvas. The Hermitage,
St Petersburg. Slabs of filleted fish hang over a wide array of marine life.

often illustrating the context in which game animals were captured.[26] Thus, while the excessive consumption of meat continued into the seventeenth century, the depiction of extravagant abundance in market and kitchen scenes was replaced by far fewer dead animals in decorative game settings, such as outside hunting pavilions.[27] The first popular gamepiece depicting animals as a subject of hunting rather than eating is attributed to Jan Fyt.[28] Fyt's characteristic paintings were of hunting trophies and dead stags and birds. Sullivan notes that in Fyt's work the fruit and vegetables have been removed, dogs have been introduced, and the setting is no longer a table indoors, but outdoors,[29] as in illus. 45.

As the gamepiece became more focused on the landscape and hunting, dead animals were increasingly depicted with hunting equipment. However, the display of hunting accessories was arbitrary and used primarily as simple props; the inclusion of numerous hunting instruments suggested that prey could be caught using several methods, and birds such as peacocks that were not normally hunted were often shown as accessories to the central theme.[30]

45 Follower of Jan Fyt (1609–1661), *Still Life with a Hare, Song Birds and a Bird Net with a Spaniel Beyond*, oil on canvas. Rafael Valls Gallery, London. Dead game painted in the natural setting of the hunt.

While many animal species were depicted in seventeenth-century dead animal paintings, birds were among the most popular, perhaps because of the large numbers that migrated into the Netherlands, and because many species were hunted at the time.[31] Several hunting methods were used to catch birds. One practice was to feed the animals wine-soaked grain, and when rendered incapable of flying the birds were simply collected up by the hunter. Another strategy was to coat small twigs with a sticky substance and use a decoy to attract birds to the twigs. Both methods were useful in the capture of live song birds which would be caged and sold at markets and fairs.[32] Many kinds of nets and snares were used to catch small birds, and when caught they would be killed and their heads stuck between a willow branch that had been twisted or partially split open, so as to arrange the birds in an orderly row.[33]

While the Dutch gamepiece art form ended in the seventeenth century, the genre continued into the eighteenth century in other parts of Europe. For example, Jean-Baptiste Oudry's paintings of dead game in elegant outdoor scenes illustrate the importance of hunting among the French aristocracy. Illus. 46 is a good example of a late decorative gamepiece. In the centre of the painting is a hunting rifle propped against a table laden with fruit and wine. On one side of the table is a single dead wolf lying on the ground; on the other side are two lively, alert-looking hunting hounds. The blood has been removed, as has any evidence of how the wolf met his fate, leaving only the assumption that the end came with a bullet from the prominently displayed rifle.

'The Dead Wolf' has a companion piece, 'The Dead Roe', which show-cases the corpse of a deer and a large bird hanging upside down with wings spread. Dogs, alive and alert, guard the game, one surveying the scene, another scaring away a large bird whose wings are also spread. While these outdoor hunting scenes are reflective of the narrative of aristocratic hunting, Oudry also painted simple still lifes of dead animals hanging against a wall, such as illus. 47. In this painting, a dead hare hangs by her foot alongside a piece of lamb, a motif similar to the early kitchen scenes of dead food animals. This painting was intended to be part of a dining room panel, and it is a particularly realistic depiction of a slab of meat and fat and of the hare's fur, vacant eyes and the small drop of blood hanging from her nose. The painting also depicts an anatomical point of view, a before-butcher and after-butcher perception of the animal body.

Representations of hunting were not confined to the gamepiece. Por-traits of hunters, richly dressed and posing with hunting dogs and weapons, were popular in the seventeenth century, illustrating once again that the sport was a privileged one.[34] Rembrandt painted some of the

46 Jean-Baptiste Oudry, *The Dead Wolf*, 1721, oil on canvas. Wallace Collection, London. Resting against a shelf bearing wine and fruit, a hunting rifle separates the live hounds from the dead wolf.

earliest examples of hunting portraiture, such as a 1639 self-portrait in which he is depicted holding a dead bittern aloft for the viewer. And while Rembrandt's hunting portrait is a particularly thoughtful one, with the bittern occupying the foreground and the hunter somewhat hidden in the background, most hunting portraits were more ostentatious celebrations of aristocratic privilege, the affection between hunter and hounds, and the accumulation of dead game. And, as in the gamepiece, hunting portraits were attempts to make statements about social status and the depiction of privileged hunters and perfect hunting hounds.

47 Jean-Baptiste Oudry, *A Hare and a Leg of Lamb*, 1742, oil on canvas. Cleveland Museum of Art, Ohio. A painting intended to form part of a dining-room panel.

Live Animal Portraiture

Artistic representations of animals in the seventeenth century were not just of animal corpses illustrating eating- or hunting-focused pictures. Many artists painted ordinary live animals such as cows, horses, deer, dogs and birds. One of the most famous pictures in The Hague for over 100 years was 'The Young Bull' painted by the Dutch artist, Paulus Potter in 1647[35] and shown in illus. 48.

For the first time since antiquity, animals are represented on their own account, in the fields and meadows where they live, and not foregrounded or backgrounded in a human context. While 'Young Bull' does include an elderly farmer standing behind the cattle and sheep, it was rare for Potter to paint human figures. His subjects were the ordinary domestic farm animals common in Holland at the time: cows, sheep, pigs and goats. One observer of Potter's work noted that while Dutch artists often included animals in their landscape paintings, the animals were there only to reinforce the rustic nature of the countryside; but Potter 'painted cattle for their own sake; they were the stars, the landscape a backdrop . . . painted in such naturalistic detail that [in some of his cattle paintings] even the manure clinging to their sides can be clearly seen'.[36]

48 Paulus Potter, *The Young Bull*, 1647, oil on canvas. Mauritshuis, The Hague. Live farm animals in their natural environment.

Potter's country cattle were representations of just that – cows in the countryside. But a very different kind of representation became common in the eighteenth century, a representation that returns us to the object-ification and corporealization of animals – prize cattle portraiture. Pedigree livestock were painted for wealthy breeders who commissioned portraits of their prized animals. Cattle were depicted with huge square bodies emphasizing size and pedigree as proof of their value, which in turn emphasized the owner's social status.[37] Harriet Ritvo writes that the purpose of livestock breeding in the late eighteenth century was to produce animals that would quickly grow very large so they could produce more meat. This 'accelerated meat production' was made possible even without special breeding skills by enclosing open fields and feeding the animals turnips, an all-year fodder that put weight on animals that was maintained throughout the winter.[38]

Cattle were not the only animals being actively bred at the time. Perfec-tion and the ideal type were also inscribed on the bodies of domesticated dogs, particularly the foxhound. While hunting dogs have been bred since antiquity, Garry Marvin notes that the modern foxhound has a short 250-year history of being manipulatively bred for speed and stamina, with a pro-portioned body capable of running 50 miles twice a week.[39] By the late seventeenth century, horses were bred to work a wide range of jobs, includ-ing war, hunting, agriculture, pulling carts, wagons, private transport and sport racing.[40] Sheep were selectively bred indoors in sheep-houses so that their wool was protected from the 'profit-damaging effects' of the outside climate.[41]

Animal portraiture was also often used to convey political messages during the seventeenth century, particularly in elaborate displays of struggle and violence. For example, intense animal struggle as predator and prey, always a popular cultural representation of animals, found much artistic expression during the Enlightenment. In a particularly graphic sculpture, illus. 49 shows a wild beast attacking a domesticated animal. Thus, although similar representations have been common since antiq-uity, the intense emotionalism and vivid details of claws tearing into skin and the graphic facial expressions of animals in life-threatening struggle were perfected in the seventeenth and eighteenth centuries.

Animals were used to represent resistance to outside aggression and defiance of tyranny, as is conveyed in Jan Asselijn's mid-seventeenth-century painting of an enraged swan defending her nest.[42] Swans were widely regarded as brave and courageous, and this characteristic is captured in the depiction of a heroic swan protecting her offspring from an approaching dog. The white swan lifts herself up in anger hissing

49 Antonio Susini (active 1572–1624) or Giovanni Francesco Susini
(*c.* 1585–*c.* 1653), *Lion Attacking a Bull*, bronze, first quarter of the seventeenth
century, after models by Giambologna (Giovanni da Bologna or Jean de Boulogne)
(1529–1608). The J. Paul Getty Museum, Los Angeles.

furiously at the dog, wings spread, feathers flying, leaving excrement on
the ground. While the creator of the work may or may not have intended
the painting to be read as symbolic of a nation under threat from invasion,
later owners did, inscribing 'Holland' over the eggs and 'The enemy of the
state' over the image of the dog (England). The swan herself was inscribed
with the title 'Pensionary, Johan de Witt' a famous public servant who was
an ardent protector of Holland's interests against England.

Dead and live animal portraiture, hunting trophies, representations of
biological perfection and political symbolism, were all to be found in
images commissioned by and for the wealthy. Few of the animals in the
lives of common people found their way into the visual record, with the
notable exception of William Hogarth's prints which are discussed later in
this chapter. Animal imagery was however an important part of community
ceremonies and rituals of the seventeenth and eighteenth centuries.

Animal Massacres as Ritual

Eighteenth-century England was, according to E. P. Thompson, a place of trouble and deep contradictions, and by the end of the century rural people were severely impoverished in spite of agricultural innovations and food surpluses.[43] In France, too, the early modern peasant was in dire straits. In the 1690s plague and famine hit northern France, forcing people to try to live on offal thrown into the street by butchers or by eating grass.[44] Peasants were in a constant struggle against hunger and death, farming strips of land in open fields, sowing and harvesting collectively, living in a world of 'inexorable, unending toil, and of brutal emotions, both raw and repressed'.[45]

Because of the disenfranchisement of the common people in Europe, rituals and ceremonies were central to their lives; as Huizinga argues, '[t]he more crushing the misery of daily life, the stronger the stimulants that will be needed to produce that intoxication' that festivals could provide.[46] E. P. Thompson writes that there is a tendency to think of eighteenth-century England as a society thriving on consumerism and politeness, with customs and rituals transformed as magic, witchcraft and oral transmission were replaced by literacy and enlightenment. But a reformation of traditional customs and rituals was resisted by the common people, creating a wide gap between the culture of aristocrats and that of the lower class throughout Europe.[47]

In addition to the time-honoured traditions of parading husband-beating wives through the streets in charivaris and finding women to accuse of witchcraft,[48] people of the seventeenth and eighteenth centuries made heavy use of animals and animal symbolism in their rituals and ceremonies. Ritualized celebrations and merriment during the Enlightenment often ended with animal-baitings[49] and were deeply embedded in animal imagery. Horns continued to be used to ritualize masculinity. Men imitated stags in a Horn Dance by 'wearing antlers' (too heavy to actually wear, the antlers were carried on stands and projected around the head and shoulders), carved animal heads or skulls, usually of a horse, ram or bull, were carried through the streets at Christmas time,[50] cocks were whipped on Shrove Tuesday,[51] dogs were whipped on St Luke's Day and if caught as strays slowly drowned for sport, wrens were hunted and plucked alive on St Stephen's Day,[52] and untold numbers of cats were tortured on all days – tied up in bags, hung from May poles, suspended from ropes, burned at the stake, chased flaming through the streets and incinerated by the sackload.[53]

Following on Lévi-Strauss's often-cited assertion that 'animals are good to think',[54] Robert Darnton writes that cats, because of their ritual value, were particularly 'good for staging ceremonies'.[55] Cat torture continued to be a popular amusement throughout Europe in the eighteenth century. Cats were tortured to the rough music of charivaris in France and in Germany (where the charivari was called '*katzenmusik*', a likely reference to the howls of cats in pain).[56] There was 'nothing unusual about the ritual killing of cats', writes Darnton, and the people of the time heard much in the wailing of a cat: witchcraft, orgy, cuckoldry, charivari and massacre, with the torture of cats always including the same three ingredients: bonfires, cats and hilarious witch-hunting.[57] Symbolic of witchcraft, cats were associated with women (the word 'pussy' has the same meaning in French slang as it does in English, and has been an obscenity for hundreds of years), and it was 'an easy jump from the sexuality of women to the cuck-olding of men'.[58] In describing popular culture in the seventeenth century, Peter Burke notes that festivals and rituals were particularly popular in Catholic cities such as Paris, Madrid, Rome and Naples, and they were usually organized by young adult men (such as the 'Abbeys of Misrule'), affirming community solidarity and civic pride, and as 'rituals of reversal . . . [they were] a symbolic turning of the world upside down which acted to some extent as a safety-valve'.[59]

A good example of the deployment of animals in a ritualized turning of the world upside down was the massacre of cats by disgruntled Parisian print-shop workers in the 1730s. Robert Darnton recounts the story as told by one of the shop workers.[60] While the printer, Jacques Vincent, and his wife doted on cats, particularly the mistress's favourite, The Gray, the workers in Vincent's shop were badly treated, required to work long hours, fed rotten pieces of meat (which the household cats refused to eat) and expected to rise early for work after sleepless nights made miserable by cats howling on the roof over the workers' bedroom. After staggering out of bed at the crack of dawn morning after morning while the master and his wife slept late, the workers decided to give the Vincents themselves a sleepless night. They positioned themselves close to the master's bedroom and howled and meowed horribly, and after several sleepless nights, the Vincents decided they were being bewitched and ordered the workers to get rid of the rowdy cats. The workers, joined by the journeymen, were glad to do so: 'with broom handles, bars of the press, and other tools of their trade, they went after every cat they could find, beginning with The Gray', smashing his spine with an iron bar[61] and stashing him in a gutter while the journeymen bludgeoned and trapped all the cats they could find, driving them across the rooftops into sacks. After dumping sackloads of half-dead cats into the courtyard, the workers staged a mock trial, pronounced the cats guilty, administered last rites and strung them up on a gallows. The events were re-enacted and accompanied by 'rough music' (the workers ran sticks across the tops of the type cases, pounded on cupboards and bleated like goats) over and over in the subsequent days when the printers wanted to take time out for amusement. Darnton notes that we have access to this narrative of animal slaughter as a ritual ceremony that reversed the social order and tested social boundaries because the compositors in print shops were among the few in the working class who were literate enough to give their own accounts of what life was like three hundred years ago.

Hunting metaphors played a central role in rituals and ceremonies during the seventeenth and eighteenth centuries, replete with representations of horses, stags and hounds. Building on hunting imagery, medieval rituals designed to humiliate and shame social offenders continued well into the Enlightenment. E. P. Thompson describes a shaming ceremony of the time that used striking hunting imagery, the Devon stag hunt.[62] A youth wearing horns and occasionally animal skins acted as the victim's proxy. He would be discovered (by design) in a nearby wooded area, chased by the hounds (village youths) through the village streets and backyards for an hour or more. Until the final kill, the 'stag' would avoid getting too close to the victim's house, but when the kill took place it was brutally realistic – the stag collapsed on the door step of the victim, a bladder of bullock's blood carried on his chest and pierced by a hunting knife spilled blood all over the stones outside the victim's house.

Animal imagery was central to the dramatic street theatre forms of charivari and rough music rituals that not only publicized scandal by mocking social offenders, but also asserted the legitimacy of authority.[63] In cases of severe sexual offences, the ritual hunts were expressions of hostility that took on magical meanings, with the community expelling the hunted from its protection when the boundaries of permissible behaviour had been violated; the stag's collapse and the spilling of blood on the victim's doorstep was a public announcement of the disgrace.[64]

Representations of horses and of sexually 'unbridled' women were common ritualized images. Morris dancers fastened the figure of a horse around their waists, imitating a small horse, and this character was known as the Hobby-horse (a term that also euphemistically refers to a promiscuous woman or a prostitute). In Kent, dancers carried Hooden Horses about to the sound of music. Similar to the Hobby-horse, the Hooden Horse was a pole upon which was mounted a wooden horse head with a hinged jaw and a hood hiding the human bearer. Riding wooden horses (and its variation Riding Stang) was a form of public punishment that required offenders to straddle a wooden horse, with weights attached to each leg, and sometimes the 'horse's back' was not a smooth set of planks but rather a sharp pointed surface, thus adding to the punishment.

Exhibition as Entertainment

In Protestant London, traditional festivals were declining and being replaced with newer forms of popular culture, such as street performances by professional entertainers, public plays held in local taverns and animal-baitings.[65] While itinerant showmen still travelled to the countryside with freaks, curiosities and peepshows (called 'raree-shows'), animal exhibitions at fairs, festivals and in sideshows were confined primarily to London in the seventeenth century.[66] Domestic animals were frequent sideshow attractions, particularly if they were monstrous, talented, or deformed, often exhibited alongside anomalous humans, such as giants, dwarves, hair-covered children and albinos.[67]

Talented animals were extremely popular attractions – dancing bears, performing birds, and trained horses (such as the famous Morocco who could return a glove to its owner after hearing the owner's name whispered in his ear) had been standard entertainment in London since the sixteenth century.[68] Spectators particularly enjoyed seeing animals trained to perform human behaviours. In addition to exhibiting birds and fleas that pulled chariots, showman offered hares that played drums, flies that duelled with pieces of straw and, as performances became more elaborate in the eighteenth century, public shows exhibited dogs and monkeys dressed as humans attacking a town, dancing, eating at a table and playing cards.[69] While Joseph Strutt had his doubts about whether some of the more spectacular animal tricks were ever 'displayed in reality', he claimed that many of his contemporaries in 1800 had witnessed an exhibition called 'The Deserter Bird', put on by a juggler in Cockspur Street opposite the Haymarket in 1775:[70]

> A number of little birds, to the amount, I believe, of twelve or fourteen, being taken from different cages, were placed upon a table in the presence of the spectators; and there they formed themselves into ranks like a company of soldiers: small cones of paper bearing some resemblance to grenadiers' caps were put upon their heads, and diminutive imitations of muskets made with wood, secured under their left wings. Thus equipped, they marched to and fro several times; when a single bird was brought forward, supposed to be a deserter,

and set between six of the musketeers, three in a row, who conducted him from the top to the bottom of the table, on the middle of which a small brass cannon charged with a little gunpowder had been previously placed, and the deserter was situated in the front part of the cannon; his guards then divided, three retiring on one side, and three on the other, and he was left standing by himself. Another bird was immediately produced; and, a lighted match being put into one of his claws, he hopped boldly on the other to the tail of the cannon, and, applying the match to the priming, discharged the piece without the least appearance of fear or agitation. The moment the explosion took place, the deserter fell down, and lay, apparently motionless, like a dead bird; but, at the command of his tutor he rose again; and the cages being brought, the feathered soldiers were stripped of their ornaments, and returned into them in perfect order.

The enthusiasm for seeing animals engaged in human activities also found its way into both written and visual art. For example, in Jean-Baptiste Oudry's drawings of a scene from a fable, 'Animals Sick of the Plague', a group of animals discuss an outbreak of plague. Believing that the scourge was sent in punishment for their sins, they decide that the most guilty among them should confess and be sacrificed for the good of all. A donkey makes a confession of a small and insignificant 'sin', and the other animals judge it as a hanging offence: 'thus human courts acquit the strong, and doom the weak, as therefore wrong'.[71]

Fights between mastiffs and bears and between bulls and lions were institutionalized entertainment in the eighteenth century through the establishment of special combat arenas in large towns, such as the Hertz Theatre in Vienna and Vauxhall in London, where in addition to staged animal combats (see illus. 50), there were also lion-tamer shows, puppeteers and wrestlers. In Paris, licensed entrepreneurs pitted dogs against wolves, deer, boars, lions, tigers, leopards, a polar bear and a mandrill.[72] Also in Paris, a bullfight was held on Sunday afternoons and public holidays at an amphitheatre where mastiffs were pitted against bulls or wild animals, and the contests ended with a fight between dogs and a donkey; these new entertainment sites 'formed part of the eighteenth-century diversification of fairground attractions'.[73] The combats were held in an arena on the northeastern edge of the city, which was temporarily closed down in the 1780s when the owner attempted to use human toreadors in the bullfight, and again in the 1790s because it was believed that the blood sport would be morally harmful for human spectators; the arena was permanently abandoned in 1833.[74]

50 Jan Collaert (1566–1628), after Jan van der Straet (Joannes Stradanus)
(1523–1605), *Noblemen Watch Combat of Wild Beasts in an Indoor Circus*,
hand-coloured engraving, Plate 12 from *Venationes Ferarum, Avium, Piscium*
('Of Hunting: Wild Beasts, Birds, Fish').

Exotics and Pets

As exploration of the world increased, more and more exotic animals were
imported into Europe for private ownership, menageries and public
display. In eighteenth-century Paris, for example, a large number of exotic
animals were kept as pets, their popularity linked to the accumulation of
personal wealth that enabled many urban dwellers to purchase and
maintain luxury animals,[75] such as monkeys and parrots.

Parrots were exotic in Europe until the nineteenth century and were
highly valued not only for their rarity but also for their ability to mimic
human speech.[76] Louise Robbins writes that male authors often associated
women with parrots (and other pets), portraying the relationship as either
lascivious or petulant, depending on whether the animal was symbolic of
the male lover or a rival of the female owner's affections; one male writer
laments the distress a young girl shows over a bird in a painting by Jean-

Baptiste Greuze, remarking 'Such pain! At her age! And for a bird!'[77]
Bruce Boehrer reads many of the images of parrots in seventeenth century
paintings as part of a larger colonial discourse that associated parrots with
ornamental backdrops and luxury consumables, exotic toys and subaltern
men such as black slaves who were the must-have luxury items of the time
for European aristocrats.[78]

There was a substantial expansion of pet-keeping in the eighteenth
century, and people doted on an ever widening variety of animals. House-
holds kept pet lambs, pet hares, pet mice, pet bats, pet toads, and pet hedge-
hogs; birds of all kinds were captured and sold in the large London bird
market, birds for singing, birds for imitating human speech and wild birds
kept as honorary pets such as the robin.[79] While the perception of pets as
property began to take hold about this time, it was not illegal to steal
animals kept only for pleasure, primarily those who were allowed to live in
the house, named and never eaten (not because some pleasure animals
weren't tasty but because they lived in close proximity to humans).[80] Indeed,
pleasure animals were sometimes eaten, but usually only under duress.
Louise Robbins recounts that on a long sea voyage carrying exotic animals
back to France, the starving captain and shipmates postponed eating the
parrots and monkeys on board by first consuming the last of the biscuit
crumbs, maggots and rat droppings that remained on the ship.[81]

Dogs and Rabies

Pet dogs were particularly popular in England. By the late 1700s almost
everyone had a dog, and the estimated one million dogs in the population
were mostly animals kept for pleasure.[82] Concern about the huge number of
dogs in the streets led authorities to try to limit the number of canines kept
by the poor, and there were numerous attempts to institute a dog tax in the
1700s. Finally, when rabies became a major concern in the late 1700s, the
tax was passed in 1796 as a means of controlling the disease, primarily by
eliminating the dogs of the poor because they were not as likely as gentlemen's dogs to be confined if they showed symptoms of the disease.[83]

As in the earlier attempts to control the spread of plague, dogs were mass-
slaughtered to halt the spread of rabies. During an outbreak of rabies in
Edinburgh in 1738, animals were clubbed to death or herded into a harbour
and drowned, and a bounty was placed on each animal killed.[84] As a direct
consequence of the 1796 licensing law, thousands of unlicensed dogs were
slaughtered throughout England.[85] The widespread destruction of suspi-
ciously rabid dogs had a rationale similar to that underlying the slaughter of
dogs and cats during outbreaks of plague discussed in the last chapter. Ritvo

writes that rabies, bubonic plague and cholera were all associated with disorder, dirt and sin.[86] In the plague-fearing slaughters, as noted in the previous chapter, roaming animals were disorderly, unsanitary and problematic because they were not part of a fixed social relationship.[87] Rabies was believed to be the result of 'unsettling social forces', and attempts to control the disease (including licensing, mandatory muzzling and rounding up vagrant dogs who were a danger to society) justified 'stigmatizing and restricting dangerous human groups', such as 'violent and disruptive' butchers, impoverished dogs and their owners who lived together in squalor, and dog owners who let their animals out daily to roam about the streets looking for food.[88] As Ritvo notes, the rabies control and prevention efforts were reinforced by the view of human dominion over other animals. This hierarchy is also pervasive in the exhibition of animals.

Exhibition as Education

With the onset of the Enlightenment, there was an increase in 'rational amusement', or education mixed with entertainment, and animal shows were considered opportunities for education in natural history.[89] In Paris, naturalists attended fairs and animal combat shows for information on the physical and behavioural characteristics of a wide range of animal species, and by the late 1700s animal show entrepreneurs were advertising the natural history value of their exhibits.[90] The exotic animals kept at the Exeter 'Change in London at the time were never exhibited as in a sideshow or a circus, but rather as examples of wildlife that might be seen in their natural habitat.[91] However, the 'natural habitat' at Exeter 'Change was only an illusion: animals were kept there in tiny cages with walls decorated with tropical foliage.[92]

Menageries and curiosity cabinets were finally opened to the public in the seventeenth century in part because of the increasing desire of aristocrats and royalty to appear powerful and cultured and to curry favour with the public.[93] While the royal menagerie in the Tower of London continued to symbolize triumph over the natural world until 1834, it also provided many with the opportunity to observe unusual animals.[94] The mix of animals at the Tower did not change much between the sixteenth and eighteenth centuries,[95] but still people travelled far and wide for the opportunity to see the lions, tigers, bears, eagles and monkeys held in the menagerie. In many cases, the animals did the travelling, particularly if they were unusual or exotic. Hansken the elephant was exhibited throughout Europe for six years in the 1600s, and Clara the rhinoceros (see illus. 51) travelled all over Europe in a horse-drawn chariot in the mid-1700s, her popularity encouraging the sale of rhinoceros prints, engravings and the invention of rhino bonnets, wigs and hairstyles.[96]

It was probably the very same Clara who was sketched as a background portrait for the *Musculorum Tabula*, a series of engravings of human bones and muscles by Jan Wandelaar (1742). Wandelaar's portraits constitute the

51 Pietro Longhi, *The Rhinoceros*, 1751, oil on canvas. Ca' Rezzonico, Museo del Settecento, Venice. This was the first to be seen in Europe since Dürer's in 1515, finally correcting the errors in that image, which was not drawn from life.

first accurate Western portrayals of a rhinoceros, finally correcting Albrecht Dürer's erroneous 1515 sketch, which, as discussed in the previous chapter, was based not on his own observation but rather on someone else's description of the animal.

The Tower of London was the only permanent exhibition of entire menageries in the city until the 1770s when wild animals were put on show at Exeter 'Change.[97] A small travelling menagerie took up residence there during the off season, and George Stubbs is reported to have bought a dead tiger from the menagerie and spent an evening 'carbonading [salting for preservation] the once tremendous tyrant of the jungle'.[98] It was common in the sixteenth and seventeenth centuries to preserve dead animals by salting, reduction to the skeleton or stuffing the dead bodies with straw.[99]

One of the best-known and well-documented menageries of all time was Versailles, built by Louis XIV in the 1660s. In fact, Louis XIV built two menageries, one at Vincennes, just outside Paris, and a more elaborate facility on the site of a royal hunting lodge in the countryside at Versailles.[100] At Vincennes, animal combats were held when the king wanted to entertain foreign visitors, but the Versailles menagerie was intended for the display of peaceful animals and exotic gifts given to the king.[101] According to Baratay and Hardouin-Fugier, the collection at Versailles was special because it was the first Western menagerie to display in one place only rare and exotic animals for viewing by visitors. A unique octagonal architectural design at Versailles allowed 'culture to enclose nature, to gather it around the monarch, who from the central salon could take everything in at a single glance, and who so dominated all he surveyed'.[102]

The octagonal design which gave the observer the ability to see everything without being seen was to be taken up again in the late 1700s by Jeremy Bentham.[103] Bentham developed what he called 'a new principle of construction', the 'panopticon', or the 'inspection house', applicable for prisons, work houses, poor houses, schools, hospitals and mad houses – 'any sort of establishment in which persons of any description are to be kept under inspection'.[104] And of course the design had proved to be very applicable to the individual animals in the Versailles menagerie. While Bentham made no reference to the germ of his idea lying in the special construction of Versailles, Michel Foucault recognized that Bentham's work was based on the old menagerie design:

Bentham does not say whether he was inspired, in his project, by Le Vaux's menagerie at Versailles: the first menagerie in which the different elements are not, as they traditionally were, distributed in a park . . . At the centre was an octagonal pavilion which, on the first floor, consisted of only a single room, the king's salon; on every side large windows looked out onto seven cages (the eighth side was reserved for the entrance), containing different species of animals. By Bentham's time, this menagerie had disappeared. But one finds in the programme of the Panopticon a similar concern with individualizing observation, with characterization and classification, with the analytical arrangement of space.[105]

There was a close connection between art and the display of nature at Versailles. Matthew Senior writes that '(l)ooking at animals at Versailles was a simultaneous looking at pictures of animals'.[106] Inventories of the exotic were documented by artists commissioned to make drawings of animals, and Louis XIV had a number of prominent artists paint each animal on arrival at the Versailles menagerie. Approximately sixty pictures were displayed in a gallery prior to entering the viewing salon, a display described by one contemporary as one that prepared visitors for what would soon be seen and to serve as a reminder of what visitors had just seen.[107] Senior notes that the Versailles animals were also used to entertain guests during royal receptions and pageants which were often held in large outdoor theatres; one ceremony in 1664 staged the representation of the four seasons of the year by displaying women riding on the backs of menagerie animals.[108]

Animals did not thrive in menagerie life. They died from the cold, unhealthy environment and from the scarce, unsuitable food, and they developed confinement deformities – such as the unusually small adult tiger whose size was compromised because of having been enclosed in a narrow cage as a cub, an emaciated, partially bald lynx with bone spurs and jaw decay, and beavers that could not swim.[109] Buffon, the famous French naturalist of the eighteenth century, lamented the imprisonment of animals in menageries and was wary about the usefulness of menageries for observing animal behaviour.[110] He preferred to study animals in as natural a setting as possible, and to this end he kept animals in a semi-free enclosure for his research.[111]

The zoo as a scientific and educational endeavour also paralleled the onset of the French Revolution and the complaint that it was shameful to feed animals in menageries (such as at Versailles) when so many people were going hungry. The Versailles animals were moved to the Jardin des Plantes as natural history collections to be dedicated to science, intended for all people to see, not just a few princes and kings and their visitors, and while other scholarly establishments (universities, academies,

faculties of medicine) were eliminated because of the fear of intellectual
tyranny, the zoological garden survived because it was open to the public,
and in 1793 it was turned into the 'national natural-history Museum'.[112] It
was also common for the animals in the Versailles menagerie to be dissected by fellows of the Académie royale des sciences, and the details of
animal structure and anatomy produced scientific publications that
described almost fifty different animal species.[113]

The advantages of dissecting recently dead animals brought increased
interest in specimens from shows and menageries, and the careful study of
animal anatomy greatly enhanced scientific illustration.[114] Continuing the
work of early anatomical enthusiasts, Albrecht Dürer and Leonardo da
Vinci, artists in the seventeenth and eighteenth centuries captured
anatomical details of a variety of animals in their work. For example, Rembrandt's drawings include numerous studies of animals, including both
domestics, such as pigs and dogs, and exotics, such as camels, lions and a
very realistic elephant (see illus. 52).

Another accomplished painter and anatomist, from a slightly later
period, was George Stubbs. Stubbs made extensive observations of a
variety of animals in private menageries, dissected horses for eighteen
months in a rented farmhouse in England,[115] and published a book on

52 Rembrandt van Rijn, *Elephant*, 1637. A study of an elephant
brought to Amsterdam from Ceylon and widely exhibited.

horse anatomy in 1766. Stubbs's close experiences with the anatomical details of horses are clearly evident in his art. He painted numerous portraits of beloved horses commissioned by their wealthy owners (such as the famous 1762 portrait of Whistlejacket), horses in domestic settings (such as mares and foals in a landscape) and wild animals (such as a series in which a lion attacks a horse).

Large animals were not the only subjects of interest to the scientists and artists of the Enlightenment. The invention of the microscope in Holland in the seventeenth century revolutionized the perception of the natural world, and for the first time insect anatomy and behaviour could be studied.[116] This new scientific gaze into the microscopic animal world was reflected in art as scientists continued to illustrate their work. In forest still life paintings of the 1600s, a breeder of reptiles and snakes painted insects and amphibians in wooded scenes, emphasizing the struggle for life in the undergrowth for toads, frogs, snakes and lizards; other scientists and painters illustrated the urinary and genital organs of molluscs and amphibians, the blood vessel structure in the tail of a tadpole, and fights between insects, reptiles and amphibians who, in their struggle, are shown destroying the surrounding plant life.[117]

Growing Opposition to Cruelty

Among the several reasons for the transition of vivisection from a public display to a private event was growing opposition to the practice on sentimental and aesthetic grounds.[118] After a particularly horrifying vivisection of a dog, Robert Hooke grumbled to his experimental partner, Robert Boyle:

> I shall hardly be induced to make any further trials of this kind, because of the torture of the creature: but certainly the enquiry would be very noble, if we could find any way so to stupify the creature, as that it might not be sensible, which I fear there is hardly any opiate will perform.[119]

There was, according to Keith Thomas, a 'new sensibility' afoot. Now, 'for the first time', influential seventeenth-century Christians began to agree with Montaigne's argument that humans had no sovereignty over other animals, and 'it became increasingly common to maintain that nature existed for God's glory and that he cared as much for the welfare of plants and animals as for man'.[120] There was a moral concern for animals that 'widened to include many living beings which had been traditionally regarded as hateful or noxious . . . [even] Worms, beetles, snails, earwigs and spiders all found their advocates; and naturalists began to seek for more humane methods of killing them'.[121]

In the eighteenth century opposition to animal experiments began in earnest. In 1764, Voltaire complained about vivisection and the 'barbarian' scientists who practised live experiments:

> This dog, so very superior to man in affection, is seized by some barbarian virtuosos, who nail him down to a table, and dissect him while living, the better to shew you the meseraic veins. All the same organs of sensation which are in yourself you perceive in him. Now, Machinist, what say you? answer me: Has Nature created all the springs of feeling in this animal, that it may not feel? has it nerves to be impassible? For shame! charge not Nature with such weakness and inconsistency.[122]

The rising opposition to the mistreatment of animals was not limited to vivisection. Cruel farm practices generated laws against bringing unnecessary harm to animals. One of the first anti-cruelty laws was established in Ireland in 1635 and prohibited using the tails of horses for ploughing, harrowing or draught and pulling the wool off living sheep instead of clipping or shearing them.[123] A few years later in the Massachusetts colony of the New World, Nathaniel Ward introduced two anti-cruelty pieces into the Body of Liberties Laws of 1641. The first prohibited any mistreatment of animals: 'No man shall exercise any Tirranny or Crueltie towards any bruite Creature which are usuallie kept for man's use' and the second required resting cattle during transport: 'If any man shall have occasion to leade or drive Cattel from place to place that is far . . . so that they be weary, or hungry, or fall sick, or . . . [lame], It shall be lawful to rest or refresh them, for a competent time, in any open place . . .'[124]

As the new sentimentality toward animals spread, animal behaviour was often anthropomorphized and described in decidedly non-mechanical ways by scientists and artists alike. Matthew Cobb wrote that Jan Swammerdam, the influential seventeenth-century biologist and natural historian, had a

> view of insect behaviour and development, [that] while lawful, was not mechanical or Cartesian. His delightfully anthropomorphic description of post-coital fatigue in the snail speaks volumes in terms of his attempt to understand animal behaviour and his conception of the factors that motivate animals.[125]

It was also common for poets to speak directly to animals in their poetry, such as William Blake's (1757–1827) query of a fly, 'Am not I, A fly like thee, Or art not thou, A man like me?'[126] David Hill notes that while many eighteenth-century writers reflected on the meaning of animals, it was primarily as representative of the human condition, such as being in love, or abstract ponderings, such as on the question of immortality – rarely was the natural world addressed for what it was. Even Blake, Wordsworth, Keats and Shelley wrote 'reflective poems which explore the generalised idea associated with the natural object . . . there is no emphasis on the particular nightingale or the particular skylark . . . there is no moment of confrontation and the train of thought that follows from it as the animal responds to the human'.[127] A rare exception was Robert Burns (1759–1796) who had a lengthy one-way conversation in his 1785 poem 'To a mouse on turning her up in her nest with a plough':[128]

> Wee, sleekit, cowrin, tim'rous beastie,
> O, what a panic's in thy breastie!
> Thou need na start awa sae hasty,
> Wi' bickering brattle!
> I wad be laith to rin an' chase thee
> Wi' murd'ring pattle!
>
> I'm truly sorry man's dominion,
> Has broken nature's social union,
> An' justifies that ill opinion,
> What makes thee startle
> At me, thy poor, earth-born companion,
> An' fellow-mortal!
>
> I doubt na, whiles, but thou may thieve;
> What then? poor beastie, thou maun live!
> A daimen icker in a thrave
> 'S a sma' request;
> I'll get a blessin wi' the lave,
> An' never miss't!
>
> Thy wee bit housie, too, in ruin!
> It's silly wa's the win's are strewin!
> An' naething, now, to big a new ane,

O' foggage green!
An' bleak December's winds ensuin,
Baith snell an' keen!

Thou saw the fields laid bare an' waste,
An' weary winter comin fast,
An' cozie here, beneath the blast,
Thou thought to dwell –
Till crash! the cruel coulter past
Out thro' thy cell.

That wee bit heap o' leaves an' stibble,
Has cost thee mony a weary nibble!
Now thou's turn'd out, for a' thy trouble,
But house or hald,
To thole the winter's sleety dribble,
An' cranreuch cauld!

But Mousie, thou art no thy lane,
In proving foresight may be vain;
The best-laid schemes o' mice an' men
Gang aft agley,
An' lea'e us nought but grief an' pain,
For promis'd joy!

Still thou art blest, compar'd wi' me;
The present only toucheth thee:
But och! I backward cast my e'e,
On prospects dreaer!
An' forward, tho' I canna see,
I guess an' fear!

Burns identified with the mouse, and compared her plight to his own misfortune, and in that respect he follows tradition in considering the mouse representative of something human. But he engaged with her, and there was emphasis on that particular mouse, as an individual, a subject of a life. Hill notes that Burns's poem is unique in that the encounter between a mouse and a man triggered a series of reflections on the animal's identity and her appearance, and what her appearance conveyed about her emotions.[129] It was also common for seventeenth-century writers to lament the captivity of cage birds, and poets wrote about the sorrow of the mother bird whose eggs were stolen or whose hatchlings were killed by hunters, and these writings about cruelty to wild birds had a substantial influence on middle-class attitudes about animals.[130] Louise Robbins argues that chained and caged exotic animals symbolized slavery, prison, and oppression in eighteenth-century France, where criticism of political tyranny, sympathy of animal slaves and awe of wildlife became standard in both natural history writings and in fiction.[131]

It is an important point that the increasing compassion of the time was not limited to other animals, but extended to exploited and mistreated humans. Keith Thomas writes:

> . . . the concern for animal welfare was part of a much wider movement which involved the spread of humane feelings towards previously despised human beings, like the criminal, the insane or the enslaved. It thus became associated with a more general demand for reform, whether the abolition of slavery, flogging and public executions or the reform of schools, prisons and the poor law. The pamphleteer who in 1656 called for a law against cruel sports also denounced torture and pressing to death as barbarous, and condemned hanging, drawing and quartering . . .[132]

The spreading humanitarian concern for exploited others was aided by what Peter Burke called a 'new culture of print' that substantially increased the amount of cheap printed materials available to the public, such as pamphlets, newspapers, broadsides and chap-books.[133] Diana Donald writes that the human–animal relationship was a recurring theme in popular mainstream publications of the early 1800s such as illustrated magazines and serial fiction, and animal cruelty served as a reminder of human social problems.[134]

Looking at Cruelty

While reading about cruelty to animals was influential in generating humanitarian public concern, *looking at* cruelty was the most compelling means of conveying the horror of animal suffering. Diana Donald argues that visual imagery was 'uniquely able to transmit the shock of first-hand experience . . . [and] painful proximity' to sites of cruelty was what actually prompted anti-cruelty protests.[135]

The most powerful eighteenth-century visual image of human brutality to animals was William Hogarth's (1697–1764) set of prints, *The Four Stages of Cruelty*, published in 1751. Hogarth's engravings conveyed not only the graphic torture and suffering of animals, but also the long-held view that it is a logical progression to move from animal cruelty to cruelty to humans.

In the first scene (illus. 53), the anti-hero, Tom Nero, an impoverished boy in the care of the Parish of St Giles, tortures a dog with an arrow,

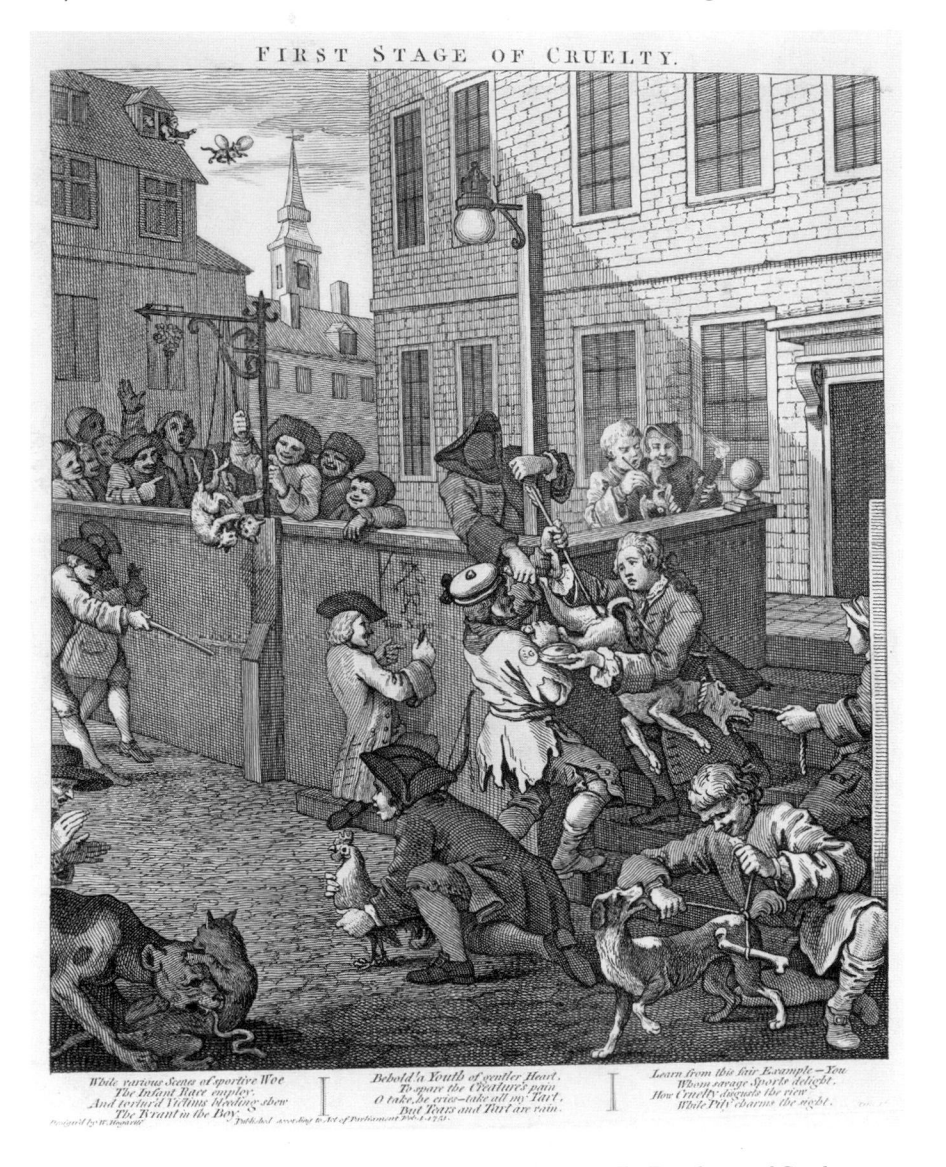

53 William Hogarth, 'First Stage of Cruelty', from *The Four Stages of Cruelty*, 1751, engraving. Animals are tortured for fun by boys in the streets of London.

assisted by a boy holding the dog's legs and another holding a rope around the dog's neck. A well-dressed young boy tries to stop Nero and offers him his tart if he will cease hurting the dog. The scene is full of animal cruelty, pain and suffering, all inflicted by youngsters: a bird's eye is gouged out, a cat is tossed from an upstairs window, sticks are thrown at a cockerel, and cats are tied together by their tails. Here is Hogarth's caption for the first illustration:

> While various Scenes of sportive Woe
> The Infant Race employ
> And tortur'd Victims bleeding shew
> The Tyrant in the boy.

> Behold a Youth of gentler Heart,
> To spare the Creature's pain
> O take, he cries – take all my Tart,
> But Tears and Tart are vain.

> Learn from this fair Example – You
> Whom savage Sports delight,
> How Cruelty disgusts the view
> While Pity charms the sight.

In the second illustration (illus. 54), Tom Nero, now a grown man, is shown savagely beating a horse who has dropped to the ground, exhausted from pulling a carriage loaded down with lawyers. The horse, emaciated and with a large sore on her chest from the rubbing harness, has her head turned away from the butt end of a whip held aloft by Nero, tears falling from her eyes, tongue hanging out. She has broken her leg in her fall. Another man beats a dying lamb with a stick, while attempting to get her to stand by pulling on her tail. In the background, an overloaded donkey is prodded with a stick, a bull is baited with a dog, and a child is run over by a wagon while playing in the street. Hogarth's caption for 'Second Stage of Cruelty' reads:

> The generous Steed in hoary Age
> Subdu'd by Labour lies,
> And mourns a cruel Master's rage,
> While Nature Strength denies.

54 William Hogarth, 'Second Stage of Cruelty', from *The Four Stages of Cruelty*,
1751, engraving. Working animals are savagely beaten,
and a bull is baited with a dog.

The tender lamb o'er drove and faint
Amidst expiring Throws
Bleats forth its innocent complaint
And dies beneath the Blows.

Inhuman Wretch! Say whence proceeds
This coward Cruelty?
What Int'rest springs from barb'rous deeds?
What Joy from Misery?

In the third stage (illus. 55), Tom Nero's cruelty has progressed from animals to humans. He is being arrested after having savagely murdered a servant girl, whom he seduced and talked into stealing from her mistress. He is to be hanged by the neck until dead.

In the final stage (illus. 56), Nero has been hanged and now lies on a dissecting table, a dog feeds on the heart removed from his flayed body. Experimental dissection after death was a fate not uncommon for those who had the misfortune of dying poor. The caption reads, in part:

Behold the Villain's dire disgrace!
Not death itself can end.
He finds no peaceful Burial Place;
His breathless Corse, no friend.

In his autobiography, Hogarth was clear in that his intention with *The Four Stages of Cruelty* was to reach the largest possible audience at the cheapest possible price:

The four stages of cruelty were done in hope of preventing in some degree that cruel treatment of poor animals which makes the streets of London more disagreeable to the human mind than anything what ever, the very describing of which gives pain. but it could not be done in too strong a manner as the most stony hearts were meant to be effected by them . . . We may only say this more, that neither correctness of drawing or fine engraving were at all necessary, but on the contrary would set the price of them out of the reach of those for whom they were chiefly intended.[136]

Katharine Rogers has noted that the image of cats in Hogarth's prints 'perpetuate the seventeenth-century representation of unvalued animals relegated to humble settings' – a shabby street scene in 'First Stage of

55 William Hogarth, 'Cruelty in Perfection', from *The Four Stages of Cruelty*,
1751, engraving. Cruelty to animals has moved on to
brutality towards other humans.

56 William Hogarth, 'The Reward of Cruelty', from *The Four Stages of Cruelty*, 1751, engraving. The murderer's corpse is dissected, the cycle of cruelty continuing beyond death.

Cruelty', a sordid garret in 'The Distressed Poet' (1737), and a barn in 'Strolling Actresses' (1738).[137] Hogarth often portrayed cats alongside 'seedy sexuality' as in the series *A Harlot's Progress* (1732) which illustrates the transition of an innocent country girl (shown in the rural setting with a goose) to a common prostitute (shown in town accompanied by a raised-hump cat in heat).[138]

The urban themes of commercialism, luxury and cruelty were, according to Diana Donald, often contrasted with rural order and reciprocity. There is an obvious connection between the girl from the country who was brutally murdered by Tom Nero and the dying lamb in the second plate, who was also an 'innocent . . . driven in from its rural pastures to form a cruel sacrifice to the devouring greed and callousness of Londoners'.[139] For humans and animals alike, country life was associated with innocence and urban life with misery. Animal exploitation was ever present in urban areas. Donald writes that the streets of London were filled with the consumption of animals: for entertainment (exhibition in zoos, mobile cages, fairs, circuses and blood sports), for food (huge numbers of rural cattle and sheep were driven into town through the streets to be marketed and slaughtered at London's Smithfield flesh market) and for riding and draught (traffic and expanding city boundaries increased the demand for draught animals so that 'the first thing that visitors noticed about London was that it smelt like a stable yard').[140]

Animals suffered untold misery in the increasing commodification of their bodies for food and labour in the seventeenth and eighteenth centuries. Making the time from birth to slaughter as short as possible for food animals was emphasized, as was the reduction of the 'proportion of unsalable bones and offal in the final carcass . . . [some pigs] were so obese that bulging flesh obscured both their legs and their foreheads'.[141] As Donald notes, 'the most shaming instance of the mercenary callousness of the age was its treatment of horses', those exhausted work animals who galloped inexorably towards an early death and the boiling house 'to be further used up in the concoction of cat's meat, candles, and compost'.[142] Keith Thomas claimed that England was 'a hell for horses . . . (t)he suffering of old . . . [horses] thought one eighteenth-century traveller, was one of the most disagreeable spectacles to be seen on the English roads'.[143] For 150 years after the Industrial Revolution, horses, donkeys and dogs continued to work in mills, breweries, coal mines and railway yards.[144] In considering the substantial monetary gain and miserable working conditions of the cows, chickens, horses, pigs and sheep over the last 300 years, Jason Hribal concludes that they labour as part of the working class:

The farms, factories, roads, forests, and mines have been their sites of production. Here, they have manufactured hair, milk, flesh, and power for the farm, factory, and mine owners. And here they are unwaged. Indeed we can think of others who operate under similar circumstances: human slaves, children, homeworkers, sex-workers, to name a few. The basic fact is that horses, cows . . . [and] or chickens have laboured, and continue to labour, under the same capitalist system as humans.[145]

Drawing similarities between the condition of animals and that of the working class (and of women) develops into a central theme over the next hundred years, as we will see in the next chapter.

Chapter 6

Modernity, 1800–2000

Looking at animals as beings worthy of ethical and moral consideration continues into the modern period. It took almost two hundred years after Ireland passed the law prohibiting ploughing with horses' tails and pulling the wool off living sheep for animal welfare concerns to coalesce into a series of anti-cruelty laws in England. The trend began with an animal protection act introduced by Richard Martin (1754–1834) and passed in 1822 along with a law 'preventing clandestine marriages'. Written as an 'Act to Prevent the Cruel and Improper Treatment of Cattle', the 1822 Martin Act prohibited the mistreatment of 'Horses, Mares, Geldings, Mules, Asses, Cows, Heifers, Steers, Oxen, Sheep, and other Cattle',[1] with the meaning of the word 'cattle' derived from 'chattel' referring to all domesticated quadrupeds held as moveable property.[2] The Society for the Prevention of Cruelty to Animals was founded in 1824 ('Royal' was added by royal decree in 1840), and animal-baiting and animal-fighting contests were banned in 1835.[3] The 1835 law against fighting or baiting bulls, bears, badgers, dogs, cocks or any domestic or wild animal was an extension of the Martin Act which had been through a series of amendments since it was first introduced in 1822.[4]

The prohibition of cruel sports, writes Keith Thomas, was based not only on the desire to protect animals from mistreatment but also on the 'distaste for the habits of the lower orders . . . middle-class opinion was as outraged by the disorder which the animal sports created as by the cruelty they involved'.[5] While many working-class games were outlawed, so also was the occasional cruel sport of the elite, such as the Eton Ram Hunt during which a ram was ceremoniously clubbed to death in Weston's Yard; but in general 'the gentlemen's fox-hunting, fishing and shooting survived unscathed'.[6]

The initial concern of reformists such as the Royal Society for the Prevention of Cruelty to Animals was not the barbarous treatment of animals in blood sports, but rather the cruelty that took place in the streets and meat markets of London.[7] Horses, donkeys and dogs were forced to pull heavy loads and beaten unmercifully, sheep and cattle destined for the meat markets suffered miserably in transit at the hands of abusive drovers and endured ever more pain and suffering as they died subjected to cruel slaughtering practices.

As transport and draught labourers, horses had a particularly abusive lot in the nineteenth century. Diana Donald writes that by the mid-1800s hundreds of old and diseased horses were slaughtered weekly in knackers' yards throughout London, their lucrative bodies providing food for pet cats and dogs, fat for grease, and bones for manure. After a prolonged waiting time of intense hunger and thirst, the horses were slaughtered at night so that their bodies could be boiled in time for the morning arrival of the tradespeople.[8]

Smithfield Market, established in London in the 900s, was a particularly problematic arena of animal abuse and a principal concern of the reformists. For nine centuries Smithfield had been the place to buy, sell and slaughter oxen, sheep, lambs, calves and pigs. Located in the centre of the city, the market had long been a target of reform efforts. But the reform of Smithfield consisted primarily of moving the operations to the suburbs,[9] consistent with the 'growing effort, not to abolish slaughter-houses, but to hide them from the public gaze'.[10] It was only with an outbreak of cholera in the 1840s that the public became concerned about the disposal of the animals' blood and offal and tainted meat emanating from the site, and Smithfield closed as a live animal market in 1855.[11]

One of the best ways to visualize how the Smithfield meat market was experienced by a nineteenth-century Londoner is to read this passage from Charles Dickens's *Oliver Twist*:

It was market-morning. The ground was covered, nearly ankle-deep, with filth and mire; and a thick steam, perpetually rising from the reeking bodies of the cattle, and mingling with the fog, which seemed to rest upon the chimney-tops, hung heavily above. All the pens in the centre of the large area, and as many temporary pens as could be crowded into the vacant space, were filled with sheep; tied up to posts by the gutter side were long lines of beasts and oxen, three or four deep. Countrymen, butchers, drovers, hawkers, boys, thieves, idlers, and vagabonds of every low grade, were mingled together in a mass; the whistling of drovers, the barking dogs, the bellowing and plunging of the oxen, the bleating of sheep, the grunting and squeaking of pigs, the cries of hawkers, the shouts, oaths, and quarrelling on all sides; the ringing of bells and roar of voices, that issued from every public-house; the crowding, pushing, driving, beating, whooping and yelling; the hideous and discordant din that resounded from every corner of the

market; and the unwashed, unshaven, squalid, and dirty figures constantly running to and fro, and bursting in and out of the throng;
rendered it a stunning and bewildering scene, which quite con-
founded the senses.[12]

How this hell was experienced by the oxen, sheep, lambs, calves and pigs
being marketed and slaughtered at Smithfield is simply unimaginable.

At the end of the nineteenth century, reform of the animal condition
was seen as part of a larger programme of reform of punishments, prisons,
wages, the poor law and the status of women.[13] In 1892 humanitarian
reformer Henry S. Salt wrote:

> Oppression and cruelty are invariably founded on a lack of imagin-
> ative sympathy; the tyrant or tormentor can have no true sense of
> kinship with the victim of his injustice. When once the sense of affinity
> is awakened, the knell of tyranny is sounded, and the ultimate conces-
> sion of 'rights' is simply a matter of time. The present condition of the
> more highly organized domestic animals is in many ways very analo-
> gous to that of the negro slaves of a hundred years ago: look back, and
> you will find in their case precisely the same exclusion from the
> common pale of humanity; the same hypocritical fallacies, to justify
> that exclusion; and, as a consequence, the same deliberate stubborn
> denial of their social 'rights'. Look back – for it is well to do so – and
> then look forward, and the moral can hardly be mistaken.[14]

It was not just a few wealthy white male intellectuals who recognized the link
between the oppression of animals and disenfranchised humans. Coral
Lansbury writes that both women and the impoverished working class in
nineteenth-century England opposed vivisection because they identified
with exploited animals. Convinced that surgeons were experimenting on
animals because they could not do so on humans, the poor lived in constant
fear that their bodies would end up on a dissector's table, either by grave-
yard theft or by dying in a workhouse or a hospital and being handed over
to surgeons who were always looking for bodies to dissect.[15] Hogarth's prints
from the *Four Stages of Cruelty* were widely distributed in Britain and beyond;
they were even nailed to the walls of inns and taverns in various towns; and
it was the last engraving (illus. 56) with Tom Nero on the dissecting table
that shaped the imagination of the working class as to what happens to the
impoverished dead.[16]

Lansbury writes that antivivisectionist women empathized with hunted,
trapped and tortured animals, seeing themselves as horses being whipped

and beaten and as dogs strapped to the vivisector's table. Some women physicians embraced the antivivisection movement after observing how poor women in need of gynecological attention were treated like animals in the charity wards – strapped to a frame that raised her pelvis, her feet held in stirrups, medical students hovering around inspecting her genit- alia.[17] Indeed, the Brown Dog Riots of 1907 began when two women medical students witnessed the vivisection of a brown dog who had a raw wound on his side indicating that he had recently been experimented on, an infringement of an 1876 law prohibiting more than one vivisection per animal – a vivisected animal could not be revived and used for another experiment, he had to be destroyed.[18] The women recorded their obser- vations as diary entries and subsequently published *The Shambles of Science* exposing the illegal vivisections going on at the University College; however, the scientist in charge at the brown dog's vivisection sued for libel and won, to the cheers of the medical students, and in 1906 anti- vivisectionists erected a drinking fountain with a statue of a large brown dog inscribed with the following memorial:

> In memory of the Brown Terrier Dog Done to Death in the Laborato- ries of University College in February, 1903, after having endured Vivisection extending over more than Two Months and having been handed over from one Vivisector to Another Till Death came to his Release. Also in Memory of the 232 dogs Vivisected at the same place during the year 1902. Men and women of England, how long shall these Things be?[19]

For three years, medical students organized riots and disturbances at women's suffrage meetings and antivivisection meetings, and in spite of the support of the local people for antivivisection, in 1910 the statue was carried away in the dead of night by four council workmen guarded by 120 police and eventually broken up in a Battersea Council yard. The anti- vivisection movement of the early twentieth century was a failure. Lansbury's view is that the concern for animals was blurred with women's rights and workers' rights, and social issues were so intermingled that it became difficult to sort antivivisection from working-class socialism or feminism. She argues that 'the cause of animals was not helped when they were seen as surrogates for women, or workers . . . If we look at animals and see only the reflection of ourselves, we deny them the reality of their own existence'.[20]

Dogcarts, Rabies and Sex

While horses continued to labour in the streets pulling heavy burdens until the 1920s, dogs were liberated relatively early from pulling carts, sleds and ploughs, at least in England. The 'Dog Cart Nuisance Act' outlawed the use of cart dogs within 15 miles of London's Charing Cross station and a national ban followed in 1854.[21]

Public criticism of the mistreatment of dogs was kindled by graphic descriptions of their abuse as cart dogs. One traveller provided an account of the cruelty inflicted on a group of dogs pulling a cart, most likely in Belgium where dogcarts were used well into the twentieth century (see illus. 57): 'Four drunken individuals were being hauled by three exhausted dogs, maltreated to the point of open wounds . . . (one) crippled animal couldn't run quickly enough, they killed it by kicking it with their feet and heavy sticks, leaving the dog's body along the road.'[22]

In England, what finally swayed public opinion to support the abolition of dogcarts was fear of rabies. Stanley Coren writes that it all began when a certain Lord Brougham made a convincing argument in Parliament that overworking cart dogs was the cause of rabies. A 'scientific' connection

57 Ferdinand Lintz, *A Dog Cart, Holland, c.* 1890, watercolour on paper.
Bourne Gallery (private collection), Reigate, Surrey. Dogs were widely used
as draught animals by those too poor to own a horse or donkey.

between rabies and cart dogs was proven with witness testimony that cart dogs were vicious because people had been snapped at or growled at upon approaching the cart, and when loads were heavy or dogs moved at a fast pace, there was frothing or foaming at the dogs' mouths.[23] Dogcarts were used mostly by the working class, grocers and bakers too poor to own a horse or even a donkey, and when the ban came into effect they no longer had the means to feed themselves, much less a non-working animal. So the only choice was to dispatch the dog. In the end, the ban on dog transportation and the imposition of a tax on service dogs resulted in the slaughter or abandonment of hundreds of thousands of dogs.[24]

The sharp increase in abandoned dogs that came with the regulation of service dogs gave rise to the first private dog refuge (and also to a series of critical editorials suggesting that it would be better to provide shelter for starving and homeless children).[25] In spite of criticism, the Temporary Home for Lost and Starving Dogs was founded in 1860 by Mary Tealby in a stable yard in North London; in 1871 it became the Battersea Dogs Home, and in 1883 it began to provide a home for abandoned cats as well as dogs.

Dogs that were taken in by Mary Tealby's shelter were the lucky ones. Thousands of dogs were regularly slaughtered by authorities on suspicion of rabies during the 1800s, much as they had been slaughtered in previous centuries on suspicion of spreading contagious 'dirty' diseases. Harriet Ritvo writes that three-quarters of the dogs destroyed during the nineteenth century in England were only epileptic or strange-looking and less than 5 per cent were mad.[26] Rabies was already in decline because of the overhunting and virtual extinction of the wolf in Western Europe,[27] and of the 150,000 dogs taken in by Mary Tealby's Temporary Home for Lost and Starving Dogs between 1860 and 1877, only one was rabid.[28]

There were numerous explanations for rabies offered up in the nineteenth century. In addition to the assertion that rabies was the inevitable result of overworking cart dogs, the disease was also blamed on the poor living conditions of the working class; the secluded, over-pampered and celibate conditions of apartment living with the bourgeoisie; mandatory muzzling which inhibited the dogs' natural impulses; coprophagia and sexual frustration.

Kathleen Kete expanded on the connection between sex and rabies in France.[29] Writing that the fear of rabies was part of the 'phobic imagination' of the time, Kete explains that the disease was regularly linked to sex, violence and repression.[30] Simultaneously fascinating and horrifying, rabies was described in research published in the 1850s as an uncontrollable, unrepressed state similar to nymphomania and satyriasis, with victims foaming at the mouth, overcome by epileptic fits, hydrophobia and an intense desire to bite.[31] Further, since nymphomania and uncontrollable sexual desire in men were considered the result of prolonged sexual abstinence, so also was rabies the spontaneous outcome of canine sexual frustration.[32]

The link between rabies and sexuality was typical in an era in which 'gender categorization overlay species differentiation', such as connecting female menstruation to canine heat cycles.[33] Sexualized links between animal bodies and women's bodies were common in nineteenth-century European visual and narrative culture. For example, women and horses were often juxtaposed in sexual imagery in paintings, as in Edwin Landseer's *The Shrew Tamed* (1861), in which a woman is depicted resting against a reclining horse in a stable. While this image is usually interpreted as one in which the woman has tamed the horse, supported by the fact that the female model used in the painting was the famous horsewoman, Annie Gilbert, there is enough ambiguity and boundary-blurring to also imply that the horse has tamed a shrewish woman.

This popular and controversial painting has been interpreted as showing the shifting relations of gender, sexuality and masculinity in Europe in the mid-1800s, building on the notion that both women and horses required frequent reining-in.[34] According to Whitney Chadwick, *The Shrew Tamed* was exhibited three years after the sensational American horse-breaker James Samuel Rarey published his *Art of Taming Horses*, which outlined his method of horse-gentling.[35] Considered the original horse whisperer, Rarey hobbled the horse with a leather harness or strap that raised one forefoot off the ground and cast the animal into a bed of straw. The horse was then 'gentled' with voice and touch; sometimes Rarey lay down beside the animal and rested his head on the horse's hooves. Causing a sensation in a culture in which the common method of horse-breaking consisted of riding the untamed horse until the animal was subdued by exhaustion, Chadwick writes that Rarey's horse-taming method was not only a challenge to the conventional master/slave relationship between man and horse, but also to male authority, generating cartoons entitled 'Husband-Taming'.[36]

The narrative arena of the nineteenth century provided even more striking links between animals, women and sex. Coral Lansbury has observed that 'the language of pornography is the language of the stable, with women being made to 'show their paces' and 'present themselves' at the command of the riding master, who flogs and seduces them into submission'.[37] Victorian pornography depicted women 'broken to the bit . . . subdued and held by straps so they can be mounted and flogged more easily, and they always end as grateful victims, trained to enjoy the whip and the straps, proud to provide pleasure for their masters'.[38] Lansbury expands on the significance of 'the bit', a constant in Victorian pornography, in which a woman, like a horse, 'must learn to take it in her mouth' overcoming fear and doubt and being sure never to bite.[39]

Vignettes of relationships between animals and humans were established means of teaching conformity and obedience to assertive women and the working class.[40] Popular fiction told stories of horses eager to work hard for their masters, and in a series of conversations in the *Girl's Own Paper*, a periodical for young women that began publication in 1880, horses learned that equality and independence were not possible because rights were determined by the master.[41]

Graphic artists also used animals to illustrate political news and opinion in nineteenth-century satiric prints and engravings. Following on the engravings produced by William Hogarth in the 1750s, James Gillray was a prolific graphic artist who used animal symbolism in his work. For example, in his 1806 cartoon, 'More Pigs than Teats', thirty-two piglets, each an identifiable political figure, are shown suckling the British sow to death. One of Gillray's favourite villains was Charles James Fox (1749–1806), known as the 'Man of the People' because he was a proponent of basic human rights, challenged the power of the king, and welcomed the French Revolution. In 'The Bear and His Leader' (illus. 58), Charles James Fox is illustrated as a bear in a muzzle and holding a emblematic red bonnet in sympathy for the French Revolution. He is being trained to dance by the Prime Minister William Wyndham Grenville, who holds a club for Disobedient Bears in one hand and rewards for Obedient Bears in his pocket. Other statesmen are caricatured in the piece, one as a blind and crippled fiddler player and another as an ape dancing and holding the bear's tail.

Nineteenth-century satire also captured the anxiety surrounding evolutionary theory in the deployment of animal bodies to represent social disorder and a world turned upside down. For example, two years after the publication of Charles Darwin's *On the Origin of Species* (1859), *Punch* ran 'The Lion of the Season', a cartoon depicting the horror expressed by a British gentleman by an ape's appearance at a social function, finely dressed up as an upper-class gentleman.[42] And twenty years later, shortly after the discovery of the Altamira cave paintings in 1879, the evolutionary theme was clearly a part of the tradition of fine art in Fernand Cormon's 1880 painting, 'Cain Fleeing with his Family', showing Cain and his kin as a tribe of prehistoric cave people walking through the desert draped in animal pelts and carrying prehistoric tools.[43]

58 James Gillray, *The Bear and His Leader*, 1806, hand-coloured etching.
The muzzled bear represents the politician Charles James Fox (1749–1806),
a supporter of the French Revolution and Britain's first Foreign Secretary.

Natural History and Hunting

Fuelled by the growing interest in natural history, increased exploration activities and the expansion of colonialism, the nineteenth century was a time of spectacular displays of animal 'specimens'. As Vernon Kisling notes, it was a time when everything in nature was considered valuable for collection and study.[44] The emphasis on combining entertainment with education that began in the late 1700s continued into the modern period with enthusiasm reinvigorated by the Industrial Revolution and the spread of museums and literary academies.[45] It was in this period of 'edutainment' that the curiosity cabinets of the Renaissance were transformed into natural history museums, with the specimen taking centre stage as a representation of the unusual, the exotic and most importantly, the spectacular.

According to the natural history museum historian, Stephen Asma, museums excite human curiosity by displaying spectacles.[46] Early museum 'spectacles' were simple dioramas of animals posed against background scenery depicting the animal's native environment,[47] such as William

BULLOCK'S MUSEUM,
22, Piccadilly.

59 Bullock's Museum, early 1800s. British Library, London. An early attempt to impart knowledge about animals and their habitat in a museum setting.

Bullock's India Museum which opened in London in 1801 (see illus. 59). By the end of the century, elaborate ecological relationships between plants and animals were common museum displays, such as territorial fights between orangutans, groups of American buffalo and other habitat collections that posed stuffed animals in action in front of sophisticated painted backgrounds.[48]

Contemporary museum visitors are as attracted to natural history spectacles as were the museum crowds of a hundred years ago. Noting that 'educational and entertainment institutions meet in the common-ground territory of the spectacular', Asma calls the violence and blood on display

in contemporary natural history museums 'melodramas' that pose stuffed animals in mock-frightening dioramas or in surprising locations, preparing to leap from around corners or dropping from the ceiling.[49]

Humans seem to be keen on imagery depicting the death of animals, particularly as the result of innovative technology or through large scale cooperation such as game drives. An early example of this fascination is a cave painting of a chase from Valltorta, Castellón, depicting hunters shooting arrows into a herd of deer and driving them over a cliff, a common hunting strategy in prehistory.[50] There is evidence of a similar kill by a group of about 150 Palaeo-Indians who drove 190 bison over a cliff in Colorado around 6500 BC.[51] A contemporary example of a drive hunt is on exhibit in the Natural History Museum in Washington, DC. The exhibit depicts a similar hunting scene with buffalo being driven over a cliff by first nation people wielding bows and arrows, and is one of the most popular dioramas in the museum's collection.

Even as it maintained the traditional engagement with images of masculinity and prowess, buffalo-hunting in the US was an activity very different from the notion of hunting as a noble sport that had characterized the hunting activities of humans for millennia. Between 1850 and 1880, tens of millions of buffalo were slaughtered mostly for their skins, tongues and rear quarters, the rest of the carcasses usually being left to rot on the Great Plains.[52] In addition to the desire to overpower the Plains Indians by eliminating their primary means of independent survival, white men slaughtered buffalo for commercial gain, and both the mass killing of the buffalo and the preservation and distribution of their hides were made possible by advancements in technology during the nineteenth century. Buffalo skins were highly lucrative: by the early 1870s hides could be effectively tanned using a lime chemical process, new powerful guns were accurate and lethal from a distance of 600 yards, and railroads allowed for the transportation of buffalo hides to distant markets.[53] Railroads also provided people with ample opportunities to slaughter buffalo from trains with relative ease and safety.

While buffalo were being slaughtered from train-side in the US, fox-hunting developed as a major part of English country life because, according to James Howe, the fox was the only animal left in the nineteenth century that could still be chased on horseback.[54] Shrinking forests and expanding urbanization decimated the 'nobler beasts of venery' such as the boar and the red deer, and hunting on horseback was a sign of high status among the English and displayed the necessary wealth it takes to maintain horses, tack and the proper riding clothes, the leisure time to hunt, and the association with life on a country estate.[55] Howe writes that hunting dominated the character of the aristocratic Englishman, generating the popular saying that upon rising each day, an English gentleman exclaims, 'Goddamn, what a beautiful morning! What shall we kill today?'[56]

Spectacles of Game Hunting

Hunting, aristocracy and displays of wealth, power and prestige are also central to the development of the natural history museum in the nineteenth century. The most spectacular crowd pleasers in the early museums were large carnivores, preferably those killed in the wild in the 'romantic, violent, and dangerous process of confrontation and conquest' in big game hunting.[57] Indeed, the stuffed animals on display in museums can be interpreted as symbolic of imperial colonization and the annexation of wild places. According to Harriet Ritvo, each dead wild animal 'represented a bloody triumph in the field . . . horns and hides, mounted heads and stuffed bodies, clearly alluded to the violent heroic underside of imperialism'.[58] The desire for trophies to fill personal holdings drove collectors to have large animals killed to complete their roster of wild specimens, while explorers financed their adventures by hunting and selling animals and by trafficking which devastated wildlife in colonial areas.[59] Even famous statesmen and politicians took part in killing and collecting wildlife. As head of a scientific expedition to Africa in 1909, Theodore Roosevelt collected 14,000 specimens of mammals, birds, reptiles and fish for the Smithsonian Institution.[60] Particularly proud of the specimens of large game animals he killed for the Smithsonian, he boasted that 'no other expedition of the kind has ever come back from Africa or Asia with a better collection of specimens than we brought back . . . the skins [and]. . . skeletons, of the square-mouthed rhinoceros, reticulated giraffe, giant eland, bongo, northern sable antelope, white-withered lechwe antelope and Vaughn's kob . . . are unrivaled in any European museum'.[61]

Animal skins and skeletons were essential elements in the reconstruction of wildlife for museum display. Early taxidermy was a scientific endeavour, a prized skill for naturalists and zoologists who were interested in preserving animal specimens for study. When introduced into the nineteenth-century museum, taxidermy provided a way to display a story about the relationship between culture and nature, a story similar to the older exhibits of ecological relationships between animals and plants. In a description of the American Museum of Natural History's African Hall, a collection of twenty-eight African dioramas representing most of the large mammals on the continent, Donna Haraway notes that taxidermy played a critical and complex role in the coordination of the exhibit, beginning in the wilderness when the animals were hunted down and ending in the museum as a finished diorama.[62]

Haraway recounts how Carl Akeley, the early twentieth-century artist, scientist, taxidermist and hunter, carefully selected wild animals to kill for mounting as natural history exhibits.[63] The search centred on finding a perfect animal, a prize trophy specimen, usually an adult male. Passed over as unremarkable were females and the young of all species (unless needed to compose a 'family' group), elephants with asymmetrical tusks, animals with less than beautiful colours and small animals. There was a hierarchy of desired game animals: lions, elephants and giraffes were the preferred species, but the most prized specimen was the gorilla. Haraway describes a few days in one of Akeley's gorilla hunt expeditions as an ongoing search for the best possible animals to photograph (for the construction of a realistic diorama) and finally kill (to be stuffed and posed according to the 'action' recorded by the camera). She notes that Akeley and his hunting party had slaughtered or attempted to slaughter every primate they had encountered since arriving in the area. On the first day of the hunt, Akeley killed and skinned a gorilla, and made a death mask of the animal, useful in a realistic reproduction of life after death. On the second day, he missed two males, but succeeded in killing a female and his attendants killed her baby. On the third day, Akeley took his camera along and photographed a group of gorillas for about 200 feet of film, but that became boring after a while, so 'finally, feeling that I had about all I could expect from that band, I picked out one that I thought to be an immature male . . . I shot and killed it and found, much to my regret, that it was a female'.[64] After Akeley had his fill of gorilla hunting, he summoned the rest of the party waiting in camp to come up to hunt gorilla, and one of the hunters killed a large silverback male, a monumental animal now stuffed and on display in the African Hall. As part of the gorilla group diorama, the Giant of Karisimbi is mounted against a naturalistic African backdrop and rises above the other gorillas in the scene 'in a chest-beating gesture of alarm and an unforgettable gaze in spite of the handicap of glass eyes'.[65]

The notion of the animal's gaze is central to the visitor's experience in the Natural History Museum. Haraway notes that each of the twenty-eight dioramas in the African Hall has at least one animal that looks directly back at the viewer. And even though a glass partition separates viewer from the viewed, the gaze invites 'visual penetration . . . The animal is frozen in a moment of supreme life.'[66] Similar attempts to stage lifelike appearances for dead animals are undertaken in trophy photography. While the Giant of Karisimbi's head was held up by the hunter and his wife for a trophy shot after the kill, it was a clearly dead body that was being photographed, the gorilla's jaw hanging slack, his body bloated and heavy.[67] In a study of the display of dead trophy animals in contemporary hunting magazines, Amy Fitzgerald and I found hundreds of images of recently killed animals carefully posed to look alive – eyes open, heads turned alertly toward the camera, legs tucked neatly under the body to simulate the appearance of resting in the field.[68] All evidence of blood and wounds was concealed, and some animals were staged as if performing live behaviours, such as the propped-up dead deer with straw stuffed in his mouth to convey the appearance of eating. Often the animal's body was superfluous – the trophy prize was a set of spectacular antlers, and the most gruesome animal images were those of severed deer heads prominently displayed as fresh 'cut-offs' being carried from the hunting site attached to the hunter's backpack or lined up on the lawn back at home. We concluded that the trophy images conveyed the message that animal bodies are highly objectified in the hunting discourse, decapitated and dismembered with body parts displayed as decoration or household objects, such as elephant tail flyswatters or elephant foot waste bins (see illus. 60).

Rarely is there any attempt to recreate or simulate the image of life for disparaged animals in the hunting discourse. For example, in our study of contemporary

60 Elephant foot being used as a waste bin.

trophy photographs, the triumph over worrisome predators was celebrated, their bodies displayed 'clearly dead . . . bobcats and foxes held
triumphantly upside down for the camera, coyotes flung across human
shoulders like bags of dirty laundry'.[69] Thus, while the big game hunting of
the early twentieth century was predicated on heroic confrontation
between hunter and prey, perceptions of predatory animals in the US
encouraged the killing of predators using any means possible. Based on
long-standing fears of wilderness areas, worries about the safety of livestock
and maintaining control over animals and land, the extermination of predators, particularly large-bodied mammals, has been common in the US
since the first settlers arrived.[70] With bounties on 'vermin' a major tool of
game management, the US Forest Service hired trappers to reduce
predator populations, and in 1915 Congress appropriated money for
predator control, directing the Bureau of Biological Survey to kill the
killers, with the new programme quickly developing into a 'semi-inde-
pendent extermination company for western ranchers'.[71] The disdain for
predators was widespread. Thomas R. Dunlap writes that Ernest Thompson
Seton, animal advocate and nature writer, depicted wolves as ravenous, dangerous outlaws; William Hornaday, an advocate of the preservation of wild
animals, claimed that falcons were at their best stuffed, owls were robbers
and murderers, and the wolf was cunning, cruel and cowardly; even the
conservationist Aldo Leopold argued in the 1920s for the total elimination
of large predators from New Mexico.[72]

Bountied and baited, the last wolf in New England was killed in Maine
in 1860, and by 1905 wolves were rare in Texas, New Mexico and Arizona.[73]
The wolf-slaughter frenzy killed other species as well. According to Jody
Emel, poisons such as strychnine and Compound 1080 (sodium fluoroac-
etate) not only killed wolves but also dogs, children and the horses who ate
the grass that the wolves had salivated on as they died.[74]

The outcomes of predator control are proudly displayed in photographs
from the 1920s. For example, in a 1921 photograph entitled 'Eagle's Nest
Catch' (illus. 61), three tiers of coyote bodies are displayed on a wood and
stone slab frame in Sweetwater County, Wyoming. Two bandoliers of rifle
cartridges are draped below a dead bobcat, and two badgers lie on the
ground near a tripod of rifles. Illus. 62, a photograph taken in 1925, is an
elaborate display of slaughtered predators that is intended to be humorous.
The bodies of dead coyotes are carefully manipulated, tied with ropes and
positioned hanging from and draped across an automobile, with one of the
bodies propped behind the steering wheel as if driving the car of carcasses.

The mass slaughter of coyotes had a devastating effect on the local
ecology. In 1927, for example, millions of mice descended upon Kern

61 Wyoming State hunters' Eagle's Nest Catch, 1921.
An entire wall is clad with the corpses of coyotes.

62 Animal carcasses on an automobile, 1925. A car is decorated with
shot coyotes, including one posed behind the steering wheel.

County, California, unchecked by any predators because two years earlier the Bureau of Biological Survey had slaughtered all of the coyotes in the area while the farmers regularly killed the local hawks and owls.[75] But it wasn't until the 1950s that public and scientific opinion challenged the predator eradication policy; until then almost everyone believed that predators would, and should, be eliminated and preserved only in special locations set aside for scientific study or public viewing,[76] places such as the zoo.

Zoo Spectacles

John Berger argued that animals are marginalized when they are put on display and observed as nothing more than spectacles, and nowhere is the marginalization of animals more evident than in the zoo.[77] While it could be argued that putting predators on display in zoos is surely preferable over their wholesale slaughter, many lament that a life in captivity is no life at all. Berger critiqued the zoo as a place of the one-way gaze, a place where animals are seen by humans but humans are never seen by animals, a place where animals are isolated from each other and without interaction between species, utterly dependent upon their keepers, passively waiting for some kind of intervention into their environment, such as feeding time. With the cage acting as a frame around the animal, visitors proceed from cage to cage observing and gazing upon the animal inside, much like visitors in an art gallery who stop in front at a painting and then move on to see the next piece on exhibit.[78] Bob Mullan and Garry Marvin have a similar view – zoos consist of a gallery of images arranged for human enjoyment and benefit that expresses the power of culture over nature.[79] Finally, Randy Malamud argues convincingly that zoos are fundamentally related to imperialism, consumerism, consumption, imprisonment, enslavement, sadism and voyeurism, and that captivity creates a perverted cultural representation of animals.[80]

Unlike the early zoological gardens which accented the space around the animal (such as plants, trees and artificial mountains) and placed animals in elaborate surroundings, the nineteenth-century zoo emphasized 'the contents of the space (zoology) rather than the space itself'.[81] The human gaze upon the animal exhibit was enhanced by small cages and circular or hexagonal arrangements, much like the special design of the Versailles menagerie in the seventeenth century that was the likely inspiration for Jeremy Bentham's panopticon, or inspection house (see Chapter 5). Michel Foucault elaborated on Bentham's panopticon and famously applied it to modern society's exercise of power and control through constant surveillance, perpetual assessment and classification:

We know the principle . . . at the periphery, an annular building; at the centre, a tower; this tower is pierced with wide windows that open onto the inner side of the ring; the peripheric building is divided into cells, each of which extends the whole width of the building; they have two windows, one on the inside, corresponding to the windows of the tower; the other, on the outside, allows the light to cross the cell from one end to the other. All that is needed, then, is to place a supervisor in a central tower and to shut up in each cell a madman, a patient, a condemned man, a worker or a schoolboy [or an animal]. By the effect of backlighting, one can observe from the tower, standing out precisely against the light, the small captive shadows in the cells of the periphery. They are like so many cages, so many small theatres, in which each actor is alone, perfectly individualized and constantly visible. The panoptic mechanism arranges spatial unities that make it possible to see constantly and to recognize immediately. In short, it reverses the principle of the dungeon; or rather of its three functions – to enclose, to deprive of light and to hide – it preserves only the first and eliminates the other two. Full lighting and the eye of a supervisor capture better than darkness, which ultimately protected. Visibility is a trap . . . Each individual, in his place, is securely confined to a cell from which he is seen from the front by the supervisor; but the side walls prevent him from coming into contact with his companions. He is seen, but he does not see; he is the object of information, never a subject in communication.[82]

Foucault's application of the principle of panopticism to disciplinary institutions such as prisons, factories, barracks, schools and hospitals is easily extrapolated to zoos, with power over those under surveillance conceptualized as a mechanism 'that insidiously objectifies those on whom it is applied'.[83]

The notion of spectacle haunts both the history of zoos and the historical treatment of the mentally ill. According to Y. F. Tuan, by the time London's Bethlehem Hospital (known as Bedlam) closed in 1770, 96,000 people had paid admission to the institution to observe the patients' entertaining behaviour, and if they were not entertaining enough the visitors would enrage inmates chained to their cells or provide them with gin to observe their drunken performances.[84] Zoo animals are similarly expected to be entertaining, and if they are not, zoo spectators have been known to torture animals into doing something. Randy Malamud writes that zoo visitors 'tend to display few of the nobler instincts of inquiry or epistemological and experiential appetite as they pass from cage to cage'.[85] Mullan and Marvin report that crocodiles have been stoned to death by spectators trying to get them to move, and in describing alligators who have had their eyes gouged out and birds with broken legs, Peter Batten concludes that it is 'doubtful whether any zoo in America has escaped vandalism in some form by sadistic, ignorant, or dimwitted humans'.[86]

One of the best ways to get captive animals to do something is to feed them. Feeding-time for wild animals has long been a favourite spectacle for humans and one that, like all animal spectacles, reaffirms the domination of culture over nature. The ancients enjoyed watching wild animals appear at certain locations for food (lured into their sight by Orpheus), ultimately making the animals easy targets to kill. Nigel Rothfels notes that the most popular animal enclosure of the nineteenth-century zoological garden was the bear pit, a deep circular hole with a tree trunk in the centre which bears could climb high enough to catch food thrown at them by the spectators observing from above the pit.[87] In the bear pit, wild, fearsome bears were reduced to comic performers willing to perform for food as four or five bears tried to reach the top of the pole for the food, greatly adding to the spectacle and the enjoyment of the humans.[88] Feeding-time for captive animals is also popular among zoo visitors because it is often a way to observe wild animals' violent behaviour. Public feeding spectacles include jaguars growling and chewing on the bones of a joint of horse, snakes eating live rats (some snakes refuse to eat dead things), and lions eating parts of a cow.[89] Encouraged by zoos in the nineteenth century, feeding animals by the public was first banned in the early 1900s, with prohibitions becoming common during the 1950s.[90]

There have been other changes in the exhibition of animals during the twentieth century. The 'illusion of liberty' was introduced by replacing the image of a captive animal with the image of one in the natural environment, and Carl Hagenbeck was the first to exhibit animals in a 'cages without bars' design.[91] Hagenbeck had a profitable business trading in exotic animals, in which huge numbers of wild animals were captured and transported for display in zoos. Over a twenty-year period beginning in the mid-1800s, the Hagenbeck company imported some 700 leopards, 1,000 lions, 400 tigers, 1,000 bears, 800 hyenas, 300 elephants, tens of thousands of monkeys and more than 100,000 birds.[92] In 1907 Hagenbeck opened Animal Park, a panorama of exotic animals and indigenous people displayed to appear as if wandering about in their natural environments. The animals were separated from each other and from visitors by a series of hidden moats and visitors could gaze on the exotic without bars or barriers, a revolutionary design that became the model for animal exhibitions throughout the twentieth century.[93]

However, the appearance of free-roaming animals in the new no-bars parks was maintained through innovations in architectural design and old-fashioned ideas about how to keep animals in their captive place. Baratay and Hardouin-Fugier write that huge ditches, some as wide as 6 metres, created impassable obstacles and when filled with water effectively enclosed certain species as if on an island, with fake rocks, mountains and valleys creating the appearance of natural landscapes. But while monkeys played on the fake rocks and herbivores grazed on a recently constructed prairie, carnivores remained in cages, glass partitions separated snakes from spectators, birds of prey were chained to rocks, water birds had clipped wings and all animal behaviour was under constant surveillance and careful control by animal trainers.[94]

Theme Park Spectacles

Controlling animal behaviour through training is central to modern animal theme parks, those spectacular displays of animals performing for human audiences. Animal theme parks are the modern equivalent of the nineteenth-century zoological gardens and pleasure parks that encour-aged promenading, the practice of walking in picturesque gardens away from civilization and into nature. As a respite from crowded, dirty urban areas, promenading was an important activity for the working class who walked on Sundays and the bourgeoisie who walked every day for recre-ation and social contact, such as meeting others and self-display.[95]

Contemporary theme parks are also marketed as democratic spaces, open to anyone who can pay the price of admission.[96] But while early twen-tieth-century amusement parks were located close to cities and attended by the urban working class, new theme parks were built in the suburbs, with audiences that were primarily white, suburban and middle-class and a single-price admission fee that shifted the meaning of the park experi-ence from casual recreation to a planned activity.[97] The Sea World chain, which opened its first park in 1964, has been particularly successful in promoting marine nature and wildlife, with human and animal entertain-ment, and highlighting of course their 'core product' – performing whales.[98] In a 'mix of museum, zoo, and carnival', Sea World emphasizes crossing species boundaries by making contact with 'animals from another world [who] are displayed in ways designed to bring forth positive emotions . . . creating closeness between people and animals'.[99] Marine World, another marine-centred theme park described as part zoo, circus and carnival, exhibits not only marine mammals, but also lions, tigers, ele-phants, chimpanzees, orangutans, rhinoceroses and birds.[100] Marine

World does not attempt to re-create realistic surroundings for the animals who are either performing in shows or walking around the landscaped grounds; they advertise an emphasis on education with entertainment, giving people opportunities to get close to exotic wildlife thus cultivating an appreciation for and conservation of wild animals.[101] Jane Desmond writes that the park's success is dependent on maintaining the 'authenticity of the natural' through strict animal training repackaged as a 'beneficial improvement on nature'.[102] The human narratives that accompany the animal shows imply that the animals are performing natural behaviours, that they are 'happy workers, well fed, and stimulated by the work they do . . . animals *want* to do these actions'.[103] Desmond argues that the implication that the animals choose to perform hides the human–animal power differentials embedded in the shows. While a 'discourse of the natural' structures the performances, animal trainers maintain control over the animals through force, restraint, confinement and domination, and any resistance on the part of the animal is carefully hidden.[104]

Bullfighting as Ritual

The very characteristics of animal behaviour kept carefully hidden in the animal performances at Sea World and Marine World – resistance, struggle, wildness – are publicly celebrated in another human-and-animal performance, the bullfight (illus. 63). Ritualized in Spain at the close of the eighteenth century, the bullfight (or the *corrida*) became a weekly event in Madrid in the nineteenth century, and, although rare in northwest Spain, Catalonia and the Balearic Islands, bullfighting is considered a national obsession.[105] Bullfights are divided into specific 'acts'. First, the bull is driven in from his pasture and kept in a dark holding area outside the arena. As the event begins, the bull is released roaring into the ring. Next, *picadors* come out on horseback and with large poles ending in spikes they weaken the bull by driving the spikes into the nape of the animal's neck. As the bull loses blood from his wounds, *banderillas* (small poles with spikes) are used by the *matador* (the killer) to stab the bull as he charges. In the last act, the *matador* uses a cloak and a sword to kill the bull, an event called the 'supreme moment'.[106] It takes less than 20 minutes from the time the bull is released until mules drag his dead body from the ring; in that short time the *matador* masters the animal by playing with the animal's instincts in successive stages, each leaving the bull ever more dominated.[107]

For centuries, Spaniards have taken every possible opportunity to hold a bullfight: to celebrate special events such as awarding doctoral degrees,

63 Francisco José de Goya y Lucientes (Francisco de Goya), *Bullfight, Suerte de Varas* [Opening act, sticking with lances], 1824, oil on canvas. The J. Paul Getty Museum, Los Angeles. The bull confronts the *picador*, whose horse is drenched with blood.

celebrating holidays and entertaining royalty.[108] The popularity of bullfighting is not confined to Spain. Certain areas of southern France also celebrate bullfight rituals and other bull (taurine) festivals, and have done so since the Middle Ages.[109] Portugal is known for bloodless bullfights, and a contemporary Portuguese community in California celebrates holidays with a bullfight in the Central Valley that employs a system of Velcro-tipped darts (replacing the traditional spikes and *banderillas*) and Velcro patches worn over the shoulders of bulls with their horns wrapped in protective coverings.[110] And in Peru, the Machu Picchu Pueblo Hotel advertises a blood fiesta held during the first week of December which highlights a primitive bullfight during which a condor is tied to the back of a bull and the two battle to the death.

Traditional bullfighting in Andalusia is a uniquely urban event. Garry Marvin writes that bringing the bull from his rural pastures to the urban environment places the animal outside his proper domain (wild untamed nature) into the city (civilized culture).[111] The bullfight is a contrived meeting between animal and men that symbolizes a confrontation between nature and culture, and through the careful control of a powerful, erratically charging bull the *matador* publicly demonstrates his domination over nature.[112] The *banderillas* are wrapped in brightly coloured paper and when they are sticking out of the bull's body the animal is thus 'decorated or adorned, a sign of the imposition of culture on nature and a further sign of the gradual denaturing of the bull . . . [who] is brought closer to those animals normally classed as domestic'.[113]

While urban spaces are ordered and controlled, the rural countryside is considered a subhuman realm of plants and animals, with country people in constant struggle with nature and thus never fully civilized.[114] The blurring of nature and culture is evident in rural festivals that often draw on the time-honoured ritual of men impersonating animals and women. For example, during the festival of the plough in the villages of the upper Maragatería in Spain, shepherds dressed as sheep attach themselves to ploughs steered by other shepherds dressed as women and together they dig a long furrow in the ground to the sound of music.[115] Later in the village the shepherds gather together and recall the events of the past year and the flaws of the village women, 'faults symbolized by the distribution of different parts of the body of a dead ass: a chatterbox received the tongue; a shameless one, the tail . . . The aim is to ensure the fertility of the soil, of the sheep and goats, but also to remind the women of their duties.'[116]

Just as the rural festivals in Spain engage with fertility rites and the re-affirmation of gendered behaviour and identity, the urban bullfight is centred by similar cultural constructs. Bullfighting is a male-focused ritual in Andalusian culture, and masculine values (sexual potency, assertiveness, independence) frame the entire event, with the bull symbolizing a combination of both the male virtues and the animal characteristics needed to ensure fertility.[117] While the participation of women in the world of bull-fighting, including performing in the ring as *matadors*, leads some scholars to question the interpretation of the bullfight as a masculine ritual,[118] Pitt-Rivers argues that the event is widely defined as 'the ritual revindication of manliness in the sense of sexual pre-eminence'.[119]

Sex, masculinity and the display of animal aggression are also the basic ingredients of other popular blood rituals, cock-fighting and dog-fighting. In a classic essay on cock-fighting in a Balinese village, Clifford Geertz wrote that Balinese men's identification with and close attachment to their cocks (same pun in Balinese as in English) is an exaggeration of the male ego.[120] The Balinese have a strong fear and hatred for anything animal-like, and they use cock-fighting in their festivals to display 'social order, abstract hatred, masculinity' and to pacify evil spirits.[121] Another ethnographic study of cock-fighting found that the human participants (primarily rural-oriented, blue-collar white males) had hypermasculine world views that emphasized the reaffirmation of masculine identity through such themes as authoritarianism, sexual animism and male bonding.[122] Finally, dog-fighting is similarly centred by the validation of masculinity, with predominantly white male working-class participants using fights between pit bull terriers (descendants of the breed used in bull-baiting until the 1800s) to attain and maintain honour and status.[123] In dog-fighting culture, as in cock-fighting, the animal is considered a reflection of the man who owns him, and dogs that quit fighting in the pit are immediately killed, providing a quick and violent end to an insufficiently aggressive canine life, with lost status regained through the speedy action to take care of 'the problem'.[124]

Killing animals is always ritualistic, argues Jonathan Burt, and even when living animals are celebrated, as in nature documentaries and sentimental family films, human–animal relationships are linked to death and loss.[125] One of the most common themes in family films that feature animals is the missing or dead parent whose orphaned offspring must move through critical rites of passage involving separation, initiation and return.[126] Killing animals in ritualized festivals was the topic of one of the first films ever made – a bullfight in Seville in 1896.[127] And animal death as a film spectacle was also the topic of Thomas Edison's 1903 short movie, *Electrocuting an Elephant*, in which Topsy, a Coney Island Luna Park elephant who had killed three men, was electrocuted with Edison's new direct current system.[128] In the late 1880s, writes Lippit, Edison had also staged the electrocution of hundreds of stray dogs and cats in New Jersey, providing the New York State Legislature with the evidence they needed to replace hanging with high-tension electricity delivered to the victim strapped to a chair as a swift and lethal killing strategy.[129] Filming the death of animals is indicative of the 'charged nature' of visual imagery, and focuses on the fascination and repulsion that comes with certain kinds of animal representations, including the 'problematic negotiation between co-existing humane and cruel impulses'.[130] According to Steve Baker, visual displays are critical to the process of 'picturing' animal abuse, as is the adoption of part-human and part-animal attributes and decentring the human form.[131] It is in the postmodern arena, with its focus on representations that destabilize the human and deobjectify the animal, that we see how disruption, fascination and repulsion promise to refashion human–animal relationships.

Looking at the Postmodern Animal

We begin by looking at vampires. We don't usually think of vampires as postmodern animals, but as the main character in Bram Stoker's 1897 novel *Dracula*. However, Stoker's image of the vampire as a being with blurred boundaries, part-human and part-animal, multiple and mysterious, is the essence of postmodernism. Donna Haraway writes that vampires transform and cross categories – they are neither good nor bad, they are polluters of the natural, including the purity of lineage, they are mobile, highly ambiguous and invoke reactions of both desire and fear.[132] For example, OncoMouse™, the first patented animal in the world, is a postmodern construct, a refiguration and an invention, and 'her status as an invention who/which remains a living animal is what makes her a vampire, subsisting in the realms of the undead'.[133] Vampires violate the integrity of body, community and kinship; they are the immigrants and the dislocated; they are those who bring about 'uninvited associations and disassociations . . . sure to undo one's sense of the self same'.[134]

The undoing of the 'self same' is central in the postmodern move away from the notions of separation, exclusion and dislike based on difference toward an emphasis on blurred boundaries and the recognition of the importance of differences. For example, Haraway argues for thinking about *affinity* rather than *identity*, placing the emphasis on making coalitions with those with whom we have a community of interest rather than a sameness of essential character. She eschews the idea of bonding through kinship and family, noting that the time has come 'to theorize an "unfamiliar" unconscious, a different primal scene, where everything does not stem from the dramas of identity and reproduction'.[135]

Very similar ideas can be found in the work of Gilles Deleuze and Félix Guattari who in 1980 proposed the concept *becoming-animal* to capture the notion of human–animal relationships based on affinity rather than identification, imitation or resemblance.[136] Deleuze and Guattari also draw on the image of the vampire, a 'multiplicity without the unity of an ancestor', a hybrid, sterile being who 'does not filiate', but rather infects, with the terms *contagion* and *epidemic* indicative of difference, heterogeneity and the anomalous.[137] One enters into alliances to become-animal with the anomalous – the odd, the peculiar, the strange, the Outsider – such as the vampire, the werewolf, Ben the Rat and Moby-Dick the Whale. Deleuze and Guattari offer us the story of Moby-Dick as a masterpiece of becoming. Moby-Dick is the Anomalous, the Outsider, the demon with whom Captain Ahab has entered into a 'monstrous alliance'. Captain Ahab stalks Moby-Dick, his becoming-whale, 'to reach the pack as a whole and pass beyond it' because it is through choosing the anomalous that one enters into a becoming-animal.[138]

Steve Baker writes that one of Deleuze and Guattari's main objectives is to avoid thinking in terms of subjects, self and individuals, with the becoming-animal concept doing away with identity (both human and animal) and subjectivity.[139] Baker argues that for Deleuze and Guattari, 'what becoming animal does is close to what art does' and thus artists (writers, painters, musicians) are directly involved in the transformation of experience that constitutes a becoming-animal.[140] Other artists have used photography to depict animals from a postmodern perspective. For example, photographer Britta Jaschinski has captured the essence of captivity and imprisonment in her photographs of zoo animals, black and white images that emphasize disembodiment, artificiality, unreality and unknowability.[141] William Wegman has spent thirty years photographing his Weimaraner dogs in images that blur the distinction between canine bodies and human bodies as he dresses his companion dogs as other species, including human models wearing the latest fashion in hats, handbags and shoes.

Baker argues that postmodern art is about creating distance from animals, producing an unsettled view of animal bodies and images that are fractured, awkward and wrong.[142] For example, some postmodern artists have exhibited shocking reworked ('botched') taxidermy – skinned dogs and cats fitted with modelled heads, a dressmaker's dummy covered in the hide of a cow, pigs and sharks preserved in formaldehyde and a sculpture of dead animals tarred, feathered and displayed hanging from a tree.[143]

A particularly macabre example of postmodernism's fascination with animal death was the 'goldfish in a blender' exhibit held at a Danish museum in Kolding in 2000. Inspired by the desire to present people with the opportunity to choose between life and death, the Chilean-born artist Marco Evaristti exhibited ten blenders each filled with water and a goldfish. Spectators were able to turn the work into 'goldfish soup' with the press of a button.[144] Two of the fish were blended to death by an anonymous visitor to the museum, and the museum director was fined €269 because he had left the blenders plugged into electrical outlets despite being warned not to do so. A technician from the blender company testified in court that it takes less than one second for the blender knife to reach between 14,000 and 15,000 rounds per minute from the time the button is pressed, killing the fish 'instantly and humanely', so the fine was dropped. During the controversy, the director of the museum said that the work was a comment on human beings often making themselves masters of (controlling) life and death, for instance through abortions and respirators. In court, he refused to pay the fine, noting that artistic licence allows for the creation of works that defy the concept of right and wrong.

Looking at animals in the postmodern world of cyberspace completes John Berger's lament that animals have been rendered absolutely marginal. A vast electronic arena of digital images, virtual reality and internet sites has now joined film and photography (and artistic exhibition) in offering new conceptions of animals and the human–animal relationship.[145] Randy Malamud writes that electronic technology provides a 'new postmodern twist' to watching animals, including the ability to look at 'something that isn't there', more control and more distance from animals and the opportunity for spectators to 'retain cultural/cognitive mastery over animals, without the smell of shit'.[146] Watching animals by way of electronic technology involves remote control cameras, telescopic lenses and other equipment that renders animals always visible,[147] a post-modern surveillance in the tradition of Foucault's panoptic mechanism discussed earlier in this chapter.

Most of all, the authenticity of animals is lost in the postmodern electronic world of virtual animals, virtual reality and digital programming. The *Webster Dictionary*'s definition of 'virtual' tells the story: being such in force or effect, though not actually or expressly such. For about $150 one can purchase (online of course) a lifesize, fully articulated robotic animatronic chimpanzee bust that, with infra-red vision and stereoscopic hearing can emulate the sounds, movements and behaviours of a live chimp, 'just like the real wild animal!' Robopet, another virtual animal and also equipped with infra-red vision and sound sensors, can be remotely controlled to express a variety of behaviours from friendly to rude, in addition to responding to commands to lie down, sit, sniff, wave, run, bark, growl, whimper, pant, 'and yes, even break wind'. And in what may be the most inauthentic animal experience of all, one can make new animals at an Internet site called Switcheroo Zoo, advertised as a boon for teachers searching for lesson plans and research resources to use in the classroom. With a digital archive of 142 species, 'zoo' visitors can switch the animals' heads, legs and tails to make new creatures. The creator can give a name to the new animal and register it with the site, establishing a host of new species, such as bunnywolf, monkeetahfly and turkephant. While hardly Promethean, these new species are, like Mary Wollstonecraft Shelley's *Frankenstein*, creations made by assembling body parts – refigurations that cross and pollute natural categories. As Donna Haraway warns us, 'it is impossible to have a settled judgment' about ambiguous beings that disrupt categories and shift boundaries.[148]

But what is clearly unsettling is the realization that while children are learning how to manipulate existing species to create their very own original animal, we humans are summarily removing untold numbers of animals from this planet every year. This situation is eerily reminiscent of Philip K. Dick's *Do Androids Dream of Electric Sheep?* In Dick's 1968 science fiction story, entire species were driven into extinction by 2021, and this forced humans to construct realistic simulations of animals to replace the living creatures in their desperate desire to experience life with animals, to have animals a part of human existence. It is clear that we don't need another 15 years to realize that dreadful narrative – our world is ever more one in which the look between humans and animals has been extinguished. Alas, this is a notion that is no science fiction.

64 Giraffe, by Britta Jaschinski

Notes

Preface

1. Joseph Meeker, cited in Theodore K. Rabb, *The Struggle for Stability in Early Modern Europe* (New York: Oxford University Press, 1975), viii.
2. John Berger, *Ways of Seeing* (London: Penguin Books, 1972).
3. Robert Darnton, *The Great Cat Massacre and Other Episodes in French Cultural History* (New York/London: Basic/Penguin, 2001).
4. Kathleen Kete, *The Beast in the Boudoir: Petkeeping in Nineteenth-Century Paris* (Berkeley: University of California Press, 1994).
5. Erica Fudge, *Perceiving Animals: Humans and Beasts in Early Modern English Culture* (Urbana: University of Illinois Press, 2002).
6. Keith Thomas, *Man and the Natural World: A History of the Modern Sensibility* (New York: Pantheon, 1983).
7. Harriet Ritvo, *The Animal Estate: The English and Other Creatures in the Victorian Age* (Cambridge, MA: Harvard University Press, 1987).
8. Coral Lansbury, *The Old Brown Dog: Women, Workers, and Vivisection in Edwardian England* (Madison: University of Wisconsin Press, 1985).
9. Esther Cohen, 'Animals in Medieval Perceptions: The Image of the Ubiquitous Other', in *Animals and Human Society: Changing Perspectives*, eds Aubrey Manning and James Serpell (London: Routledge, 1994), 59–80.
10. Scott A. Sullivan, *The Dutch Gamepiece* (Totowa, NJ: Rowman & Allanheld Publishers, 1984).
11. Paul G. Bahn and Jean Vertut, *Journey through the Ice Age* (Berkeley: University of California Press, 1997).
12. Juliet Clutton-Brock, *A Natural History of Domesticated Mammals* (New York: Cambridge University Press, 1999). (Originally published in 1987.)
13. Eric Baratay and Elisabeth Hardouin-Fugier, *Zoo: A History of Zoological Gardens in the West* (London: Reaktion, 2002).
14. Lynn White, Jr., *Medieval Religion and Technology: Collected Essays* (Berkeley: University of California Press, 1978).
15. Bruno Latour, 'A Prologue in Form of a Dialogue between a student and his (somewhat) Socratic Professor' (http://www.ensmp.fr/~latour/articles/article/090.html).

Chapter 1

1. Randall White, *Prehistoric Art: The Symbolic Journey of Humankind* (New York: Harry N. Abrams, 2003).
2. Paul G. Bahn and Jean Vertut, *Journey through the Ice Age* (Berkeley: University of California Press, 1997).
3. Jean Clottes and Jean Courtin, *The Cave beneath the Sea: Paleolithic Images at Cosquer*, trans. Marilyn Garner (New York: Harry N. Abrams, 1996).
4. Helene Valladas and Jean Clottes, 'Style, Chauvet and Radiocarbon,' *Antiquity* 77 (2003), 142–5.
5. H. W. Janson and Joseph Kerman, *A History of Art and Music* (Englewood Cliffs, NJ: Prentice Hall, 1968).
6. Bahn and Vertut, *Ice Age*, 183–5. Regarding fertility interpretations, Bahn and Vertut also reject the idea that the art was primarily about human sexuality, a popular theory since the early 1900s. They conclude that 'the theory that the art is about the male preoccupations of hunting, fighting and girls comes from twentieth-century male scholars' (189).
7. White, *Prehistoric Art*, 57.
8. David Lewis-Williams, *The Mind in the Cave: Consciousness and the Origins of Art* (London: Thames & Hudson, 2002).
9. Bahn and Vertut, *Ice Age*, 181.
10. Bahn and Vertut, *Ice Age*, 181.
11. White, *Prehistoric Art*, 15–16.
12. Bahn and Vertut write that specific interpretations of the cave art are rooted in particular historical and cultural contexts. For example, the idea that the art was produced for 'art's sake' was popular at the end of the nineteenth century, magical and spiritual interpretations were taken from the ethnographical work of the early twentieth century, structural and sexual interpretations were important in the mid-twentieth century, astronomical interpretations developed during the age of space exploration and hallucinogenic interpretations were popular in the New Age of recent decades (see Bahn and Vertut, *Ice Age*, 207–8).
13. Steven Mithen, 'The Hunter-Gatherer Prehistory of Human–Animal Interactions', *Anthrozoos* 12 (1999), 195–204.
14. Mithen, 'Hunter-Gatherer Prehistory', 197.
15. Bahn and Vertut, *Ice Age*, 177–9. Bahn and Vertut also note that Roman artists followed a similar pattern of painting wild species on their pottery but eating domesticated animals.
16. Clottes and Courtin, *Cave beneath the Sea*, 87.
17. Bahn and Vertut, *Ice Age*, 190.
18. Bahn and Vertut, *Ice Age*, 195.

19. Juliet Clutton-Brock, *A Natural History of Domesticated Mammals* (New York: Cambridge University Press, 1999). (Originally published in 1987.)

20. Bahn and Vertut, *Ice Age*, 152–3.

21. Jean Clottes, *Chauvet Cave: The Art of Earliest Times*, trans. Paul G. Bahn (Salt Lake City: University of Utah Press, 2003).

22. Anne-Catherine Welté, 'An Approach to the Theme of Confronted Animals in French Palaeolithic Art', in *Animals into Art*, ed. Howard Morphy (London: Unwin Hyman, 1989).

23. Welté, 'Confronted Animals', 230.

24. Bahn and Vertut, *Ice Age*, 139; Welté, 'Confronted Animals', 230.

25. Bahn and Vertut, *Ice Age*, 175.

26. White, *Prehistoric Art*, 119.

27. Nicholas J. Conard, 'Palaeolithic Ivory Sculptures from Southwestern Germany and the Origins of Figurative Art', *Nature* 426 (2003), 830–2.

28. Anthony Sinclair, 'Archaeology: Art of the Ancients', *Nature* 426, 774–5 (2003).

29. Conard, 'Palaeolithic ivory sculptures', 830.

30. Steven Mithen, *After the Ice: A Global Human History, 20,000–5000 BC* (Cambridge, MA: Harvard University Press, 2004).

31. Lewis-Williams, *Mind in the Cave*, 286.

32. Clottes, *Chauvet Cave*, 193, 204.

33. Clottes, *Chauvet Cave*, 204.

34. Mithen, *After the Ice*, 148.

35. Mithen, *After the Ice*, 148–9.

36. Clutton-Brock, *Domesticated Mammals*, 3.

37. Mithen, 'Hunter-gatherer prehistory', 200; Clutton-Brock, *Domesticated Mammals*, 5.

38. Bahn and Vertut, *Ice Age*, 142. This assertion is controversial; see Clutton-Brock, *Domesticated Mammals*, 10.

39. Clottes and Courtin, *Cave beneath the Sea*, 89.

40. Clutton-Brock, *Domesticated Mammals*, 40.

41. Juliet Clutton-Brock ed., *The Walking Larder: Patterns of Domestication, Pastoralism, and Predation* (London: Unwin Hyman, 1989).

42. Mithen, *After the Ice*, 34.

43. Clutton-Brock, *Domesticated Mammals*, 58 (see also Mithen, *After the Ice*, 519).

44. Clutton-Brock, *Domesticated Mammals*, 7.

45. Douglas Brewer, Terence Clark and Adrian Phillips, *Dogs in Antiquity: Anubis to Cerberus, the Origins of the Domestic Dog* (Warminster: Aris & Phillips, 2001).

46. Thomas Veltre, 'Menageries, Metaphors, and Meanings', in *New Worlds,*

New Animals: From Menagerie to Zoological Park in the Nineteenth Century, eds R. J. Hoage and William A. Deiss (Baltimore: Johns Hopkins University Press, 1996), 19–29.

47. L. Chaix, A. Bridault and R. Picavet, 'A Tamed Brown Bear (Ursus Arctos L.) of the Late Mesolithic from La Grande-Rivoire (Isère, France)?', *Journal of Archaeological Science* 24 (1997), 1067–74.

48. Bahn and Vertut, *Ice Age*, 25, 87–99.

49. Bahn and Vertut, *Ice Age*, 87, 96, 99.

50. Bahn and Vertut, *Ice Age*, 103.

51. White, *Prehistoric Art*, 71.

52. White, *Prehistoric Art*, 135.

53. Mithen, 'Hunter-gatherer prehistory', 199. This is another controversial issue in prehistory. One scholar argues that 'no potentially meaningful objects of any kind were placed with or offered to the dead' in what are believed to be Neanderthal burials (see White, *Prehistoric Art*, 64).

54. Clottes, *Chauvet Cave*, 48.

55. White, *Prehistoric Art*, 8.

56. John Berger, *About Looking* (New York: Pantheon Books, 1980).

Chapter 2

1. Juliet Clutton-Brock, *A Natural History of Domesticated Mammals* (New York: Cambridge University Press, 1999). (Originally published in 1987.)

2. Clutton-Brock, *Domesticated Mammals*, 78.

3. Calvin W. Schwabe, 'Animals in the Ancient World', in *Animals and Human Society: Changing Perspectives*, eds Aubrey Manning and James Serpell (London: Routledge, 1994), 36–58.

4. Paul Collins, 'A Goat Fit for a King', *ART News* (2003), 106–8.

5. Schwabe, 'Ancient world', 37–8.

6. Schwabe, 'Ancient world', 40–1.

7. Schwabe, 'Ancient world', 53.

8. Schwabe, 'Ancient world', 53.

9. Patrick F. Houlihan, *The Animal World of the Pharaohs* (London: Thames and Hudson, 1996).

10. Kenneth Clark, *Animals and Men: Their Relationship as Reflected in Western Art from Prehistory to the Present Day* (New York: William Morrow, 1977).

11. E. H. Gombrich, *The Story of Art* (New York: Phaidon Press, 1995).

12. Francis Klingender, *Animals in Art and Thought to the End of the Middle Ages*, eds Evelyn Antal and John Harthan (Cambridge, MA: MIT Press, 1971).

13. Klingender, *Animals in Art*, 44–6.

14. Donald P. Hansen, 'Art of the Royal Tombs of Ur: A Brief Interpretation',

in *Treasures from the Royal Tombs of Ur*, eds Richard L. Zettler and Lee Horne (Philadelphia: University of Pennsylvania Museum, 1998), 43–59.

15. Hansen, 'Art of the royal tombs', 45–6.
16. Collins, 'Goat', 108; Hansen, 'Art of the royal tombs', 62.
17. Hansen, 'Art of the royal tombs', 49, 62. On the tree-climbing behaviour of goats, see J. Donald Hughes, *Pan's Travail: Environmental Problems of the Ancient Greeks and Romans* (Baltimore: Johns Hopkins University Press, 1994), 31.
18. Hansen, 'Art of the royal tombs', 61.
19. Hansen, 'Art of the royal tombs', 54.
20. Stephen Mitchell, *Gilgamesh* (New York: Free Press, 2004).
21. Some scholars argue that the hero and bull-man theme depicted on the Mesopotamian cylinder seals do not in fact represent the Gilgamesh epic at all because episodes of the story, with one exception of a particular battle scene, have not been found among the preserved visual artefacts in the Ur tombs (see Hansen, 'Art of the royal tombs', 50).
22. Schwabe, 'Ancient world', 41.
23. Klingender, *Animals in Art*, 54–5.
24. Gombrich, *Story of Art*, 64.
25. Houlihan, *Animal World of the Pharaohs*, 98.
26. Clutton-Brock, *Domesticated Mammals*, 126.
27. Schwabe, 'Ancient world', 40.
28. Houlihan, *Animal World of the Pharaohs*, 19.
29. Schwabe, 'Ancient world', 49–50.
30. Hughes, *Pan's Travail*, 135.
31. Clutton-Brock, *Domesticated Mammals*, 108–13.
32. Clutton-Brock, *Domesticated Mammals*, 111.
33. Clutton-Brock, *Domesticated Mammals*, 110.
34. Clutton-Brock, *Domesticated Mammals*, 111.
35. Lynn White, Jr., *Medieval Technology and Social Change* (London: Oxford University Press, 1962).
36. Clutton-Brock, *Domesticated Mammals*, 40.
37. Clutton-Brock, *Domesticated Mammals*, 60; Clutton-Brock notes that this was probably not an unbroken line of ancestry but rather manipulation by artificial selection of the natural diversity in the species.
38. Dorothy Phillips, *Ancient Egyptian Animals* (New York: Metropolitan Museum of Art Picture Books, 1948).
39. Katharine M. Rogers, *The Cat and the Human Imagination: Feline Images from Bast to Garfield* (Ann Arbor: University of Michigan Press, 1998).
40. Clutton-Brock, *Domesticated Mammals*, 138–9.
41. Clutton-Brock, *Domesticated Mammals*, 138.

42. Bob Brier, 'Case of the Dummy Mummy', *Archaeology* 54 (2001), 28–9.

43. Pierre Levêque, *The Birth of Greece* (New York: Harry M. Abrams, 1994).

44. Clark, *Animals and Men*, 104.

45. H. H. Scullard, *The Elephant in the Greek and Roman World* (Ithaca: Cornell University Press, 1974).

46. Clutton-Brock, *Domesticated Mammals*, 149.

47. J. M. C. Toynbee, *Animals in Roman Life and Art* (London, The Camelot Press, 1973).

48. Jo-Ann Shelton, 'Dancing and Dying: The Display of Elephants in Ancient Roman Arenas', in *Daimonopylai: Essays in Classics and the Classical Tradition Presented to Edmund G. Berry*, eds Rory B. Egan and Mark Joyal (Winnipeg: University of Manitoba, 2004), 363–82.

49. David Matz, *Daily Life of the Ancient Romans* (Westport: Greenwood Press, 2002).

50. Jo Marceau, Louise Candlish, Fergus Day and David Williams eds, *Art: A World History* (New York: DK Publishing, 1997).

51. Gombrich, *Story of Art*, 73.

52. Christine E. Morris, 'In Pursuit of the White Tusked Boar: Aspects of Hunting in Mycenaean Society', in *Celebrations of Death and Divinity in the Bronze Age Argolid*, eds Robin Hagg and Gullog C. Nordquist (Stockholm: Paul Astroms Forlag, 1990), 151–6.

53. Ephraim David, 'Hunting in Spartan Society and Consciousness', *Echos du Monde Classique/Classical Views* 37 (1993), 393–413.

54. Judith M. Barringer, *The Hunt in Ancient Greece* (Baltimore: Johns Hopkins University Press, 2001).

55. Barringer, *Hunt in Ancient Greece*, 123. The link between hunting and sexuality has remarkable resilience. A similar link is documented in the visual and narrative discourses of contemporary sport hunting (see Linda Kalof, Amy Fitzgerald and Lori Baralt, 'Animals, Women and Weapons: Blurred Sexual Boundaries in the Discourse of Sport Hunting', *Society and Animals* 12(3) (2004), 237–51).

56. Barringer, *Hunt in Ancient Greece*, 204.

57. Houlihan, *Animal World of the Pharaohs*, 42–3.

58. Egyptians also occasionally depicted gazelle as a domesticated animal, but while it is possible they kept gazelle as curiosities or for sacrifice, gazelle cannot be truly domesticated. Clutton-Brock notes that gazelle are extremely nervous, and if corralled they batter themselves to death against their enclosures in efforts to escape; they are also territorial, and males are not likely to breed well in captivity. While gazelle can be tamed and driven into pens for short periods, unlike sheep, goats and cattle (which can be driven in the direction humans wish to travel), humans have to follow the

migrating gazelle herds because of the rigidity of the animals' migration routes (see Clutton-Brock, *Domesticated Mammals*, 19, 21).

59. John K. Anderson, *Hunting in the Ancient World* (Berkeley: University of California Press, 1985).

60. Suetonius, 'Domitianus XIX (Translated by J. C. Rolfe)' (http://www.fordham.edu/halsall/ancient/suet-domitian-rolfe.html).

61. Thomas Veltre, 'Menageries, Metaphors, and Meanings', in *New Worlds, New Animals: From Menagerie to Zoological Park in the Nineteenth Century*, eds R. J. Hoage and William A. Deiss (Baltimore: Johns Hopkins University Press, 1996), 19–29.

62. Varro, cited in Anderson, *Hunting in the Ancient World*, 86.

63. Shelton, 'Dancing and dying', 368.

64. Shelton, 'Dancing and dying', 368.

65. Toynbee, *Animals in Roman Life and Art*, 20.

66. Keith Hopkins, *Death and Renewal: Sociological Studies in Roman History* (New York: Cambridge University Press, 1983).

67. Hopkins, *Death and Renewal*, 15–16.

68. Paul Veyne, *Bread and Circuses: Historical Sociology and Political Pluralism*, trans. Brian Pearce (London: Penguin Press, 1990).

69. Veyne, *Bread and Circuses*, 400–1.

70. K. M. Coleman, 'Fatal Charades: Roman Executions Staged as Mythological Enactments', *Journal of Roman Studies* 80 (1990), 44–73.

71. Alison Futrell, *Blood in the Arena: The Spectacle of Roman Power* (Austin: University of Texas Press, 1997).

72. Shelby Brown, 'Death as Decoration: Scenes from the Arena on Roman Domestic Mosaics', in *Pornography and Representation in Greece and Rome*, ed. Amy Richlin (New York: Oxford University Press, 1992), 180–211.

73. Thomas Wiedemann, *Emperors and Gladiators* (London: Routledge, 1992).

74. George Jennison, *Animals for Show and Pleasure in Ancient Rome* (Manchester: Manchester University Press, 1937).

75. David L. Bomgardner, 'The Trade in Wild Beasts for Roman Spectacles: A Green Perspective', *Anthropozoologica* 16 (1992), 161–6.

76. Futrell, *Blood in the Arena*, 24–6.

77. Shelton, 'Dancing and dying', 367.

78. Donald G. Kyle, *Spectacles of Death in Ancient Rome* (New York: Routledge, 1998).

79. Shelton, 'Dancing and dying', 367.

80. J. M. C. Toynbee is the authority on the Latin and Greek works that reference animals in Roman life. The major literary sources are Varro, Columella, Pliny the Elder, Martial, Plutarch, Arrian, Oppian and Aelian (see Toynbee, *Animals in Roman Life and Art*, 23).

81. Toynbee, *Animals in Roman Life and Art*, 19.
82. William M. Johnson, *The Rose-Tinted Menagerie: A History of Animals in Entertainment, from Ancient Rome to the 20th Century* (London: Héretic, 1990).
83. Kyle, *Spectacles of Death*, 13, 19.
84. Anderson, *Hunting in the Ancient World*, 149.
85. Claudian, 'De Consulate Stilichonis, Book III' (http://penelope. uchicago.edu/Thayer/E/Roman/Texts/Claudian/De_Consulatu_ Stilichonis/3*.html).
86. Jennison, *Animals for Show*, 141–9.
87. Jennison, *Animals for Show*, 149.
88. Jennison, *Animals for Show*, 159–62.
89. Claudian, quoted in Jennison, *Animals for Show*, 160. The unwillingness of animals to attack martyrs in the arena was commonly noted in Christian writings as a sign of the martyr's innocence (Wiedemann, *Emperors and Gladiators*, 89).
90. Roland Auguet, *Cruelty and Civilization: The Roman Games* (New York: Routledge, 1972).
91. Dio Cassius, 'Book XXXIX', (http://penelope.uchicago.edu/Thayer/ E/Roman/Texts/Cassius_Dio/39*.html).
92. Hopkins, *Death and Renewal*, 28.
93. Hopkins, *Death and Renewal*, 29. On the use of public punishment as a strategy of social control, see Michel Foucault, *Discipline and Punish* (New York: Vintage, 1977/1995).
94. Brown, 'Death as decoration', 181; Coleman, 'Fatal charades', 57–8.
95. Coleman, 'Fatal charades', 59.
96. Brown, 'Death as decoration', 208.
97. Brown, 'Death as decoration', 194. This human serenity is shown in illus. 13.
98. Brown, 'Death as decoration', 198.
99. Coleman, 'Fatal charades', 54.
100. Coleman, 'Fatal charades', 54.
101. Wiedemann, *Emperors and Gladiators*, 56.
102. Futrell, *Blood in the Arena*, 15.
103. Nigel Spivey, *Etruscan Art* (London: Thames and Hudson, 1997).
104. Jose M. Galan, 'Bullfight Scenes in Ancient Egyptian Tombs', *Journal of Egyptian Archaeology* 80 (1994), 81–96.
105. Pliny the Elder, *Natural History: A Selection*, trans. John F. Healy (London: Penguin, 2004).
106. Veltre, 'Menageries', 20.
107. Veltre, 'Menageries', 20.
108. Houlihan, *Animal World of the Pharaohs*, 195.

109. Houlihan, *Animal World of the Pharaohs*, 196.
110. Pliny the Elder, *Natural History*, 108–9.
111. Houlihan, *Animal World of the Pharaohs*, 199.
112. Houlihan, *Animal World of the Pharaohs*, 200.
113. Houlihan, *Animal World of the Pharaohs*, 200–3.
114. Hughes, *Pan's Travail*, 108.
115. Hughes, *Pan's Travail*, 109.
116. Paul Plass, *The Game of Death in Ancient Rome* (Madison: University of Wisconsin Press, 1995).
117. Hughes, *Pan's Travail*, 109.
118. Michael Lahanas, 'Galen' (www.mlahanas.de/Greeks/Galen.htm (accessed 18 November 2004)).
119. Hughes, *Pan's Travail*, 108. On Aristotle and dissections, see also H. H. Scullard, *The Elephant in the Greek and Roman World* (Ithaca: Cornell University Press, 1974).
120. Hoage, R. J., Anne Roskell and Jane Mansour, 'Menageries and Zoos to 1900', in *New Worlds, New Animals: From Menagerie to Zoological Park in the Nineteenth Century*, eds R. J. Hoage and William A. Deiss (Baltimore: Johns Hopkins University Press, 1996), 8–18, at 10.
121. Hoage, Roskell and Mansour, 'Menageries and zoos', 10.
122. Pliny the Elder, *Natural History*, 129.
123. Kyle, *Spectacles of Death*, 17.
124. K. M. Coleman, 'Launching into History: Aquatic Displays in the Early Empire', *The Journal of Roman Studies* 83 (1993), 48–74.
125. Coleman, 'Launching into history', 56.
126. K. M. Coleman, 'Ptolemy Philadelphus and the Roman Amphitheater', in *Roman Theater and Society: E. Togo Salmon Papers I*, ed. William J. Slater (Ann Arbor: University of Michigan Press, 1996), 49–68.
127. Coleman, 'Launching into history', 67.
128. Coleman, 'Ptolemy', 66.
129. Elder Pliny, 'The Natural History, Book VIII. The Nature of the Terrestrial Animals', eds John Bostock and H. T. Riley (http://www.perseus. tufts.edu/cgi-bin/ptext?doc=Perseus%3Atext%3A1999.02.0137&query= toc:head%3D%23333, accessed 14 November 2005).
130. For a description of a similar cooperative fishing endeavour between contemporary dolphins and humans in Santa Catarina, Brazil, see Eugene Linden, *The Parrots Lament: And Other True Tales of Animals Intrigue, Intelligence, and Ingenuity* (New York: Penguin, 1999).
131. Elder Pliny, 'The Natural History, Book IX. The Natural History of Fishes', eds John Bostock and H. T. Riley (http://www.perseus.tufts.edu/cgi-bin/ ptext?doc=Perseus%3Atext%3A1999.02.0137&query=toc:head%3D%234 18, accessed 14 November 2005).

132. John F. Healy, 'The Life and Character of Pliny the Elder', in *Pliny the Elder, Natural History: A Selection*, ed. John F. Healy (London: Penguin, 2004), ix–xxxx.

Chapter 3

1. Lynn White, Jr., *Medieval Technology and Social Change* (London: Oxford University Press, 1962). While there is much controversy among historians over this book and over White's theories that connect social change to technological innovation (i.e. technological determination) in the Middle Ages, some scholars argue that there is no better overview of the period: 'the broad outlines of his paradigms still stand', and we should keep using the book until it is replaced by something better (Alex Roland, 'Once More into the Stirrups: Lynn White Jr., *Medieval Technology and Social Change*', *Technology and Culture* 44 (2003), 574–85, at 583).
2. White, *Medieval Technology*, 4.
3. Vito Fumagalli, *Landscapes of Fear: Perceptions of Nature and the City in the Middle Ages*, trans. Shayne Mitchell (Cambridge: Polity Press, 1994).
4. Fumagalli, Landscapes of Fear, 138, 142.
5. Walter of Henley, cited in White, *Medieval Technology*, 65.
6. White, *Medieval Technology*, 57–69.
7. White, *Medieval Technology*, 59.
8. White, *Medieval Technology*, 59–60.
9. White, *Medieval Technology*, 66–8.
10. White, *Medieval Technology*, 69, 73.
11. Lynn White, Jr., *Medieval Religion and Technology: Collected Essays* (Berkeley: University of California Press, 1978).
12. White, *Medieval Religion*, 146–7.
13. Fumagalli, *Landscapes of Fear*, 146–8.
14. David Herlihy, *The Black Death and the Transformation of the West* (Cambridge, MA: Harvard University Press, 1997).
15. Norman F. Cantor, *In the Wake of the Plague: The Black Death and the World It Made* (New York: Free Press, 2001).
16. Rob Meens, 'Eating Animals in the Early Middle Ages: Classifying the Animal World and Building Group Identities', in *The Animal/Human Boundary: Historical Perspectives*, eds Angela N. H. Creager and William Chester Jordan (Rochester, NY: University of Rochester Press, 2002), 3–28.
17. Keith Thomas, *Man and the Natural World: A History of the Modern Sensibility* (New York: Pantheon, 1983).
18. Thomas, *Man and the Natural World*, 116.
19. Meens, 'Eating animals', 16.

20. Meens, 'Eating animals', 16–18.

21. Esther Cohen, 'Animals in Medieval Perceptions: The Image of the Ubiquitous Other', in *Animals and Human Society: Changing Perspectives*, eds Aubrey Manning and James Serpell (London: Routledge, 1994), 59–80.

22. Cohen, 'Animals in medieval perceptions', 63.

23. Bartholomeus, cited in Cohen, 'Animals in medieval perceptions', 61.

24. Janetta Rebold Benton, 'Gargoyles: Animal Imagery and Artistic Individuality in Medieval Art', in *Animals in the Middle Ages: A Book of Essays*, ed. Nona C. Flores (New York and London: Garland Publishing, 1996), 147–65.

25. Janetta Rebold Benton, *The Medieval Menagerie: Animals in the Art of the Middle Ages* (New York: Abbeville Press, 1992).

26. Nona C. Flores (ed.) *Animals in the Middle Ages: A Book of Essays* (New York: Garland, 1996).

27. Some authorities consider Physiologus to have been the writer of the text, rather than the title of the work, perhaps someone who lived in the period of early Christianity, with 'the Physiologus' probably referring to 'the natural historian' (see Kenneth Clark, *Animals and Men: Their Relationship as Reflected in Western Art from Prehistory to the Present Day* (New York: William Morrow, 1977), 20).

28. Debra Hassig, 'Sex in the Bestiaries', in *The Mark of the Beast: The Medieval Bestiary in Art, Life and Literature*, ed. Debra Hassig (New York: Garland, 1999), 71–93.

29. Hassig, 'Sex in the bestiaries', 72–9.

30. Anna Wilson, 'Sexing the Hyena: Intraspecies Readings of the Female Phallus', *Signs* 28 (2003), 755–90.

31. Wilson, 'Sexing the hyena', 764.

32. Hassig, 'Sex in the bestiaries', 74.

33. Hassig, 'Sex in the bestiaries', 82.

34. Hassig, 'Sex in the bestiaries', 80–1.

35. Paul H. Freedman, 'The Representation of Medieval Peasants as Bestial and as Human', in *The Animal/Human Boundary: Historical Perspectives*, eds Angela N. H. Creager and William Chester Jordan (Rochester, NY: University of Rochester Press, 2002), 29–49.

36. Freedman, 'Medieval peasants as bestial', 33.

37. Janet Backhouse, *Medieval Rural Life in the Luttrell Psalter* (Toronto: University of Toronto Press, 2000).

38. Thomas, *Man and the Natural World*, 95.

39. Robert S. Gottfried, *The Black Death: Natural and Human Disaster in Medieval Europe* (New York: Free Press, 1983), at 3.

40. Gottfried, *Black Death*, 7.

41. Gottfried, *Black Death*, 24–6. While I am aware of some criticism of Gottfried's book (see Stuart Jenks's review in *The Journal of Economic History*, 46(3) 1986, 815–23) other scholars find Gottfried's work a well-informed and useful synthesis on the Black Death of the Middle Ages, see for example, Cantor, *Wake of the Plague*, 224.

42. Clive Ponting, *A Green History of the World* (Middlesex: Penguin, 1991).

43. Ponting, *Green History*, 104–5. Ponting also asserts that in some famine-ravaged areas people resorted to cannibalism – bodies were dug up for food in Ireland in 1318 and executed criminals were eaten in Silesia.

44. Graham Twigg, *The Black Death: A Biological Reappraisal* (London: Batsford, 1984).

45. Cantor, *Wake of the Plague*, 15–16.

46. Cantor, *Wake of the Plague*, 15.

47. John M. Gilbert, *Hunting and Hunting Reserves in Medieval Scotland* (Edinburgh: John Donald Publishers, 1979).

48. Jean Birrell, 'Deer and Deer Farming in Medieval England', *Agricultural History Review* 40 (1991), 112–26.

49. Birrell, 'Deer farming in medieval England', 119.

50. Birrell, 'Deer farming in medieval England', 122.

51. Marcelle Thiébaux, 'The Mediaeval Chase', *Speculum* 42 (1967), 260–74.

52. Thiébaux, 'The mediaeval chase', 262.

53. Joseph Strutt, *The Sports and Pastimes of the People of England*, ed. J. C. Cox (London and New York: Augustus M. Kelley, 1903).

54. Marcelle Thiébaux, *The Stag of Love: The Chase in Medieval Literature* (Ithaca: Cornell University Press, 1974).

55. Thomas, *Man and the Natural World*, 105–6.

56. Ian MacInnes, 'Mastiffs and Spaniels: Gender and Nation in the English Dog', *Textual Practice* 17 (2003), 21–40.

57. Douglas Brewer, Terence Clark and Adrian Phillips, *Dogs in Antiquity: Anubis to Cerberus, the Origins of the Domestic Dog* (Warminster: Aris & Phillips, 2001).

58. Gilbert, *Hunting Reserves in Medieval Scotland*, 65.

59. William Secord, *Dog Painting, 1840–1940: A Social History of the Dog in Art* (Suffolk: Antique Collectors' Club, 1992).

60. Thomas, *Man and the Natural World*, 101; Secord, *Dog Painting*, 64.

61. Oscar Brownstein, 'The Popularity of Baiting in England before 1600: A Study in Social and Theatrical History', *Educational Theatre Journal* 21 (1969), 237–50.

62. Brownstein, 'Baiting in England before 1600', 243.

63. Fumagalli, *Landscapes of Fear*, 136.

64. Fumagalli, *Landscapes of Fear*, 40.

65. Fumagalli, *Landscapes of Fear*, 147.

66. Herlihy, *Black Death and the Transformation of the West*, 17.

67. Gottfried, *Black Death*, 98.

68. Fumagalli, *Landscapes of Fear*, 133; Gottfried, *Black Death*, 82.

69. J. Huizinga, *The Waning of the Middle Ages: A Study of the Forms of Life, Thought and Art in France and the Netherlands in the XIVth and XVth Centuries* (New York: St Martins, 1949).

70. Gottfried, *Black Death*, 90–2; Herlihy, *Black Death and the Transformation of the West*, 63.

71. William G. Naphy and Penny Roberts, eds, *Fear in Early Modern Society* (Manchester: Manchester University Press, 1997).

72. Herlihy, *Black Death and the Transformation of the West*, 67–8.

73. Cohen, 'Animals in medieval perceptions', 65–8.

74. In the ritual of scapegoating, a priest took two goats, killed one and ceremoniously placed the sins of the people on the head of the second goat, who then carried those sins away as he was driven into the wilderness or sent plunging to his death over a steep cliff.

75. Cohen, 'Animals in medieval perceptions', 66–7.

76. Ronald Hutton, *The Rise and Fall of Merry England: The Ritual Year 1400–1700* (New York: Oxford, 1994).

77. In the next chapter, I elaborate on the use of animals to shame women for 'unrestrained' sexual behaviour.

78. Strutt, *Sports and Pastimes of the People of England*, 201.

79. Cohen, 'Animals in medieval perceptions', 68.

80. Cohen, 'Animals in medieval perceptions', 68.

81. Cohen, 'Animals in medieval perceptions, 69–71.

82. Fumagalli, *Landscapes of Fear*, 143.

83. Ruth Mellinkoff, 'Riding Backwards: Theme of Humiliation and Symbol of Evil', *Viator* 4 (1973), 154–66.

84. Mellinkoff, 'Riding backwards', 175.

85. Huizinga, *Waning of the Middle Ages*, 24.

86. Esther Cohen, 'Symbols of Culpability and the Universal Language of Justice: The Ritual of Public Executions in Late Medieval Europe', *History of European Ideas* 11 (1989), 407–16.

87. Cohen, 'Symbols of culpability', 412–13.

88. Cohen, 'Symbols of culpability', 411.

89. Pieter Spierenberg, *The Spectacle of Suffering: Executions and the Evolution of Repression from a Preindustrial Metropolis to the European Experience* (Cambridge: Cambridge University Press, 1984).

90. Piers Beirnes, 'The Law is an Ass: Reading E.P. Evans' the Medieval Prosecution and Capital Punishment of Animals', *Society and Animals* 2 (1994), 27–46.

91. Cohen, 'Animals in medieval perceptions', 73.

92. Peter Dinzelbacher, 'Animal Trials: A Multidisciplinary Approach', *Journal of Interdisciplinary History* 32 (2002), 405–21.

93. Peter Mason, 'The Excommunication of Caterpillars: Ethno-Anthropological Remarks on the Trial and Punishment of Animals', *Social Science Information* 27 (1988), 265–73.

94. Cohen, 'Animals in medieval perceptions', 74.

95. Biernes, 'The law is an ass', 31.

96. Cohen, 'Animals in medieval perceptions', 74.

97. Cohen, 'Animals in medieval perceptions, 75.

98. Cohen, 'Law, folklore and animal lore', 35.

99. Dinzelbacher, 'Animal trials', 405–6.

100. William M. Johnson, *The Rose-Tinted Menagerie: A History of Animals in Entertainment, from Ancient Rome to the 20th Century* (London: Heretic, 1990).

101. Vernon N. Kisling, Jr., 'Ancient Collections and Menageries', in *Zoo and Aquarium History: Ancient Animal Collections to Zoological Gardens*, ed. Vernon N. Kisling, Jr. (Boca Raton: CRC Press, 2001), 1–47.

102. Johnson, *The Rose-Tinted Menagerie*, 31.

103. Strutt, *Sports and Pastimes of the People of England*, 195.

104. Strutt, *Sports and Pastimes of the People of England*, 196–7.

105. Strutt, *Sports and Pastimes of the People of England*, 197.

106. Secord, *Dog Painting*, 94.

107. Secord, *Dog Painting*, 91.

108. Thomas Moffet, cited in Brownstein, 'Popularity of baiting in England before 1600', 242.

109. Brownstein, 'Baiting in England before 1600', 241–2.

110. Thomas Veltre, 'Menageries, Metaphors, and Meanings', in *New Worlds, New Animals: From Menagerie to Zoological Park in the Nineteenth Century*, eds R. J. Hoage and William A. Deiss (Baltimore: Johns Hopkins University Press, 1996), 19–29.

111. Daniel Hahn, *The Tower Menagerie: Being the Amazing True Story of the Royal Collection of Wild and Ferocious Beasts* (London: Simon & Schuster, 2003).

112. Hahn, *Tower Menagerie*, 16.

113. Derek Wilson, *The Tower of London: A Thousand Years* (London: Allison & Busby, 1998).

114. Wilson, *Tower of London*, 23.

115. Hahn, *Tower Menagerie*, 27.

116. Clinton H. Keeling, 'Zoological Gardens of Great Britain', in *Zoo and Aquarium History: Ancient Animal Collections to Zoological Gardens*, ed. Vernon N. Kisling, Jr. (Boca Raton: CRC Press, 2001), 49–74.

117. Clark, *Animals and Men*, 107.

118. Veltre, 'Menageries, metaphors, and meanings', 25.

119. White, *Medieval Religion*, 28.

120. Herlihy, *Black Death and the Transformation of the West*, 72.

121. Joyce E. Salisbury, *The Beast Within* (New York & London: Routledge, 1994).

122. Thomas, *Man and the Natural World*, 151.

123. Thomas, *Man and the Natural World*, 152–3.

124. Geoffrey Chaucer, 'The Manciple's Tale of the Crow', (1380) (http://www. 4literature.net/Geoffrey_Chaucer/Manciple_s_Tale/ (accessed 28 November 2005)).

125. Francis of Assisi, *The Little Flowers of St Francis of Assisi*, trans. W. Heywood (New York: Vintage, 1998).

126. Adrian House, *Francis of Assisi* (Mahwah, NJ: HiddenSpring, 2001).

127. House, *Francis of Assisi*, 179.

128. Thomas, *Man and the Natural World*, 153.

129. White, *Medieval Religion*, 31–2.

130. Clark, *Animals and Men*, 26.

131. Nona C. Flores, 'The Mirror of Nature Distorted: The Medieval Artist's Dilemma in Depicting Animals', in *The Medieval World of Nature: A Book of Essays*, ed. Joyce E. Salisbury (New York: Garland Publishing, 1993), 3–45.

132. Flores, 'Mirror of nature distorted', 9.

133. White, *Medieval Religion*, 32, 41.

Chapter 4

1. Stephen T. Asma, *Stuffed Animals and Pickled Heads: The Culture and Evolution of Natural History Museums* (New York: Oxford University Press, 2001).

2. Albrecht Dürer, *Nature's Artist: Plants and Animals*, ed. Christopher Wynne, trans. Michael Robinson (Munich: Prestel, 2003).

3. E. H. Gombrich, *The Story of Art* (New York: Phaidon Press, 1995).

4. Eric Baratay and Elisabeth Hardouin-Fugier, *Zoo: A History of Zoological Gardens in the West* (London: Reaktion, 2002).

5. Dürer, *Nature's Artist*, 62.

6. Asma, *Stuffed Animals*, 70–2.

7. Oliver Impey and Arthur MacGregor, 'Introduction', in *The Origins of Museums: The Cabinet of Curiosities in Sixteenth- and Seventeenth-Century Europe*, eds Oliver Impey and Arthur MacGregor (Oxford: Clarendon Press, 1985), 1–4.

8. Baratay and Hardouin-Fugier, *Zoo*, 31.

9. Baratay and Hardouin-Fugier, *Zoo*, 31–2.

10. Baratay and Hardouin-Fugier, *Zoo*, 32.

11. Vernon N. Kisling, Jr., 'Ancient Collections and Menageries', in *Zoo and Aquarium History: Ancient Animal Collections to Zoological Gardens*, ed. Vernon N. Kisling, Jr. (Boca Raton: CRC Press, 2001), 1–47.

12. Kisling, 'Ancient collections and menageries', 28, 30.

13. Kenneth Clark, *Animals and Men: Their Relationship as Reflected in Western Art from Prehistory to the Present Day* (New York: William Morrow, 1977).

14. Charles Nicholl, *Leonardo Da Vinci: Flights of the Mind* (New York: Viking Penguin, 2004).

15. Nicholl, *Leonardo da Vinci*, 42.

16. Leonardo da Vinci, 'Fables on Animals, from the Notebooks of Leonardo Da Vinci, Volume 1, Trans Jean Paul Richter, 1888' (http://www.schulers. com/books/science/Notebooks_of_Leonardo/Notebooks_of_Leonardo1 29.htm).

17. Kenneth Clark, *Leonardo Da Vinci: An Account of His Development as an Artist* (London: Penguin, 1959).

18. Giorgio Vasari, quoted in Clark, *Leonardo da Vinci*, 127.

19. Nicholl, *Leonardo da Vinci*, 43.

20. Clark, *Leonardo da Vinci*, 89. It is known that Leonardo conducted human dissections in Florence at the Santa Maria Nuova hospital (see Clark, *Leonardo da Vinci*, 147.)

21. Thomas Veltre, 'Menageries, Metaphors, and Meanings', in *New Worlds, New Animals: From Menagerie to Zoological Park in the Nineteenth Century*, eds R. J. Hoage and William A. Deiss (Baltimore: Johns Hopkins University Press, 1996), 19–29.

22. Anita Guerrini, 'The Ethics of Animal Experimentation in Seventeenth-Century England', *Journal of the History of Ideas* 50 (1989), 391–407.

23. Daniel Garrison, ' Animal Anatomy in Vesalius's *on the Fabric of the Human Body*' (2003)(http://vesalius.northwestern.edu/essays/animalanatomy. html, accessed 5 October 2004).

24. Robert S. Gottfried, *The Black Death: Natural and Human Disaster in Medieval Europe* (New York: Free Press, 1983).

25. Gottfried, *Black Death*, 135–6.

26. Gottfried, *Black Death*, 138.

27. Keith Thomas, *Man and the Natural World: A History of the Modern Sensibility* (New York: Pantheon, 1983).

28. Gottfried, *Black Death*, 138.

29. Gottfried, *Black Death*, 90.

30. Norbert Schneider, *Still Life: Still Life Painting in the Early Modern Period* (Köln: Taschen, 1999).

31. Norman Bryson, *Looking at the Overlooked: Four Essays on Still Life Painting* (London: Reaktion Books, 1990), at 147.

32. Bryson, *Looking at the Overlooked*, 149.
33. Bryson, *Looking at the Overlooked*, 149.
34. Schneider, *Still Life*, 34, 41.
35. Nathaniel Wolloch, 'Dead Animals and the Beast-Machine: Seventeenth-Century Netherlandish Paintings of Dead Animals, as Anti-Cartesian Statements', *Art History* 22 (1999), 705–27.
36. Schneider, *Still Life*, 28.
37. Clark, *Animals and Men*, 118.
38. Schneider, *Still Life*, 12.
39. Bryson, *Looking at the Overlooked*, 160–1.
40. Scott A. Sullivan, *The Dutch Gamepiece* (Totowa, NJ: Rowman & Allanheld Publishers, 1984).
41. Roger B. Manning, 'Poaching as a Symbolic Substitute for War in Tudor and Early Stuart England', *Journal of Medieval and Renaissance Studies* 22 (1992), 185–210.
42. Manning, 'Poaching', 191.
43. Manning, 'Poaching', 193.
44. Roger B. Manning, *Village Revolts: Social Protest and Popular Disturbances in England, 1509–1640* (Oxford: Clarendon Press, 1988).
45. Manning, *Village Revolts*, 287–8.
46. Manning, 'Poaching', 189.
47. Manning, 'Poaching', 186.
48. Manning, 'Poaching', 208–9.
49. Manning, 'Poaching', 201–2.
50. Schneider, *Still Life*, 51.
51. Wolloch, 'Dead animals and the beast-machine', 705.
52. Schneider, *Still Life*, 28.
53. Anonymous, cited in Clive Ponting, *A Green History of the World* (London: Penguin, 1991), 105.
54. Gottfried, *Black Death*, 89.
55. Garthine Walker, *Crime, Gender and Social Order in Early Modern England* (Cambridge: Cambridge University Press, 2003).
56. Richard D. Ryder, *Animal Revolution: Changing Attitudes Towards Speciesism* (Oxford: Berg, 2000). (Originally published in 1989.)
57. Robert Darnton, *The Great Cat Massacre and Other Episodes in French Cultural History* (NY/London: Basic/Penguin, 2001). (Originally published in 1984.)
58. Katharine M. Rogers, *The Cat and the Human Imagination: Feline Images from Bast to Garfield* (Ann Arbor: University of Michigan Press, 1998).
59. Mark S. R. Jenner, 'The Great Dog Massacre', in *Fear in Early Modern Society*, eds William G. Naphy and Penny Roberts (Manchester: Manchester University Press, 1997), 44–61.

60. Jenner, 'Great dog massacre', 49–50.

61. David Underdown, *Revel, Riot, and Rebellion: Popular Politics and Culture in England 1603–1660* (Oxford: Clarendon Press, 1985).

62. Jenner, 'Great dog massacre', 56.

63. Thomas, *Man and the Natural World*, 110.

64. Thomas, *Man and the Natural World*, 104.

65. Katharine MacDonogh, *Reigning Cats and Dogs* (New York: St Martin's Press, 1999).

66. Thomas, *Man and the Natural World*, 183.

67. Oscar Brownstein, 'The Popularity of Baiting in England before 1600: A Study in Social and Theatrical History', *Educational Theatre Journal* 21 (1969), 237–50.

68. Tobias Hug, '"You Should Go to Hockley in the Hole, and to Marybone, Child, to Learn Valour": On the Social Logic of Animal Baiting in Early Modern London', *Renaissance Journal* 2 (2004) (http://www2.warwick. ac.uk/fac/arts/ren/publications/journal/nine/hug.doc, accessed 28 July 2005).

69. William Secord, *Dog Painting, 1840–1940: A Social History of the Dog in Art* (Suffolk: Antique Collectors' Club, 1992).

70. Secord, *Dog Painting*, 95.

71. Rebecca Ann Bach, 'Bearbaiting, Dominion, and Colonialism', in *Race, Ethnicity, and Power in the Renaissance*, ed. Joyce Green MacDonald (London: Associated University Presses, 1997), 19–35.

72. Jason Scott-Warren, 'When Theaters Were Bear-Gardens; or, What's at Stake in the Comedy of Humors', *Shakespeare Quarterly* 54 (2003), 63–82.

73. James Stokes, 'Bull and Bear Baiting in Somerset: The Gentles' Sport', in *English Parish Drama*, eds Alexandra F. Johnston and Wim Husken (Amsterdam: Rodopi, 1996), 65–80.

74. Stokes, 'Bull and bear baiting in Somerset', 68–9.

75. Bruce Boehrer, *Shakespeare Among the Animals* (New York: Palgrave, 2002); Stephen Dickey, 'Shakespeare's mastiff comedy', *Shakespeare Quarterly* 42 (1991), 255–75; Erica Fudge, *Perceiving Animals* (Urbana: University of Illinois Press, 2002) (Originally published in 1999.).

76. Hug, 'You should go to Hockley', 7.

77. Stokes, 'Bull and bear baiting in Somerset', 65.

78. Bach, 'Bearbaiting, dominion, and colonialism', 20; Scott-Warren, 'When theaters were bear-gardens', 63; Leslie Hotson, *The Commonwealth and Restoration Stage* (New York: Russell & Russell, 1962).

79. Dickey, 'Shakespeare's mastiff comedy', 255, 262.

80. Scott-Warren, 'When theaters were bear-gardens', 64.

81. Scott-Warren, 'When theaters were bear-gardens', 74.

82. Scott-Warren, 'When theaters were bear-gardens', 74, 77.

83. Scott-Warren, 'When theaters were bear-gardens', 78.

84. Ian MacInnes, 'Mastiffs and Spaniels: Gender and Nation in the English Dog', *Textual Practice* 17 (2003), 21–40.

85. MacInnes, 'Mastiffs and spaniels', 30.

86. Dickey, 'Shakespeare's mastiff comedy', 256–9.

87. S. P. Cerasano, 'The Master of the Bears in Art and Enterprise', *Medieval and Renaissance Drama in England* V (1991), 195–209, at 199.

88. Hug, 'You should go to Hockley', 6.

89. Dickey, 'Shakespeare's mastiff comedy', 259.

90. Dickey, 'Shakespeare's mastiff comedy', 260.

91. Fudge, *Perceiving Animals*, 19.

92. Bach, 'Bearbaiting, dominion, and colonialism', 21.

93. Stokes, 'Bull and bear baiting in Somerset', 76.

94. Gottfried, *Black Death*, 103.

95. Theodore K. Rabb, *The Struggle for Stability in Early Modern Europe* (New York: Oxford University Press, 1975).

96. Rabb, *Struggle for Stability*, 94–5.

97. J. Huizinga, *The Waning of the Middle Ages: A Study of the Forms of Life, Thought and Art in France and the Netherlands in the XIVth and XVth Centuries* (New York: St. Martins, 1949).

98. David Herlihy, *The Black Death and the Transformation of the West* (Cambridge, MA: Harvard University Press, 1997).

99. Rabb, *Struggle for Stability*, 40–1.

100. Rabb, *Struggle for Stability*, 40.

101. Peter Clark, *The English Alehouse: A Social History, 1200–1830* (New York: Longman, 1983).

102. Clark, *The English Alehouse*, 152.

103. Clark, *The English Alehouse*, 153, 155.

104. Clark, *The English Alehouse*, 234.

105. Underdown, *Revel, Riot, and Rebellion*, 101.

106. Underdown, *Revel, Riot, and Rebellion*, 100–101.

107. E. Cobham Brewer, 'Dictionary of Phrase and Fable' (1898) (http://www.bartleby.com/81/8465.html, accessed 8 June 2005).

108. Anton Blok, 'Rams and Billy-Goats: A Key to the Mediterranean Code of Honour', *Man* 16 (1981), 427–40.

109. Blok, 'Rams and billy-goats', 431–2.

110. Blok, 'Rams and billy-goats', 430.

111. Underdown, *Revel, Riot, and Rebellion*, 101–2.

112. Underdown, *Revel, Riot, and Rebellion*, 102.

113. Michel de Montaigne, 'An Apologie de Raymond Sebond', Chapter 12

from Montaigne's Essays: Book II (trans. John Florio)' (1580) (http://www.uoregon.edu/%7Erbear/montaigne/2xii.htm, accessed 5 July 2005).

Chapter 5

1. Peter Harrison, 'Virtues of Animals in Seventeenth-Century Thought', *Journal of the History of Ideas* 59 (1998), 463–84, at 463.
2. René Descartes, 'Letter to Marquess of Newcastle, 23 November 1646', in *Descartes: Philosophical Letters*, ed. Anthony Kenny (Oxford: Clarendon Press, 1970), 206–7.
3. René Descartes, 'Letter from Descartes to More, 5 February 1649', in *Descartes: Philosophical Letters*, ed. Anthony Kenny (Oxford: Clarendon Press, 1970), 245.
4. Peter Harrison, 'Descartes on Animals', *The Philosophical Quarterly*, 42 (1992), 220. Harrison notes that Richard Ryder was mistaken in writing that Descartes alienated his wife by experimenting on their dog (see Richard Ryder, *Animal Revolution* (Oxford: Berg, 2000)). It was the French physiologist Claude Bernard who so mistreated his wife and the family pet.
5. George Heffernan, 'Preface', to *Discourse on the Method*, by René Descartes, 1637, ed. George Heffernan (Notre Dame: University of Notre Dame Press, 1994), 2.
6. René Descartes, *Discourse on the Method of Conducting One's Reason Well and of Seeking the Truth in the Sciences* (1637), ed. George Heffernan (Notre Dame: University of Notre Dame Press, 1994).
7. Theodore Brown, cited in Theodore K. Rabb, *The Struggle for Stability in Early Modern Europe* (New York: Oxford, 1975), 111.
8. Ruth Perry, 'Radical Doubt and the Liberation of Women', *Eighteenth-Century Studies* 18 (1985), 472–93.
9. Anita Guerrini, 'The Ethics of Animal Experimentation in Seventeenth-Century England', *Journal of the History of Ideas* 50 (1989), 391–407.
10. Guerrini, 'Ethics of animal experimentation', 392.
11. Guerrini, 'Ethics of animal experimentation', 395.
12. Nathaniel Wolloch, 'Dead Animals and the Beast-Machine: Seventeenth-century Netherlandish Paintings of Dead Animals, as Anti-Cartesian Statements', *Art History* 22 (1999), 705–27 at 721–2. The assertion that death and dying has an aesthetic appeal in artistic representations of animals was also proposed by Shelby Brown in her analysis of the visual representation of the Roman arena scenes in decorative mosaics from the third century (see Chapter 2 this volume).
13. E. H. Gombrich, *The Story of Art* (New York: Phaidon Press, 1995).
14. Gombrich, *Story of Art*, 379.

15. Gombrich, *Story of Art*, 380–1.
16. Scott A. Sullivan, *The Dutch Gamepiece* (Totowa, NJ: Rowman & Allanheld Publishers, 1984).
17. Sullivan, *Dutch Gamepiece*, 40–1.
18. Sullivan, *Dutch Gamepiece*, 79.
19. Sullivan, *Dutch Gamepiece*, 2, 4.
20. Sullivan, *Dutch Gamepiece*, 17.
21. Wolloch, 'Dead animals and the beast-machine', 713–14.
22. Norbert Schneider, *Still Life: Still Life Painting in the Early Modern Period* (Köln: Taschen, 1999).
23. Sullivan, *Dutch Gamepiece*, 17.
24. J. Huizinga, *The Waning of the Middle Ages* (New York: St. Martins, 1949) 250, 253.
25. Schneider, *Still Life*, 52–3.
26. Sullivan, *Dutch Gamepiece*, 21, 78.
27. Schneider, *Still Life*, 54.
28. Sullivan, *Dutch Gamepiece*, 20.
29. Sullivan, *Dutch Gamepiece*, 20.
30. Sullivan, *Dutch Gamepiece*, 56.
31. Wolloch, 'Dead animals and the beast-machine', 713, 726.
32. Sullivan, *Dutch Gamepiece*, 38. This method of catching birds was also used in antiquity, when birds were lured or decoyed (by imitation or attracted by mirrors) to a rod or branch covered with sticky birdlime (see J. Donald Hughes, *Pan's Travail: Environmental Problems of the Ancient Greeks and Romans* (Baltimore: Johns Hopkins University Press, 1994), 104).
33. Sullivan, *Dutch Gamepiece*, 38.
34. Sullivan, *Dutch Gamepiece*, 42.
35. Kenneth Clark, *Animals and Men: Their Relationship as Reflected in Western Art from Prehistory to the Present Day* (New York: William Morrow, 1977).
36. M. Therese Southgate, 'Two Cows and a Young Bull Beside a Fence in a Meadow', *Journal of the American Medical Association* 284 (2000), 279.
37. John Berger, *Ways of Seeing* (London: Penguin Books, 1972).
38. Harriet Ritvo, *The Animal Estate: The English and Other Creatures in the Victorian Age* (Cambridge, MA: Harvard University Press, 1987).
39. Garry Marvin, 'Cultured Killers: Creating and Representing Foxhounds', *Society and Animals* 9, np (2001) (www.psyeta.org/sa/sa9.3/marvin.shtml, accessed 16 July 2004).
40. Keith Thomas, *Man and the Natural World: A History of the Modern Sensibility* (New York: Pantheon, 1983).
41. Jason Hribal, 'Animals Are Part of the Working Class: A Challenge to Labor History', *Labor History* 44 (2003), 435–53.

42. Clark, *Animals and Men*, 21–2.

43. E. P. Thompson, *Customs in Common* (London: Merlin Press, 1991).

44. Robert Darnton, *The Great Cat Massacre and Other Episodes in French Cultural History* (New York/London: Basic/Penguin, 2001). (Originally published in 1984.)

45. Darnton, *Great Cat Massacre*, 29–30.

46. Huizinga, *Waning of the Middle Ages*, 250.

47. Thompson, *Customs in Common*, 1, 18.

48. Peter Burke, 'Popular Culture in Seventeenth-Century London', *The London Journal* 3 (1977), 143–62.

49. Thompson, *Customs in Common*, 54.

50. Ronald Hutton, *The Rise and Fall of Merry England: The Ritual Year 1400–1700* (New York: Oxford University Press, 1994).

51. Burke, 'Popular culture in seventeenth-century London', 145.

52. Coral Lansbury, *The Old Brown Dog: Women, Workers, and Vivisection in Edwardian England* (Madison: University of Wisconsin Press, 1985), 61.

53. Darnton, *Great Cat Massacre*, 83.

54. Claude Lévi-Strauss, *Totemism*, trans. Rodney Needham (Boston, MA: Beacon Press, 1963), 89.

55. Darnton, *Great Cat Massacre*, 89–90.

56. Darnton, *Great Cat Massacre*, 83.

57. Darnton, *Great Cat Massacre*, 85, 92, 96.

58. Darnton, *Great Cat Massacre*, 95.

59. Burke, 'Popular culture in seventeenth-century London', 146.

60. Darnton, *Great Cat Massacre*, 75–82.

61. Keith Thomas notes that it was common for the poor to mutilate the animals of the aristocracy in 'some defiant gesture of social protest . . . [perceiving] the gentry's dogs, horses and deer as symbols of aristocratic privilege . . . [and] threats to their customary rights.' (see Thomas, *Man and the Natural World*, 184).

62. Thompson, *Customs in Common*, 470–1.

63. Thompson, *Customs in Common*, 478.

64. Thompson, *Customs in Common*, 487, 489.

65. Burke, 'Popular culture in seventeenth-century London', 148.

66. Richard D. Altick, *The Shows of London* (Cambridge, MA: Belknap Press, 1978).

67. Altick, *Shows of London*, 39; Eric Baratay and Elisabeth Hardouin-Fugier, *Zoo: A History of Zoological Gardens in the West* (London: Reaktion, 2002), 60–1.

68. Altick, *Shows of London*, 40.

69. Baratay and Hardouin-Fugier, *Zoo*, 60.

70. Joseph Strutt, *The Sports and Pastimes of the People of England* (New York: Augustus M. Kelley Publishers, 1970), 200–1. (Originally published in 1801.)

71. Jean de La Fontaine, 'The Animals Sick of the Plague', in *Jean La Fontaine Fables Online on Windsor Castle* (http://oaks.nvg.org/lg2ra12.html, accessed 5 June 2005).

72. Louise E. Robbins, *Elephant Slaves and Pampered Parrots: Exotic Animals in Eighteenth-Century Paris* (Baltimore: Johns Hopkins University Press, 2002).

73. Baratay and Hardouin-Fugier, *Zoo*, 61.

74. Robbins, *Elephant Slaves and Pampered Parrots*, 71–2.

75. Robbins, *Elephant Slaves and Pampered Parrots*, 8.

76. Robbins, *Elephant Slaves and Pampered Parrots*, 126.

77. Robbins, *Elephant Slaves and Pampered Parrots*, 142.

78. Bruce Boehrer, *Shakespeare among the Animals: Nature and Society in the Drama of Early Modern England* (New York: Palgrave, 2002), at 100–1.

79. Thomas, *Man and the Natural World*, 110–11.

80. Thomas, *Man and the Natural World*, 112–15.

81. Robbins, *Elephant Slaves and Pampered Parrots*, 12.

82. Thomas, *Man and the Natural World*, 105.

83. John D. Blaisdell, 'The Rise of Man's Best Friend: The Popularity of Dogs as Companion Animals in Late Eighteenth-Century London as Reflected by the Dog Tax of 1796', *Anthrozoos* 12 (1999), 76–87.

84. Blaisdell, 'Rise of man's best friend', 77–8.

85. Katharine MacDonogh, *Reigning Cats and Dogs* (New York: St. Martin's Press, 1999).

86. Ritvo, *Animal Estate*, 174.

87. Mark S. R. Jenner, 'The Great Dog Massacre', in *Fear in Early Modern Society*, eds William G. Naphy and Penny Roberts (Manchester: Manchester University Press, 1997), 44–61.

88. Ritvo, *Animal Estate*, 170, 177, 179, 188.

89. Altick, *Shows of London*, 39; Robbins, *Elephant Slaves and Pampered Parrots*, 87–8.

90. Robbins, *Elephant Slaves and Pampered Parrots*, 87–8.

91. Altick, *Shows of London*, 39.

92. Baratay and Hardouin-Fugier, *Zoo*, 58.

93. Baratay and Hardouin-Fugier, *Zoo*, 55.

94. Thomas, *Man and the Natural World*, 277.

95. Baratay and Hardouin-Fugier, *Zoo*, 39.

96. Baratay and Hardouin-Fugier, *Zoo*, 59.

97. Altick, *Shows of London*, 38.

98. Altick, *Shows of London*, 39.

 99. Baratay and Hardouin-Fugier, *Zoo*, 65.

100. Robbins, *Elephant Slaves and Pampered Parrots*, 37.

101. Robbins, *Elephant Slaves and Pampered Parrots*, 37–8.

102. Baratay and Hardouin-Fugier, *Zoo*, 51.

103. This is the same Bentham who is best known for posing the famous question concerning the rationality of animals: 'The question is not, can they reason? Nor, can they talk? But, can they suffer?' (see Jeremy Bentham, *Principles of Morals and Legislation*, 1789 (http://www.la.utexas. edu/research/poltheory/bentham/ipml/ipml.c17.s01.n02.html, accessed 26 July 2005)).

104. Jeremy Bentham, 'Panopticon', in *The Panopticon Writings*, ed. Miran Bozovic (London: Verso, 1787/1995), 29–95 (http://cartome.org/panopticon2.htm, accessed 26 July 2005).

105. Michel Foucault, *Discipline and Punish: The Birth of the Prison*, trans. Alan Sheridan (New York: Vintage, 1995) (http://cartome.org/foucault.htm, accessed 16 July 2005).

106. Matthew Senior, 'The Menagerie and the Labyrinthe: Animals at Versailles, 1662–1792', in *Renaissance Beasts: Of Animals, Humans, and Other Wonderful Creatures*, ed. Erica Fudge (Urbana: University of Illinois Press, 2004), 208–32, at 212.

107. Baratay and Hardouin-Fugier, *Zoo*, 51, 62.

108. Senior, 'Menagerie and the labyrinthe', 221.

109. Baratay and Hardouin-Fugier, *Zoo*, 69; Robbins, *Elephant Slaves and Pampered Parrots*, 65–6.

110. Robbins, *Elephant Slaves and Pampered Parrots*, 66–7.

111. Baratay and Hardouin-Fugier, *Zoo*, 68.

112. Baratay and Hardouin-Fugier, *Zoo*, 75.

113. Robbins, *Elephant Slaves and Pampered Parrots*, 45.

114. Baratay and Hardouin-Fugier, *Zoo*, 67.

115. www.kfki.hu/~arthp/bio/s/stubbs/biograph.html, accessed 27 April 2004.

116. Matthew Cobb, 'Reading and Writing the Book of Nature: Jan Swammerdam (1637–1680)', *Endeavour* 24 (2000), 122–8.

117. These forest still life painters were Otto Marseus van Schrieck, Jan Swammerdam, Antoni van Leeuwenhoek and Rachel Ruysch (see Schneider, *Still Life*, 195–7).

118. Guerrini, 'Ethics of animal experimentation', 406–7.

119. Robert Hooke, quoted in Guerrini, 'Ethics of animal experimentation', 401.

120. Thomas, *Man and the Natural World*, 166.

121. Thomas, *Man and the Natural World*, 173. I should note Anita Guerrini's

argument that, while a new sensibility toward animals was taking form in the seventeenth century, there was no moral opposition to vivisection, only isolated sentimental and aesthetic complaints (see Guerrini, 'Ethics of animal experimentation', 407).

122. Voltaire, 'Beasts', in *The Philosophical Dictionary, for the Pocket* (Catskill: T. & M. Croswel, J. Fellows & E. Duyckinck, 1796), 29. (Originally published in 1764.)

123. Thomas Wentworth, 'Act against Plowing by the Tayle, and Pulling the Wooll Off Living Sheep, 1635', in *The Statutes at Large, Passed in the Parliaments Held in Ireland* (Dublin: George Grierson, 1786), ix.

124. Nathaniel Ward, '"Off the Bruite Creature", Liberty 92 and 93 of the Body of Liberties of 1641', in *A Bibliographical Sketch of the Laws of the Massachusetts Colony from 1630 to 1686*, ed. William H. Whitmore (Boston, 1890). (Originally published in 1856.)

125. Cobb, 'Book of Nature', 127.

126. William Blake, (1789), 'The Fly', Project Gutenberg EText of Poems of William Blake (www.gutenberg.org/catalog/world/readfile?pageno=21+f K-files=36357.

127. David Hill, 'Of Mice and Sparrows: Nature and Power in the Late Eighteenth Century', *Forum for Modern Language Studies* 38 (2002), 1–13 at 3–4.

128. Robert Burns, 'To a Mouse on Turning Her up in Her Nest with a Plough', (1785) (http://www.robertburns.org/works/75.shtml).

129. Hill, 'Mice and sparrows', 6. Leonardo's fables discussed in the last chapter also show an engagement with the emotions of particular animals.

130. Thomas, *Man and the Natural World*, 280.

131. Robbins, *Elephant Slaves and Pampered Parrots*, 233.

132. Thomas, *Man and the Natural World*, 184.

133. Burke, 'Popular culture in seventeenth-century London', 154–5.

134. Diana Donald, '"Beastly Sights": The Treatment of Animals as a Moral Theme in Representations of London, 1820–1850', *Art History* 22 (1999), 514–44.

135. Donald, 'Beastly sights', 516, 523.

136. William Hogarth, quoted in I. R. F. Gordon, 'The Four Stages of Cruelty (1750)', in *The Literary Encyclopedia*, eds Robert Clark, Emory Elliott and Janet Todd (London: The Literary Dictionary Company, 2003) (http://www.litencyc.com/php/sworks.php?rec=true&UID=807, accessed 25 May 2005).

137. Katharine M. Rogers, *The Cat and the Human Imagination: Feline Images from Bast to Garfield* (Ann Arbor: University of Michigan Press, 1998), 41.

138. Rogers, *Cat and the Human Imagination*, 42.

139. Donald, 'Beastly sights', 525–6.

140. Donald, 'Beastly sights', 515.
141. Ritvo, *Animal Estate*, 67, 75.
142. Donald, 'Beastly sights', 521–2.
143. Thomas, *Man and the Natural World*, 100.
144. Thomas, *Man and the Natural World*, 182.
145. Hribal, 'Animals are part of the working class', 436.

Chapter 6

1. Richard Martin, Act to Prevent the Cruel and Improper Treatment of Cattle, in *United Kingdom Parliament Legislation* (Leeds, 1822).
2. While older English sources, such as the King James version of the Bible, refer to livestock in general as cattle, the contemporary use of the word 'cattle' generally refers to bovines.
3. Keith Thomas, *Man and the Natural World: A History of the Modern Sensibility* (New York: Pantheon, 1983).
4. Brian Harrison, 'Animals and the State in Nineteenth-Century England', *The English Historical Review* 99 (1973), 786–820.
5. Thomas, *Man and the Natural World*, 186.
6. Thomas, *Man and the Natural World*, 186.
7. Harrison, 'Animals and the state', 788.
8. Diana Donald, "Beastly sights': The Treatment of Animals as a Moral Theme in Representations of London, 1820–1850', *Art History* 22 (1999), 514–44.
9. Donald, 'Beastly sights', 530.
10. Thomas, *Man and the Natural World*, 299.
11. Donald, 'Beastly sights', 530.
12. Charles Dickens, *Oliver Twist* (London: Penguin, 2002), 171. (Originally published in 1838.)
13. Thomas, *Man and the Natural World*, 185.
14. Henry S. Salt. *Animals' Rights* (New York and London, 1892), 16–17.
15. Coral Lansbury, *The Old Brown Dog: Women, Workers, and Vivisection in Edwardian England* (Madison: University of Wisconsin Press, 1985).
16. Lansbury, *Old Brown Dog*, 54.
17. Lansbury, *Old Brown Dog*, 85.
18. Lansbury, *Old Brown Dog*, 9–10, 16–21.
19. Lansbury, *Old Brown Dog*, 14.
20. Lansbury, *Old Brown Dog*, 188.
21. Stanley Coren, *The Pawprints of History: Dogs and the Course of Human Events* (Free Press, 2003), 152; Harrison, 'Animals and the State', 789.
22. Anonymous quoted in William Secord, *Dog Painting: The European Breeds* (Suffolk: Antique Collectors' Club, 2000), 23.

23. Coren, *Pawprints of History*, 153.
24. M. B. McMullan, 'The Day the Dogs Died in London', *London Journal* 23 (1)(1998), 32–40, at 39.
25. Coren, *Pawprints of History*, 155.
26. Harriet Ritvo, *The Animal Estate: The English and Other Creatures in the Victorian Age* (Cambridge, MA: Harvard University Press, 1987).
27. Katharine MacDonogh, *Reigning Cats and Dogs* (New York: St. Martin's Press, 1999).
28. Ritvo, *Animal Estate*, 170.
29. Kathleen Kete, *The Beast in the Boudoir: Petkeeping in Nineteenth-Century Paris* (Berkeley: University of California Press, 1994).
30. Kete, *Beast in the Boudoir*, 98.
31. Kete, *Beast in the Boudoir*, 101–2.
32. Kete, *Beast in the Boudoir*, 103–4.
33. Kete, *Beast in the Boudoir*, 104.
34. Whitney Chadwick, 'The Fine Art of Gentling: Horses, Women and Rosa Bonheur in Victorian England', in *The Body Imaged: The Human Form and Visual Culture since the Renaissance*, eds Kathleen Adler and Marcia Pointon, 89–107 (Cambridge: Cambridge University Press, 1993).
35. Chadwick, 'Art of gentling', 100–1.
36. Chadwick, 'Art of gentling', 102.
37. Lansbury, *Old Brown Dog*, 99.
38. Lansbury, *Old Brown Dog*, 99.
39. Lansbury, *Old Brown Dog*, 101–2.
40. Lansbury, *Old Brown Dog*, 69.
41. Lansbury, *Old Brown Dog*, 69.
42. Martha Lucy, 'Reading the Animal in Degas's *Young Spartans*', *Nineteenth-Century Art Worldwide: A Journal of Nineteenth-Century Visual Culture* Spring (2003), 1–18 (http://www.19thc-artworldwide.org/spring_03/articles/lucy.html, accessed 16 July 2004).
43. Lucy, 'Reading the animal', 11.
44. Vernon N. Kisling, Jr., 'Ancient Collections and Menageries', in *Zoo and Aquarium History: Ancient Animal Collections to Zoological Gardens*, ed. Vernon N. Kisling, Jr. (Boca Raton: CRC Press, 2001), 1–47.
45. Eric Baratay and Elisabeth Hardouin-Fugier, *Zoo: A History of Zoological Gardens in the West* (London: Reaktion, 2002).
46. Stephen T. Asma, *Stuffed Animals & Pickled Heads: The Culture and Evolution of Natural History Museums* (New York: Oxford University Press, 2001).
47. Ritvo, *Animal Estate*, 248.
48. Asma, *Stuffed Animals*, 42.
49. Asma, *Stuffed Animals*, 37–8.

50. Francis Klingender, *Animals in Art and Thought to the End of the Middle Ages* eds Evelyn Antal and John Harthan (Cambridge, MA: MIT Press, 1971).

51. J. B. Wheat, cited in Juliet Clutton-Brock, *A Natural History of Domesticated Mammals* (New York: Cambridge University Press, 1999), 21.

52. Jody Emel, 'Are You Man Enough, Big and Bad Enough? Wolf Eradication in the US', in *Animal Geographies: Place, Politics, and Identity in the Nature-Culture Borderlands*, eds Jennifer Wolch and Jody Emel (London: Verso, 1998), 91–116.

53. Keith Miller, 'The West: Buffalo Hunting on the Great Plains: Promoting One Society While Supplanting Another' (2002) (http://hnn.us/articles/531.html, accessed 9 October 2005).

54. James Howe, 'Fox Hunting as Ritual', *American Ethnologist* 8 (1981), 278–300.

55. Howe, 'Fox hunting', 284, 294.

56. Henry Charles Fitz-Roy Somerset, eighth Duke of Beaufort, cited in Howe, 'Fox hunting', 279.

57. Ritvo, *Animal Estate*, 243.

58. Ritvo, *Animal Estate*, 248.

59. Baratay and Hardouin-Fugier, *Zoo*, 114–15.

60. Theodore Roosevelt, 'Wild Man and Wild Beast in Africa', *The National Geographic Magazine* 22 (1911), 1–33.

61. Roosevelt, 'Wild man', 4.

62. Donna Haraway, *Primate Visions: Gender, Race, and Nature in the World of Modern Science* (New York: Routledge, 1989).

63. Haraway, *Primate Visions*, 30–41.

64. Carl Akeley, cited in Haraway, *Primate Visions*, 33.

65. Haraway, *Primate Visions*, 31.

66. Haraway, *Primate Visions*, 30.

67. Haraway, *Primate Visions*, 34.

68. Linda Kalof and Amy Fitzgerald, 'Reading the Trophy: Exploring the Display of Dead Animals in Hunting Magazines', *Visual Studies* 18 (2003), 112–22.

69. Kalof and Fitzgerald, 'Reading the trophy', 118.

70. Thomas R. Dunlap, 'The Coyote Itself: Ecologists and the Value of Predators, 1900–1972', *Environmental Review* 7 (1983), 54–70.

71. Dunlap, 'Coyote', 55.

72. Dunlap, 'Coyote', 55–6.

73. Emel, 'Man enough', 96, 99.

74. Emel, 'Man enough', 98.

75. Dunlap, 'Coyote', 58.

76. Dunlap, 'Coyote', 57–8.

77. Berger, *About Looking* (New York: Pantheon Books, 1980).

78. Berger, *About Looking*, 23.

79. Bob Mullan and Garry Marvin, *Zoo Culture* (London: Weidenfeld & Nicolson, 1987).

80. Randy Malamud, *Reading Zoos: Representations of Animals and Captivity* (New York: New York University Press, 1998).

81. Baratay and Hardouin-Fugier, *Zoo*, 80.

82. Michel Foucault, *Discipline and Punish: The Birth of the Prison*, trans. Allan Sheridan (New York: Vintage Books, 1995), at 200. (Originally published in 1977).

83. Foucault, *Discipline and Punish*, 220.

84. Yi-Fu Tuan, *Dominance and Affection: The Making of Pets* (New Haven: Yale University Press, 1984).

85. Malamud, *Reading Zoos*, 226.

86. Peter Batten, cited in Mullan and Marvin, *Zoo Culture*, 135.

87. Nigel Rothfels, *Savages and Beasts: The Birth of the Modern Zoo* (Baltimore: Johns Hopkins University Press, 2002).

88. Ritvo, *Animal Estate*, 220; Rothfels, *Savages and Beasts*, 23–4.

89. Malamud, *Reading Zoos*, 231–5.

90. Baratay and Hardouin-Fugier, *Zoo*, 185.

91. Baratay and Hardouin-Fugier, *Zoo*, 237.

92. Herman Reichenbach, cited in Mullan and Marvin, *Zoo Culture*, 112. It has been estimated that for every animal visible in a nineteenth-century zoo, ten others were killed – mothers and other adults were regularly slaughtered to capture the young, and innumerable animals died during transport (see Baratay and Hardouin-Fugier, *Zoo*, 118).

93. Rothfels, *Savages and Beasts*, 9.

94. Baratay and Hardouin-Fugier, *Zoo*, 238–42.

95. Baratay and Hardouin-Fugier, *Zoo*, 100–1.

96. Susan G. Davis, *Spectacular Nature: Corporate Culture and the Sea World Experience* (Berkeley: University of California Press, 1997).

97. Davis, *Spectacular Nature*, 22–3.

98. Davis, *Spectacular Nature*, 25–8.

99. Davis, *Spectacular Nature*, 35.

100. Jane C. Desmond, *Staging Tourism: Bodies on Display from Waikiki to Sea World* (Chicago: University of Chicago Press, 1999).

101. Desmond, *Staging Tourism*, 193.

102. Desmond, *Staging Tourism*, 200.

103. Desmond, *Staging Tourism*, 204–5.

104. Desmond, *Staging Tourism*, 150, 197.

105. Bartolomé Bennassar, *The Spanish Character: Attitudes and Mentalities from the*

Sixteenth to the Nineteenth Century, trans. Benjamin Keen (Berkeley: University of California Press, 1979).

106. José Luis Acquaroni, *Bulls and Bullfighting*, trans. Charles David Ley (Barcelona: Editorial Noguer, 1966).

107. Juan Belmonte, *Killer of Bulls: The Autobiography of a Matador* (Garden City, NY: Doubleday, Doran & Co., 1937).

108. Bennassar, *Spanish Character*, 158–60.

109. Julian Pitt-Rivers, 'The Spanish Bull-Fight and Kindred Activities', *Anthropology Today* 9 (1993), 11–15.

110. Jennifer Reese, 'Festa', *Via* May (2003) (http://www.viamagazine.com/top_stories/articles/festa03.asp, accessed 10 October 2005).

111. Garry Marvin, *Bullfight* (Urbana: University of Illinois Press, 1994).

112. Marvin, *Bullfight*, 134–6.

113. Marvin, *Bullfight*, 138.

114. Marvin, *Bullfight*, 130.

115. Bennassar, *Spanish Character*, 158.

116. Bennassar, *Spanish Character*, 158.

117. Marvin, *Bullfight*, 132–3, 142; Pitt-Rivers, 'Spanish bull-fight', 12.

118. Sarah Pink, *Women and Bullfighting: Gender, Sex and the Consumption of Tradition* (Oxford: Berg, 1997).

119. Pitt-Rivers, 'Spanish bull-fight', 12.

120. Clifford Geertz, *The Interpretation of Cultures* (New York: Basic Books, 1973).

121. Geertz, *Interpretation of Cultures*, 442.

122. Fred Hawley, 'The Moral and Conceptual Universe of Cockfighters: Symbolism and Rationalization', *Society and Animals* 1 (1993), 159–68.

123. Rhonda Evans, DeAnn K. Gauthier and Craig J. Forsyth, 'Dogfighting: Symbolic Expression and Validation of Masculinity', *Sex Roles* 39 (1998), 825–38.

124. Evans, Gauthier and Forsyth, 'Dogfighting', 833.

125. Jonathan Burt, *Animals in Film* (London: Reaktion, 2002).

126. Burt, *Animals in Film*, 177.

127. Jonathan Burt, 'The Illumination of the Animal Kingdom: The Role of Light and Electricity in Animal Representation', *Society and Animals* 9 (2001), 203–28.

128. Akira Mizuta Lippit, 'The Death of an Animal', *Film Quarterly* 56 (2002), 9–22.

129. Lippit, 'Death of an Animal', 12.

130. Burt, 'Illumination of the Animal Kingdom', 212.

131. Steve Baker, *Picturing the Beast: Animals, Identity, and Representation* (Urbana: University of Illinois Press, 2001). (Originally published in 1993.)

132. Donna J. Haraway, Modest_Witness@Second_Millennium.FemaleMan©_ Meets_OncoMouse™ (New York: Routledge, 1997).

133. Haraway, *Modest _Witness*, 79.

134. Haraway, *Modest_Witness*, 215.

135. Haraway, *Modest_Witness*, 265.

136. Gilles Deleuze and Félix Guattari, *A Thousand Plateaus: Capitalism and Schizophrenia*, trans. Brian Massumi (Minneapolis: University of Minnesota Press, 1987).

137. Deleuze and Guattari, *Thousand Plateaus*, 241–3.

138. Deleuze and Guattari, *Thousand Plateaus*, 244–5.

139. Steve Baker, *The Postmodern Animal* (London: Reaktion, 2000).

140. Baker, *Postmodern Animal*, 104, 138.

141. Malamud, *Reading Zoos*, 275.

142. Baker, *Postmodern Animal*, 54, 189.

143. Baker, *Postmodern Animal*, 61, 106–7, 112.

144. Anonymous, 'Liquidising Goldfish "Not a Crime"', (http://news.bbc. co.uk/1/hi/world/europe/3040891.stm, accessed 28 October 2005).

145. Gail Davies, 'Virtual Animals in Electronic Zoos: The Changing Geographies of Animal Capture and Display', in *Animal Spaces, Beastly Places: New Geographies of Human–Animal Relations*, eds Chris Philo and Chris Wilbert (London: Routledge, 2000), 243–67.

146. Malamud, *Reading Zoos*, 258.

147. Davies, 'Virtual animals', 258.

148. Haraway, *Modest_Witness*, 215.

Bibliography

Acquaroni, José Luis, *Bulls and Bullfighting*, trans. Charles David Ley (Barcelona: Editorial Noguer, 1966).

Altick, Richard D., *The Shows of London* (Cambridge, MA: Belknap Press, 1978).

Anderson, John K., *Hunting in the Ancient World* (Berkeley: University of California Press, 1985).

Anonymous, 'Liquidising Goldfish "Not a Crime"' (http://news.bbc.co.uk/1/hi/world/europe/3040891.stm, accessed 28 October 2005).

Asma, Stephen T., *Stuffed Animals and Pickled Heads: The Culture and Evolution of Natural History Museums* (New York: Oxford University Press, 2001).

Assisi, Francis of, *The Little Flowers of St. Francis of Assisi*, trans. W. Heywood (New York: Vintage, 1998).

Auguet, Roland, *Cruelty and Civilization: The Roman Games* (New York: Routledge, 1972).

Bach, Rebecca Ann, 'Bearbaiting, Dominion, and Colonialism', in *Race, Ethnicity, and Power in the Renaissance*, ed. Joyce Green MacDonald (London: Associated University Presses, 1997), 19–35.

Backhouse, Janet, *Medieval Rural Life in the Luttrell Psalter* (Toronto: University of Toronto Press, 2000).

Bahn, Paul G. and Jean Vertut, *Journey through the Ice Age* (Berkeley: University of California Press, 1997).

Baker, Steve, *The Postmodern Animal* (London: Reaktion, 2000).

Baker, Steve, *Picturing the Beast: Animals, Identity, and Representation* (Urbana: University of Illinois Press, 2001). (Originally published in 1993.)

Baratay, Eric and Elisabeth Hardouin-Fugier, *Zoo: A History of Zoological Gardens in the West* (London: Reaktion, 2002). (Originally published in 1993).

Barringer, Judith M., *The Hunt in Ancient Greece* (Baltimore: Johns Hopkins University Press, 2001).

Beirnes, Piers, 'The Law Is an Ass: Reading E. P. Evans' the Medieval Prosecution and Capital Punishment of Animals', *Society and Animals* 2 (1994), 27–46.

Belmonte, Juan, *Killer of Bulls: The Autobiography of a Matador* (Garden City, NY: Doubleday, Doran, 1937).

Bennassar, Bartolomé, *The Spanish Character: Attitudes and Mentalities from the Sixteenth to the Nineteenth Century*, trans. Benjamin Keen (Berkeley: University of California Press, 1979).

Bentham, Jeremy, 'Panopticon', in *The Panopticon Writings*, ed. Miran Bozovic (London: Verso, 1787/1995), 29–95 (http://cartome.org/panopticon2. htm, accessed 26 July 2005).

Bentham, Jeremy, *Principles of Morals and Legislation* (1789) (http://www.la. utexas.edu/research/poltheory/bentham/ipml/ipml.c17.s01.n02.html, accessed 26 July 2005).

Benton, Janetta Rebold, *The Medieval Menagerie: Animals in the Art of the Middle Ages* (New York: Abbeville Press, 1992).

Benton, Janetta Rebold, 'Gargoyles: Animal Imagery and Artistic Individuality in Medieval Art', in *Animals in the Middle Ages: A Book of Essays*, ed. Nona C. Flores (New York and London: Garland Publishing, 1996), 147–65.

Berger, John, *Ways of Seeing* (London: Penguin Books, 1972).

Berger, John, *About Looking* (New York: Pantheon Books, 1980).

Birrell, Jean, 'Deer and Deer Farming in Medieval England', *Agricultural History Review* 40 (1991), 112–26.

Blaisdell, John D., 'The Rise of Man's Best Friend: The Popularity of Dogs as Companion Animals in Late Eighteenth-Century London as Reflected by the Dog Tax of 1796', *Anthrozoos* 12 (1999), 76–87.

Blake, Robert (1789), 'The Fly', Project Gutenberg EText of Poems of Robert Blake (www.gutenberg.org/catalog/world/readfile?pageno=21+fK-files= 36357).

Blok, Anton, 'Rams and Billy-Goats: A Key to the Mediterranean Code of Honour', *Man* 16 (1981), 427–40.

Boehrer, Bruce, *Shakespeare among the Animals: Nature and Society in the Drama of Early Modern England* (New York: Palgrave, 2002).

Bomgardner, David L., 'The Trade in Wild Beasts for Roman Spectacles: A Green Perspective', *Anthropozoologica* 16 (1992), 161–6.

Brewer, Douglas, Terence Clark and Adrian Phillips, *Dogs in Antiquity: Anubis to Cerberus, the Origins of the Domestic Dog* (Warminster: Aris & Phillips, 2001).

Brewer, E. Cobham, 'Dictionary of Phrase and Fable', (1898) (http://www. bartleby.com/81/8465.html, accessed 8 June 2005).

Brier, Bob, 'Case of the Dummy Mummy', *Archaeology* 54 (2001), 28–9.

Brown, Shelby, 'Death as Decoration: Scenes from the Arena on Roman

Domestic Mosaics', in *Pornography and Representation in Greece and Rome*, ed. Amy Richlin (New York: Oxford University Press, 1992), 180–211.

Brownstein, Oscar, 'The Popularity of Baiting in England before 1600: A Study in Social and Theatrical History', *Educational Theatre Journal* 21 (1969), 237–50.

Bryson, Norman, *Looking at the Overlooked: Four Essays on Still Life Painting* (London: Reaktion Books, 1990).

Burke, Peter, 'Popular Culture in Seventeenth-Century London', *The London Journal* 3 (1977), 143–62.

Burns, Robert, 'To a Mouse on Turning Her up in Her Nest with a Plough', (1785) (http://www.robertburns.org/works/75.shtml).

Burt, Jonathan, 'The Illumination of the Animal Kingdom: The Role of Light and Electricity in Animal Representation', *Society and Animals* 9 (2001), 203–28.

Burt, Jonathan, *Animals in Film* (London: Reaktion, 2002).

Cantor, Norman F., *In the Wake of the Plague: The Black Death and the World It Made* (New York: Free Press, 2001).

Cerasano, S. P., 'The Master of the Bears in Art and Enterprise', *Medieval and Renaissance Drama in England* V (1991), 195–209.

Chadwick, Whitney, 'The Fine Art of Gentling: Horses, Women and Rosa Bonheur in Victorian England', in *The Body Imaged: The Human Form and Visual Culture since the Renaissance*, eds Kathleen Adler and Marcia Pointon (Cambridge: Cambridge University Press, 1993), 89–107.

Chaix, L., A. Bridault and R. Picavet, 'A Tamed Brown Bear (Ursus Arctos L.) of the Late Mesolithic from La Grande-Rivoire (Isère, France)?', *Journal of Archaeological Science* 24 (1997), 1067–74.

Chaucer, Geoffrey, 'The Manciple's Tale of the Crow' (1380) (http://www.4literature.net/Geoffrey_Chaucer/Manciple_s_Tale/, accessed 28 November 2005).

Clark, Kenneth, *Leonardo Da Vinci: An Account of His Development as an Artist* (London: Penguin, 1959).

Clark, Kenneth, *Animals and Men: Their Relationship as Reflected in Western Art from Prehistory to the Present Day* (New York: William Morrow, 1977).

Clark, Peter, *The English Alehouse: A Social History, 1200–1830* (New York: Longman, 1983).

Claudian, 'De Consulate Stilichonis, Book III', (http://penelope.uchicago.edu/Thayer/E/Roman/Texts/Claudian/De_Consulatu_Stilichonis/3*.html).

Clottes, Jean, *Chauvet Cave: The Art of Earliest Times*, trans. Paul G. Bahn (Salt

Lake City: University of Utah Press, 2003).

Clottes, Jean and Jean Courtin, *The Cave beneath the Sea: Paleolithic Images at Cosquer*, trans. Marilyn Garner (New York: Harry N. Abrams, 1996).

Clutton-Brock, Juliet, *A Natural History of Domesticated Mammals* (New York: Cambridge University Press, 1999). (Originally published in 1987.)

Clutton-Brock, Juliet ed., *The Walking Larder: Patterns of Domestication, Pastoralism, and Predation* (London: Unwin Hyman, 1989).

Cobb, Matthew, 'Reading and Writing the Book of Nature: Jan Swammerdam (1637–1680)', *Endeavour* 24 (2000), 122–8.

Cohen, Ester, 'Law, Folklore, and Animal Lore', *Past and Present* 110 (1986), 6–37.

Cohen, Esther, 'Symbols of Culpability and the Universal Language of Justice: The Ritual of Public Executions in Late Medieval Europe', *History of European Ideas* 11 (1989), 407–16.

Cohen, Esther, 'Animals in Medieval Perceptions: The Image of the Ubiquitous Other', in *Animals and Human Society: Changing Perspectives*, eds Aubrey Manning and James Serpell (London: Routledge, 1994), 59–80.

Coleman, K. M., 'Fatal Charades: Roman Executions Staged as Mythological Enactments', *Journal of Roman Studies* 80 (1990), 44–73.

Coleman, K. M., 'Launching into History: Aquatic Displays in the Early Empire', *Journal of Roman Studies* 83 (1993), 48–74.

Coleman, K. M., 'Ptolemy Philadelphus and the Roman Amphitheater', in *Roman Theater and Society: E. Togo Salmon Papers I*, ed. William J. Slater (Ann Arbor: University of Michigan Press, 1996), 49–68.

Collins, Paul, 'A Goat Fit for a King', *ART News* 102(7) (2003), 106–8.

Conard, Nicholas J., 'Palaeolithic Ivory Sculptures from Southwestern Germany and the Origins of Figurative Art', *Nature* 426 (2003), 830–2.

Coren, Stanley, *The Pawprints of History: Dogs and Course of Human Events* (New York: Free Press, 2003).

Da Vinci, Leonardo, 'Fables on Animals, from the Notebooks of Leonardo Da Vinci, Volume 1, trans. Jean Paul Richter, 1888' (http://www.schulers. com/books/ science/Notebooks_of_Leonardo/Notebooks_of_Leonardo129.htm).

Darnton, Robert, *The Great Cat Massacre and Other Episodes in French Cultural History* (New York/London: Basic/Penguin, 2001). (Originally published in 1984.)

David, Ephraim, 'Hunting in Spartan Society and Consciousness', *Echos du Monde Classique/Classical Views* 37 (1993), 393–413.

Davies, Gail, 'Virtual Animals in Electronic Zoos: The Changing Geographies of Animal Capture and Display', in *Animal Spaces, Beastly Places: New Geographies of Human–Animal Relations*, eds Chris Philo and Chris Wilbert (London: Routledge, 2000), 243–67.

Davis, Susan G., *Spectacular Nature: Corporate Culture and the Sea World Experience* (Berkeley: University of California Press, 1997).

Deleuze, Gilles and Félix Guattari, *A Thousand Plateaus: Capitalism and Schizophrenia*, trans. Brian Massumi (Minneapolis: University of Minnesota Press, 1987).

Descartes, René, 'Letter to Marquess of Newcastle, 23 November 1646', in *Descartes: Philosophical Letters*, ed. Anthony Kenny (Oxford: Clarendon Press, 1970).

Descartes, René, 'Letter from Descartes to More, 5 February 1649', in *Descartes: Philosophical Letters*, ed. Anthony Kenny (Oxford: Clarendon Press, 1970).

Descartes, René, *Discourse on the Method of Conducting One's Reason Well and of Seeking the Truth in the Sciences (1637)*, ed. George Heffernan, trans. George Heffernan (Notre Dame: University of Notre Dame Press, 1994).

Desmond, Jane C., *Staging Tourism: Bodies on Display from Waikiki to Sea World* (Chicago: University of Chicago Press, 1999).

Dickens, Charles, *Oliver Twist, or the Parish Boy's Progress (1837)* (London: Penguin, 2002). (Originally published in 1838.)

Dickey, Stephen, 'Shakespeare's Mastiff Comedy', *Shakespeare Quarterly* 42 (1991), 255–75.

Dinzelbacher, Peter, 'Animal Trials: A Multidisciplinary Approach', *Journal of Interdisciplinary History* 32 (2002), 405–21.

Dio, Cassius, 'Book XXXIX', (http://penelope.uchicago.edu/Thayer/E/Roman/Texts/Cassius_Dio/39*.html).

Donald, Diana, '"Beastly Sights": The Treatment of Animals as a Moral Theme in Representations of London, 1820–1850', *Art History* 22 (1999), 514–44.

Dunlap, Thomas R., 'The Coyote Itself: Ecologists and the Value of Predators, 1900–1972', *Environmental Review* 7 (1983), 54–70.

Dürer, Albrecht, *Nature's Artist: Plants and Animals*, ed. Christopher Wynne, trans. Michael Robinson (Munich: Prestel, 2003).

Emel, Jody, 'Are You Man Enough, Big and Bad Enough? Wolf Eradication in the US', in *Animal Geographies: Place, Politics, and Identity in the Nature-Culture Borderlands*, eds Jennifer Wolch and Jody Emel (London: Verso, 1998), 91–116.

Evans, Rhonda, DeAnn K. Gauthier and Craig J. Forsyth, 'Dogfighting: Symbolic Expression and Validation of Masculinity', *Sex Roles* 39 (1998), 825–38.

Flores, Nona C., 'The Mirror of Nature Distorted: The Medieval Artist's Dilemma in Depicting Animals', in *The Medieval World of Nature: A Book of Essays*, ed. Joyce E. Salisbury (New York: Garland Publishing, 1993), 3–45.

Flores, Nona C. (ed.) *Animals in the Middle Ages: A Book of Essays* (New York: Garland, 1996).

Foucault, Michel, *Discipline and Punish: the Birth of the Prison*, trans. Allan Sheridan (New York: Vintage Books, 1995). (Originally published in 1977).

Freedman, Paul H., 'The Representation of Medieval Peasants as Bestial and as Human', in *The Animal/Human Boundary: Historical Perspectives*, eds Angela N. H. Creager and William Chester Jordan (Rochester: University of Rochester Press, 2002), 29–49.

Fudge, Erica, *Perceiving Animals: Humans and Beasts in Early Modern English Culture* (Urbana: University of Illinois Press, 2002). (Originally published in 1999.)

Fumagalli, Vito, *Landscapes of Fear: Perceptions of Nature and the City in the Middle Ages*, trans. Shayne Mitchell (Cambridge: Polity Press, 1994).

Futrell, Alison, *Blood in the Arena: The Spectacle of Roman Power* (Austin: University of Texas Press, 1997).

Galan, Jose M., 'Bullfight Scenes in Ancient Egyptian Tombs', *Journal of Egyptian Archaeology* 80 (1994), 81–96.

Garrison, Daniel, '"Animal Anatomy" in Vesalius's *On the Fabric of the Human Body*' (2003) (http://vesalius.northwestern.edu/essays/animalanatomy.html, accessed 5 October 2004).

Geertz, Clifford, *The Interpretation of Cultures* (New York: Basic Books, 1973).

Gilbert, John M., *Hunting and Hunting Reserves in Medieval Scotland* (Edinburgh: John Donald Publishers, 1979).

Gombrich, E. H., *The Story of Art* (New York: Phaidon Press, 1995).

Gordon, I. R. F., 'The Four Stages of Cruelty (1750)', in *The Literary Encyclopedia*, eds Robert Clark, Emory Elliott and Janet Todd (London: The Literary Dictionary Company, 2003) (http://www.litencyc.com/php/sworks.php?rec=true&UID=807, accessed 25 May 2005).

Gottfried, Robert S., *The Black Death: Natural and Human Disaster in Medieval Europe* (New York: Free Press, 1983).

Guerrini, Anita, 'The Ethics of Animal Experimentation in Seventeenth-Century England', *Journal of the History of Ideas* 50 (1989), 391–407.

Hahn, Daniel, *The Tower Menagerie: Being the Amazing True Story of the Royal Collection of Wild and Ferocious Beasts* (London: Simon & Schuster, 2003).

Hansen, Donald P., 'Art of the Royal Tombs of Ur: A Brief Interpretation', in *Treasures from the Royal Tombs of Ur*, eds Richard L. Zettler and Lee Horne

(Philadelphia: University of Pennsylvania Museum, 1998), 43–59.

Haraway, Donna, *Primate Visions: Gender, Race, and Nature in the World of Modern Science* (New York: Routledge, 1989).

Haraway, Donna J., Modest_Witness@Second_Millennium.FemaleMan©_ Meets_OncoMouse' (New York: Routledge, 1997).

Harrison, Brian, 'Animals and the State in Nineteenth-Century England', *English Historical Review* 99 (1973), 786–820.

Harrison, Peter, 'Descartes on Animals', *Philosophical Quarterly* 42 (1992), 219–27.

Harrison, Peter, 'Virtues of Animals in Seventeenth-Century Thought', *Journal of the History of Ideas* 59 (1998), 463–84.

Hassig, Debra, 'Sex in the Bestiaries', in *The Mark of the Beast: The Medieval Bestiary in Art, Life and Literature*, ed. Debra Hassig (New York: Garland, 1999), 71–93.

Hawley, Fred, 'The Moral and Conceptual Universe of Cockfighters: Symbolism and Rationalization', *Society and Animals* 1 (1993), 159–68.

Healy, John F., 'The Life and Character of Pliny the Elder', in *Pliny the Elder, Natural History: A Selection*, ed. John F. Healy (London: Penguin, 2004), ix–xxxx.

Heffernan, George, 'Preface', in *Discourse on the Method, by René Descartes (1637)*, ed. George Heffernan (Notre Dame: University of Notre Dame Press, 1994), 1–8.

Herlihy, David, *The Black Death and the Transformation of the West* (Cambridge, MA: Harvard University Press, 1997).

Hill, David, 'Of Mice and Sparrows: Nature and Power in the Late Eighteenth Century', *Forum for Modern Language Studies* 38 (2002), 1–13.

Hoage, R. J., Anne Roskell and Jane Mansour, 'Menageries and Zoos to 1900', in *New Worlds, New Animals: From Menagerie to Zoological Park in the Nineteenth Century*, eds R. J. Hoage and William A. Deiss (Baltimore: Johns Hopkins University Press, 1996), 8–18.

Hopkins, Keith, *Death and Renewal: Sociological Studies in Roman History* (New York: Cambridge University Press, 1983).

Hotson, Leslie, *The Commonwealth and Restoration Stage* (New York: Russell & Russell, 1962).

Houlihan, Patrick F., *The Animal World of the Pharaohs* (London: Thames and Hudson, 1996).

House, Adrian, *Francis of Assisi* (Mahwah, NJ: HiddenSpring, 2001).

Howe, James, 'Fox Hunting as Ritual', *American Ethnologist* 8 (1981), 278–300.

Hribal, Jason, '"Animals Are Part of the Working Class": A Challenge to Labor History', *Labor History* 44 (2003), 435–53.

Hug, Tobias, '"You Should Go to Hockley in the Hole, and to Marybone, Child, to Learn Valour": On the Social Logic of Animal Baiting in Early Modern London', *Renaissance Journal* 2 (2004) (http://www2.warwick.ac.uk/fac/arts/ren/publications/journal/nine/hug.doc, accessed 28 July 2005).

Hughes, J. Donald, *Pan's Travail: Environmental Problems of the Ancient Greeks and Romans* (Baltimore: Johns Hopkins University Press, 1994).

Huizinga, J., *The Waning of the Middle Ages: A Study of the Forms of Life, Thought and Art in France and the Netherlands in the XIVth and XVth Centuries* (New York: St. Martins, 1949).

Hutton, Ronald, *The Rise and Fall of Merry England: The Ritual Year 1400–1700* (New York: Oxford, 1994).

Impey, Oliver and Arthur MacGregor, 'Introduction', in *The Origins of Museums: The Cabinet of Curiosities in Sixteenth- and Seventeenth-Century Europe*, eds Oliver Impey and Arthur MacGregory (Oxford: Clarendon Press, 1985), 1–4.

Janson, H. W. and Joseph Kerman, *A History of Art and Music* (Englewood Cliffs, NJ: Prentice Hall, 1968).

Jenks, Stuart, 'Review of the Black Death: Natural and Human Disaster in Medieval Europe (by Robert Gottfried)', *Journal of Economic History* 46, (1986) 815–23.

Jenner, Mark S. R., 'The Great Dog Massacre', in *Fear in Early Modern Society*, eds William G. Naphy and Penny Roberts (Manchester: Manchester University Press, 1997), 44–61.

Jennison, George, *Animals for Show and Pleasure in Ancient Rome* (Manchester University Press, 1937).

Johnson, William M., *The Rose-Tinted Menagerie: A History of Animals in Entertainment, from Ancient Rome to the 20th Century* (London: Heretic, 1990).

Kalof, Linda and Amy Fitzgerald, 'Reading the Trophy: Exploring the Display of Dead Animals in Hunting Magazines', *Visual Studies* 18 (2003), 112–22.

Kalof, Linda, Amy Fitzgerald and Lori Baralt, 'Animals, Women and Weapons: Blurred Sexual Boundaries in the Discourse of Sport Hunting', *Society and Animals* 12(3), 2004), 237–51.

Keeling, Clinton H., 'Zoological Gardens of Great Britain', in *Zoo and Aquarium History: Ancient Animal Collections to Zoological Gardens*, ed. Vernon N. Kisling, Jr. (Boca Raton: CRC Press, 2001), 49–74.

Kete, Kathleen, *The Beast in the Boudoir: Petkeeping in Nineteenth-Century Paris* (Berkeley: University of California Press, 1994).

Kisling, Vernon N., Jr., 'Ancient Collections and Menageries', in *Zoo and Aquarium History: Ancient Animal Collections to Zoological Gardens*, ed. Vernon N. Kisling, Jr. (Boca Raton: CRC Press, 2001), 1–47.

Klingender, Francis, *Animals in Art and Thought to the End of the Middle Ages*, eds Evelyn Antal and John Harthan (Cambridge, MA: MIT Press, 1971).

Kyle, Donald G., *Spectacles of Death in Ancient Rome* (New York: Routledge, 1998).

La Fontaine, Jean de, 'The Animals Sick of the Plague', in 'Jean La Fontaine Fables Online on Windsor Castle' (http://oaks.nvg.org/lg2ra12.html, accessed 5 June 2005).

Lahanas, Michael, 'Galen' (www.mlahanas.de/Greeks/Galen.htm, accessed 18 November 2004).

Lansbury, Coral, *The Old Brown Dog: Women, Workers, and Vivisection in Edwardian England* (Madison: University of Wisconsin Press, 1985).

Latour, Bruno, 'A Prologue in Form of a Dialogue between a Student and his (somewhat) Socratic Professor' (http://www.ensmp.fr/~latour/articles/article/090.html).

Leveque, Pierre, *The Birth of Greece* (New York: Harry M. Abrams, 1994).

Lévi-Strauss, Claude, *Totemism*, trans. Rodney Needham (Boston: Beacon Press, 1963).

Lewis-Williams, David, *The Mind in the Cave: Consciousness and the Origins of Art* (London: Thames & Hudson, 2002).

Linden, Eugene, *The Parrot's Lament: And Other True Tales of Animals' Intrigue, Intelligence, and Ingenuity* (New York: Penguin, 1999).

Lippit, Akira Mizuta, 'The Death of an Animal', *Film Quarterly* 56 (2002), 9–22.

Lucy, Martha, 'Reading the Animal in Degas's *Young Spartans*', *Nineteenth-Century Art Worldwide: A Journal of Nineteenth-Century Visual Culture* Spring(2003), 1–18 (http://www.19thc-artworldwide.org/spring_03/articles/lucy.html, accessed 16 July 2004).

MacDonogh, Katharine, *Reigning Cats and Dogs* (New York: St. Martin's Press, 1999).

MacInnes, Ian, 'Mastiffs and Spaniels: Gender and Nation in the English Dog', *Textual Practice* 17 (2003), 21–40.

Malamud, Randy, *Reading Zoos: Representations of Animals and Captivity* (New York: New York University Press, 1998).

Manning, Roger B., *Village Revolts: Social Protest and Popular Disturbances in England, 1509–1640* (Oxford: Clarendon Press, 1988).

Manning, Roger B., 'Poaching as a Symbolic Substitute for War in Tudor and Early Stuart England', *Journal of Medieval and Renaissance Studies* 22 (1992), 185–210.

Marceau, Jo, Louise Candlish, Fergus Day and David Williams, eds, *Art: A World History* (New York: DK Publishing, 1997).

Martin, Richard, Act to Prevent the Cruel and Improper Treatment of Cattle, in *United Kingdom Parliament Legislation*, (Leeds, 1822).

Marvin, Garry, *Bullfight* (Urbana: University of Illinois Press, 1994).

Marvin, Garry, 'Cultured Killers: Creating and Representing Foxhounds', *Society and Animals* 9, np (2001) (www.psyeta.org/sa/sa9.3/marvin.shtml, accessed 16 July 2004).

Mason, Peter, 'The Excommunication of Caterpillars: Ethno-Anthropological Remarks on the Trial and Punishment of Animals', *Social Science Information* 27, 265–73 (1988).

Matz, David, *Daily Life of the Ancient Romans* (Westport: Greenwood Press, 2002).

McMullan, M. B., 'The Day the Dogs Died in London', *London Journal* 23(1) (1998), 32–40.

Meens, Rob, 'Eating Animals in the Early Middle Ages: Classifying the Animal World and Building Group Identities', in *The Animal/Human Boundary: Historical Perspectives*, eds Angela N. H. Creager and William Chester Jordan (Rochester, NY: University of Rochester Press, 2002), 3–28.

Mellinkoff, Ruth, 'Riding Backwards: Theme of Humiliation and Symbol of Evil', *Viator* 4 (1973), 154–66.

Miller, Keith, 'The West: Buffalo Hunting on the Great Plains: Promoting One Society While Supplanting Another', (2002) (http://hnn.us/articles/531.html, accessed 9 October 2005).

Mitchell, Stephen, *Gilgamesh* (New York: Free Press, 2004).

Mithen, Steven, 'The Hunter-Gatherer Prehistory of Human–Animal Interactions', *Anthrozoos* 12 (1999), 195–204.

Mithen, Steven, *After the Ice: A Global Human History, 20,000–5000 BC* (Cambridge, MA: Harvard University Press, 2004).

Montaigne, Michel de, 'An Apologie de Raymond Sebond', Chapter 12 from Montaigne's Essays: Book II, trans. John Florio (1580) (http://www.uoregon.edu/%7Erbear/montaigne/2xii.htm, accessed 5 July 2005).

Morris, Christine E., 'In Pursuit of the White Tusked Boar: Aspects of Hunting in Mycenaean Society', in *Celebrations of Death and Divinity in the Bronze Age Argolid*, eds Robin Hagg and Gullog C. Nordquist (Stockholm: Paul Astroms Forlag, 1990), 151–6.

Mullan, Bob and Garry Marvin, *Zoo Culture* (London: Weidenfeld & Nicolson, 1987).

Naphy, William G. and Penny Roberts, eds, *Fear in Early Modern Society* (Manchester:

Manchester University Press, 1997).

Nicholl, Charles, *Leonardo Da Vinci: Flights of the Mind* (New York: Viking Penguin, 2004).

Perry, Ruth, 'Radical Doubt and the Liberation of Women', *Eighteenth-Century Studies* 18 (1985), 472–93.

Phillips, Dorothy, *Ancient Egyptian Animals* (New York: Metropolitan Museum of Art Picture Books, 1948).

Pink, Sarah, *Women and Bullfighting: Gender, Sex and the Consumption of Tradition* (Oxford: Berg, 1997).

Pitt-Rivers, Julian, 'The Spanish Bull-Fight and Kindred Activities', *Anthropology Today* 9 (1993), 11–15.

Plass, Paul, *The Game of Death in Ancient Rome* (Madison: University of Wisconsin Press, 1995).

Pliny, Elder, 'The Natural History, Book IX. The Natural History of Fishes', eds John Bostock and H. T. Riley (http://www.perseus.tufts.edu/cgi-bin/ptext?doc=Perseus%3Atext%3A1999.02.0137&query=toc:head%3D%2341, accessed 14 November 2005).

Pliny, Elder, 'The Natural History, Book VIII. The Nature of the Terrestrial Animals', eds John Bostock and H. T. Riley (http://www.perseus.tufts.edu/cgi-bin/ptext?doc=Perseus%3Atext%3A1999.02.0137&query=toc:head%3D%23333, accessed 14 November 2005).

Pliny, Elder, *Natural History: A Selection*, trans. John F. Healy (London: Penguin, 2004).

Ponting, Clive, *A Green History of the World* (Harmondsworth: Penguin, 1991).

Rabb, Theodore K., *The Struggle for Stability in Early Modern Europe* (New York: Oxford University Press, 1975).

Reese, Jennifer, 'Festa', *Via* May (2003) (http://www.viamagazine.com/top_stories/articles/festa03.asp, accessed 10 October 2005).

Ritvo, Harriet, *The Animal Estate: The English and Other Creatures in the Victorian Age* (Cambridge, MA: Harvard University Press, 1987).

Robbins, Louise E., *Elephant Slaves and Pampered Parrots: Exotic Animals in Eighteenth-Century Paris* (Baltimore: Johns Hopkins University Press, 2002).

Rodale, J., ed. *The Synonym Finder* (Emmaus, PA: Rodale Press, 1978).

Rogers, Katharine M., *The Cat and the Human Imagination: Feline Images from Bast to Garfield* (Ann Arbor: University of Michigan Press, 1998).

Roland, Alex, 'Once More into the Stirrups: Lynn White Jr., *Medieval Technology and Social Change*', *Technology and Culture* 44 (2003), 574–85.

Roosevelt, Theodore, 'Wild Man and Wild Beast in Africa', *National Geographic Magazine* XXII (1911), 1–33.

Rothfels, Nigel, *Savages and Beasts: The Birth of the Modern Zoo* (Baltimore: Johns Hopkins University Press, 2002).

Ryder, Richard D., *Animal Revolution: Changing Attitudes Towards Speciesism* (Oxford: Berg, 2000). (Originally published in 1989.)

Salisbury, Joyce E., *The Beast Within* (New York & London: Routledge, 1994).

Salt, Henry S., *Animals' Rights* (New York & London, 1892).

Schneider, Norbert, *Still Life: Still Life Painting in the Early Modern Period* (Köln: Taschen, 1999).

Schwabe, Calvin W., 'Animals in the Ancient World', in *Animals and Human Society: Changing Perspectives*, eds Aubrey Manning and James Serpell (London: Routledge, 1994), 36–58.

Scott-Warren, Jason, 'When Theaters Were Bear-Gardens; or, What's at Stake in the Comedy of Humors', *Shakespeare Quarterly* 54 (2003), 63–82.

Scullard, H. H., *The Elephant in the Greek and Roman World* (Ithaca: Cornell University Press, 1974).

Secord, William, *Dog Painting, 1840–1940: A Social History of the Dog in Art* (Suffolk: Antique Collectors' Club, 1992).

Senior, Matthew, 'The Menagerie and the Labyrinthe: Animals at Versailles, 1662–1792', in *Renaissance Beasts: Of Animals, Humans, and Other Wonderful Creatures*, ed. Erica Fudge (Urbana: University of Illinois Press, 2004), 208–232.

Shelton, Jo-Ann, 'Dancing and Dying: The Display of Elephants in Ancient Roman Arenas', in *Daimonopylai: Essays in Classics and the Classical Tradition Presented to Edmund G. Berry*, eds Rory B. Egan and Mark Joyal (Winnipeg: University of Manitoba, 2004), 363–82.

Sinclair, Anthony, 'Archaeology: Art of the Ancients', *Nature* 426 (2003), 774–5.

Southgate, M. Therese, 'Two Cows and a Young Bull Beside a Fence in a Meadow', *Journal of the American Medical Association* 284 (2000), 279.

Spierenberg, Pieter, *The Spectacle of Suffering: Executions and the Evolution of Repression from a Preindustrial Metropolis to the European Experience* (Cambridge: Cambridge University Press, 1984).

Spivey, Nigel, *Etruscan Art* (London: Thames and Hudson, 1997).

Stokes, James, 'Bull and Bear Baiting in Somerset: The Gentles' Sport', in *English Parish Drama*, eds Alexandra F. Johnston and Wim Husken (Amsterdam: Rodopi, 1996), 65–80.

Strutt, Joseph, *The Sports and Pastimes of the People of England*, ed. J. C. Cox

(London and New York: Augustus M. Kelley, 1970). (Originally published in 1801.)

Suetonius, 'Domitianus XIX', trans. J. C. Rolfe (http://www.fordham.edu/halsall/ancient/suet-domitian-rolfe.html).

Sullivan, Scott A., *The Dutch Gamepiece* (Totowa, NJ: Rowman & Allanheld Publishers, 1984).

Thiébaux, Marcelle, 'The Mediaeval Chase', *Speculum* 42 (1967), 260–74.

Thiébaux, Marcelle, *The Stag of Love: The Chase in Medieval Literature* (Ithaca: Cornell University Press, 1974).

Thomas, Keith, *Man and the Natural World: A History of the Modern Sensibility* (New York: Pantheon, 1983).

Thompson, E. P., *Customs in Common* (London: Merlin Press, 1991).

Toynbee, J. M. C., *Animals in Roman Life and Art* (London: Camelot Press, 1973).

Tuan, Yi-Fu, *Dominance and Affection: The Making of Pets* (New Haven: Yale University Press, 1984).

Twigg, Graham, *The Black Death: A Biological Reappraisal* (London: Batsford, 1984).

Underdown, David, *Revel, Riot, and Rebellion: Popular Politics and Culture in England 1603–1660* (Oxford: Clarendon Press, 1985).

Valladas, Helene and Jean Clottes, 'Style, Chauvet and Radiocarbon', *Antiquity* 77 (2003), 142–5.

Veltre, Thomas, 'Menageries, Metaphors, and Meanings', in *New Worlds, New Animals: From Menagerie to Zoological Park in the Nineteenth Century*, eds R. J. Hoage and William A. Deiss (Baltimore: Johns Hopkins University Press, 1996), 19–29.

Veyne, Paul, *Bread and Circuses: Historical Sociology and Political Pluralism*, trans. Brian Pearce (London: Penguin Press, 1990).

Voltaire, 'Beasts', in *The Philosophical Dictionary, for the Pocket*, (Catskill: T & M Croswel, J. Fellows & E. Duyckinck, 1796), 29. (Originally published in 1764.)

Walker, Garthine, *Crime, Gender and Social Order in Early Modern England* (Cambridge: Cambridge University Press, 2003).

Ward, Nathaniel, '"Off the Bruite Creature", Liberty 92 and 93 of the Body of Liberties of 1641', in *A Bibliographical Sketch of the Laws of the Massachusetts Colony from 1630 to 1686*, ed. William H. Whitmore (Boston, 1890). (Originally published in 1856.)

Welté, Anne-Catherine, 'An Approach to the Theme of Confronted Animals in

French Palaeolithic Art', in *Animals into Art*, ed. Howard Morphy, (London: Unwin Hyman, 1989).

Wentworth, Thomas, 'Act against Plowing by the Tayle, and Pulling the Wooll Off Living Sheep, 1635', in *The Statutes at Large, Passed in the Parliaments Held in Ireland* (Dublin: George Grierson, 1786), ix.

White, Lynn, Jr., *Medieval Technology and Social Change* (London: Oxford University Press, 1962).

White, Lynn, Jr., *Medieval Religion and Technology: Collected Essays* (Berkeley: University of California Press, 1978).

White, Randall, *Prehistoric Art: The Symbolic Journey of Humankind* (New York: Harry N. Abrams, 2003).

Wiedemann, Thomas, *Emperors and Gladiators* (London: Routledge, 1992).

Wilson, Anna, 'Sexing the Hyena: Intraspecies Readings of the Female Phallus', *Signs* 28 (2003), 755–790.

Wilson, Derek, *The Tower of London: A Thousand Years* (London: Allison & Busby, 1998).

Wolloch, Nathaniel, 'Dead Animals and the Beast-Machine: Seventeenth-Century Netherlandish Paintings of Dead Animals, as Anti-Cartesian Statements', *Art History* 22 (1999), 705–27.

Photo Acknowledgements

1 Giraudon/Art Resource, NY, ART80361.
2 Art Resource, NY/ART99863.
3 American Library Color Slide Company, 26989.
4 American Library Color Slide Company, 45195.
5 American Library Color Slide Company, 15415.
6 American Library Color Slide Company, 62901.
7 American Library Color Slide Company, 4531.
8 American Library Color Slide Company, 21498.
9 Erich Lessing/Art Resource, NY, ART178776.
10 Art Resource 10742.
11 American Library Color Slide Company, 63978.
12 Photo Linda Kalof.
13 American Library Color Slide Company, 27237.
14 Giraudon/Art Resource, NY, ART21265.
15 © Walters Art Museum, Baltimore, Maryland. Bridgeman Art Library, 204675.
16 Scala/Art Resource, NY, ART42513.
17 British Library 21611.
18 Lauros/Giraudon. Bridgeman Art Library, XIR173605.
19 Scala/Art Resource, NY, ART39051.
20 Victoria and Albert Museum, London/Art Resource, NY, ART19866.
21 The J. Paul Getty Museum, Los Angeles.
22 British Library c2169-06.
23 British Library 20679.
24 British Library 10099.
25 Victoria and Albert Museum, London/Art Resource, NY, ART181085.
26 Bridgeman Art Library, XTD 068707.
27 British Library 18926.
28 MS 146. Giraudon/Art Resource, NY, ART60368.
29 British Library 12067.
30 Giraudon. Bridgeman Art Library, 154680.
31 British Library 001084.

32 British Library 001614.

33 Private collection; Bridgeman Art Library, 168591.

34 American Library Color Slide Company, 1726.

35 Bridgeman Art Library, 166366.

36 Bridgeman Art Library, 58236.

37 Lauros/Giraudon. Bridgeman Art Library, 93879.

38 American Library Color Slide Company, 1938.

39 The J. Paul Getty Museum, Los Angeles.

40 Giraudon. Bridgeman Art Library, 47570.

41 Bridgeman Art Library, 34886.

42 Bridgeman Art Library, 23447.

43 Bridgeman Art Library, 62702.

44 Bridgeman Art Library, 167058.

45 Bridgeman Art Library, 35764.

46 Bridgeman Art Library, TWC62205.

47 © Cleveland Museum of Art, John L. Severance Fund, 1969.53.

48 Bridgeman Art Library, 30247.

49 The J. Paul Getty Museum, Los Angeles (001463).

50 Published by Phillipus Gallaeus of Amsterdam. Bridgeman Art Library, 161106 71.

51 Alinari. Bridgeman Art Library, 227102 74.

52 American Library Color Slide Company, 25199.

53 Trustees of the Weston Park Foundation, UK. Bridgeman Art Library, WES67099.

54 Trustees of the Weston Park Foundation, UK. Bridgeman Art Library, WES67100.

55 Trustees of the Weston Park Foundation, UK. Bridgeman Art Library, WES67101.

56 Trustees of the Weston Park Foundation, UK. Bridgeman Art Library, WES67102.

57 Bridgeman Art Library, BOU203009.

58 Courtesy of the Warden and Scholars of New College, Oxford, Oxford. Bridgeman Art Library, NCO193178.

59 British Library 21552.

60 Photo Linda Kalof.

61 Denver Public Library, Western History Collection, photographer unknown (Z1567).

62 Bureau of Biological Survey. Denver Public Library, Western History Collection, photographer unknown (Z1566).

63 The J. Paul Getty Museum, Los Angeles (001041).

64 Photo copyright by Britta Jaschinski, reproduced with permission of the artist.

Index